"Not many financial journalists' columns repay a reading months or years later. Caroline Baum's knack for making complex ideas understandable and her irreverent style make her book one of the rare exceptions."

DR. ALLAN H. MELTZER
The Allan H. Meltzer University Professor of Political Economy,
Carnegie Mellon University

"Caroline Baum demonstrates that economics (the "dismal science") can be made lively, humorous, creative, and professional. The book *Just What I Said* is economics in action. It is beautifully written and well argued and is always on the mark. Complex subjects are made simple through Baum's masterful application of the basic principles of economics. Read it, you will like it and learn a lot."

DR. JACOB A. FRENKEL
Vice Chairman, American International Group, Inc.
Former Governor of the Bank of Israel

Just What I Said

CAROLINE BAUM

Just What I Said

BLOOMBERG ECONOMICS COLUMNIST
TAKES ON BONDS, BANKS, BUDGETS,
AND BUBBLES

BLOOMBERG PRESS
NEW YORK

BLOOMBERG, BLOOMBERG ANYWHERE, BLOOMBERG.COM, BLOOMBERG MARKET ESSENTIALS, *Bloomberg Markets*, BLOOMBERG NEWS, BLOOMBERG PRESS, BLOOMBERG PROFESSIONAL, BLOOMBERG RADIO, BLOOMBERG TELEVISION, and BLOOMBERG TRADEBOOK are trademarks and service marks of Bloomberg Finance L.P. ("BFLP"), a Delaware limited partnership, or its subsidiaries. The BLOOMBERG PROFESSIONAL service (the "BPS") is owned and distributed locally by BFLP and its subsidiaries in all jurisdictions other than Argentina, Bermuda, China, India, Japan, and Korea (the "BLP Countries"). BFLP is a wholly-owned subsidiary of Bloomberg L.P. ("BLP"). BLP provides BFLP with all global marketing and operational support and service for these products and distributes the BPS either directly or through a non-BFLP subsidiary in the BLP Countries. All rights reserved.

This publication contains the author's opinions and is designed to provide accurate and authoritative information. It is sold with the understanding that the author, publisher, and Bloomberg L.P. are not engaged in rendering legal, accounting, investment-planning, or other professional advice. The reader should seek the services of a qualified professional for such advice; the author, publisher, and Bloomberg L.P. cannot be held responsible for any loss incurred as a result of specific investments or planning decisions made by the reader.

First edition published 2005

11 13 15 17 18 16 14 12

ISBN-13: 978-1-57660-219-5

The Library of Congress has cataloged the earlier printing
as follows:

Baum, Caroline
  Just what I said : Bloomberg economics columnist takes on bonds, banks, budgets,
and bubbles / by Caroline Baum. -- 1st. ed.
       p. cm.
  Summary: "Analysis and commentary on economics, the Federal Reserve, monetary policy, the bond markets, and politics, selected from among 1,300 columns written by Caroline Baum since 1998 for Bloomberg News, the electronic business and financial news service"--Provided by publisher.
  Includes index.
  ISBN 1-57660-219-2 (alk. paper)
  1. United States--Economic conditions. 2. Finance. 3. Economics. I. Title.

HC106.83.B38 2005
330.973'0931--dc22   2005016435

To the memory of my father,
who always believed in me
even when I didn't believe in myself

Contents

P r e f a c e

JOURNALISTS HAVE a love/hate relationship with their work. We love the process—coming up with an idea, reporting the story, following its twists and turns, unearthing new details along the way, crafting the lead and the kicker—but we hate the result.

Not at the time, of course. A week or a month later, when we reread the story, what jumps out at us is all the ways we could have made it better.

Perhaps that's why I declined previous overtures to produce a book of columns, which I've been writing for 18 years, the last seven for Bloomberg News. I was afraid I'd be so critical of my work that I would be unable to see its long-term value, no less to present it in a manner that would be compelling to readers so many years after the fact.

By the time Bill Inman, editor of Bloomberg Publishing, and Jared Kieling, Bloomberg Press's acquisitions editor, approached me last year, I was ready to take the plunge. I suspect their solicitousness had something to do with it.

First I had some questions. Who would buy this book? All my columns are archived on the Bloomberg Professional service. Why would any regular reader of my column buy the book?

Bill had the answer. Plenty of people, especially pre-Internet dinosaurs, like books. They like to touch and hold them. They like to carry a book around, read it on the train, plane, or in front of a crackling fire.

What's more, Bill said my ability to make thorny subjects simple, not to mention lively, would have broader appeal in a world where a basic understanding of economics and financial markets is necessary in everyday life.

I was warming to the idea, even though I was dreading wading through the entire Baum "oeuvre": the 1,300 columns I'd written since joining Bloomberg in February 1998 (I wrote a column for Dow Jones for 11 years prior to joining Bloomberg News).

Bill told me how well the columns held up, how their value transcended the time and circumstances in which they were written, how their themes were as relevant today as when they first appeared. He wanted the best of those columns collected in one volume for people who, like my regular readers, follow the financial markets and value my perspective.

What follows, then, is a compilation of my columns on the macro-economy, bond market, interest rates and policies that affect them. I arranged them by theme—and was surprised as the chapters started to accumulate. Here I thought I wrote the same six columns over and over, and somehow I managed to come up with 19 different themes.

Readers tell me they sense the joy I get from writing my columns. I hope you experience the same joy reading them.

CAROLINE BAUM
West Tisbury, Massachusetts

Acknowledgments

THIS IS A BOOK OF COLUMNS, so any debt of gratitude must start with those individuals who make my column happen several times each week.

I owe so much to my longtime editor, Steve Dickson, whose steady hand keeps me on course. Steve respects my voice, and I respect his. It doesn't get any better between writer and editor.

Steve is a great wordsmith, and many of the catchy column headlines bear his stamp.

Bill Ahearn oversees the work of all the Bloomberg News columnists with the wisdom and judgment acquired from years of experience. Bill has taught me patience (no mean feat since I live in real time), to trust myself to get it right even when it's coming out wrong.

I want to thank Matt Winkler, editor in chief of Bloomberg News, who recruited me in 1998. Matt has supported me and promoted my work for the last seven years, giving me some time off from my day job to devote my full attention to the book.

Thanks also to my Bloomberg News colleagues, who are always willing to offer their expertise—and expert sources—in their respective fields when I venture outside of mine. This is true of Bloomberg reporters and editors around the globe, who treat me like royalty when I travel.

I'm grateful to the economists who took me under their wing early on and educated me. An inquisitive student who wants to get it right is irresistible to a teacher, but some folks went beyond the call of duty. I'm indebted to Paul Kasriel, the late Bob Laurent, and Tim Schiller for teaching me to use economics to think about the world; and to Jim Glassman and Joe Carson for always having time to walk me through hard concepts and help me translate theory into something practical and readable.

Thanks also to Jim Bianco, who's never too busy to unearth some arcane data series to help prove a point.

With these people as my teachers and the market as my classroom, you could say I've had one hell of an education. If, over the years, I've managed to convey ideas to my readers with the same infectious enthusiasm with which they were conveyed to me, then I will consider myself successful.

This book would not have been possible without the efforts of Bill Inman at Bloomberg Publishing, who approached me with the idea, and Jared Kieling of Bloomberg Press, who turned the idea into reality with his astute suggestions and editing. Barbara Diez Goldenberg, Bloomberg Press design director, shepherded the project from beginning to end, which greatly enhanced my peace of mind.

I would not be able to do the work I do with the intensity it requires without balance in my life. I'm blessed to have such a wonderful circle of friends, sources and colleagues who listened patiently as I rattled on about the book project.

I'm especially grateful for the love and friendship of Steve Cary over the years and for the guidance and grounding of Pat Hill.

And thanks to my mother, who has never understood the concepts of "online" or "newswire" (and probably harbors suspicions about how I earn a living). Finally she'll have something in hard copy to adorn her cocktail table.

I n t r o d u c t i o n

IN THE OLD DAYS, business and financial news was relegated to—where else?—the business and financial section of the newspaper.

Every once in a while a big leveraged buyout or merger would hit the front pages. But business news mostly played second fiddle to the major political stories of the day.

The 1990s changed all that. During the latter part of the decade— the real go-go years—everyone was interested in the daily ebb and flow (mostly flow) of the stock market. And it wasn't the staid Dow Jones Industrial Average or the Standard and Poor's 500 Index that captured people's attention. The public was interested in the high-flying Nasdaq, which rose 571 percent from the start of 1995 to its high close of 5048.62 on March 10, 2000.

The stock market drove the economy, not the other way around. At its peak in March 2000, total stock market capitalization was 1.8 times the size of the U.S. economy. The wealth generated by the appreciation in equity prices from 1995 through 1999, even if unrealized, encouraged consumers to spend more of their earned income. Venture capital beck-oned to anyone with a half-baked idea and "dot com" after the name. Businesses took advantage of inflated share prices to raise capital and invest in more plants and equipment than they could realistically utilize.

The stock market became the filter through which we viewed the world. Anything that affected equity prices immediately became big news.

When a series of rolling economic and financial crises hit Asia, Latin America and Russia starting in 1997—compounded by a homegrown crisis at mega–hedge fund Long Term Capital Management—it roiled stock markets around the world and was front-page news for days and weeks at a time.

Alan Greenspan became the central banker to the world. And because the Federal Reserve had lifted its veil of secrecy in 1994, pub-licly announcing policy changes in real time, ordinary folks were able to follow along with the pros. Monetary policy had gone mainstream.

Business news became big business. Television executives pounced on the opportunity.

First came FNN, the Financial News Network, which was acquired by General Electric Co.'s CNBC. CNN, the first 24-hour all-news cable channel, begat CNNfn, dedicated to financial news (CNNfn is now defunct). Bloomberg L.P. started its own business-news cable channel. And News Corp. Chairman Rupert Murdoch has announced his intention to launch a Fox business-news cable channel.

Business anchors became household names. Then they became stars.

Reporters took us onto the floor of the New York Stock Exchange and into Chicago's futures-trading pits, where men and women in brightly colored waiters' coats made peculiar hand signals and screamed at one another.

It may have looked like reality TV, but it was capitalism in action.

There was just one problem with this round-the-clock business and financial coverage: There wasn't enough real news to fill the airwaves 24/7. So the shows, which tried to differentiate themselves from one another via catchy names, devoted more and more time to chitchat. Viewers could listen to Myron the money manager hawk tech stocks or Henry the hedge fund operator talk about opportunities in "busted converts."

Back then, before New York Attorney General Eliot Spitzer cracked down on the financial services industry, the guests didn't have to reveal whether they had a position in whatever they happened to be pitching. (You could be pretty sure that most of them did—and were looking to sell at higher prices.)

Small-cap value fund managers opined about Fed policy. Economists handicapped geopolitical risks. Youthful Internet CEOs offered investors "return on vision" in place of actual profits.

Experts were in demand, their expertise compressed into a three- to five-minute segment. (As long as they were an expert in *something*, it didn't matter if the subject under discussion was their particular area of expertise.)

And there's the rub: With so much time to fill, most of the filler was sound bites.

What business anchors and reporters lacked in knowledge they made up for in enthusiasm. CNBC was known as the cheerleader for the Nasdaq bubble. The network threw a party when the Dow closed above 10,000 for the first time in April 1999. The anchors looked as if they were attending a wake when the index broke through 10,000 on its way south.

Anyone hoping to get real insight into how the markets and the economy operate and interact from these snippets would have been disappointed. TV makes it all look quite glam, what with Internet IPOs soaring several hundred percent the day after the sale. But there's plenty of humdrum stuff that gets lost in the glitter.

That's where I come in. Humdrum, in the right hands, can be exciting.

The operation of the Federal Reserve—how the central bank creates reserves out of thin air and destroys them in the same way—would normally make for dry, scholarly reading. It wouldn't even fly as a PBS series.

What if the Fed chairman could be disrobed to reveal an ordinary human being under the sphinxlike facade? What if the emperor has no clothes? It would sure make all that stuff about the sources and uses of reserves easier to swallow.

That's my job: to make knotty subjects understandable and fun.

I once wrote a column comparing Alan Greenspan to Alfred Hitchcock. The connection may not be immediately apparent, but after reading every word Greenspan has uttered since he became Fed chairman in 1987 and seeing most of Hitchcock's films, it was to me. The column was light; it was deep. (It's in chapter 8.) It'll give you a unique perspective on how Greenspan operates.

I had another flight of fancy (no pun intended) as I was watching birds flock to my new bird feeder. Could the avian world shed any new light on the law of supply and demand? Bird-watching became a lesson in economics. (See chapter 5.)

Then there's mop technology. Isn't it time someone applied Moore's Law—the observation that the memory capacity of computer chips doubles every 18 months—to the vast home-products market, where most of the 111 million households surely own a mop? You'll read about that, too, in this book (chapter 11).

In the midst of the late 1990s productivity boom, like most consumers I spent hours on the phone with tech support trying to get help with my home computer. While I was on perma-hold, it dawned on me that the degradation of services was a particularly insidious, albeit unmeasured, form of inflation. That realization became the basis for my belief and analysis that we are understating service-sector inflation.

Economics, in other words, can be demystified and explained via the raw material of daily life.

I didn't come to this line of work with pre-formed ideas. Most of my education and training was on the job, not in the classroom.

I was pretty green when I started out in 1987, reporting on the daily happenings in the U.S. Treasury market and injecting some flavor into my copy. I asked a lot of questions. I talked to a lot of people. I read and studied on my own and even went back to school to take some economics courses.

My views on how the economy works evolved over the years. With increased understanding came a fundamental belief in free markets, which infuses all my writing.

Like the agora of ancient Greece, modern-day markets are the forum where buyers and sellers come together (not necessarily in a physical sense) to exchange something, be it goods, services, financial assets or contracts to buy or sell assets in the future. They engage in voluntary transactions at a price they determine.

This is the basis of the free-market capitalist system, which has proved to be the superior method of organizing an economy.

Command economies, where the state controls the means of production and distribution and sets prices, can't possibly deliver the goods and services consumers want because they have no price signals to guide them. That's why "Soviet Union" is preceded by the qualifier "former."

Just thinking about how markets miraculously perform so many functions—Chinese manufacturers know exactly what consumers in Chicago want—inspires a sense of awe. I hope I impart that sense to readers.

I've organized this book thematically rather than chronologically. The columns in each chapter may not be topically consistent, but they all exemplify a common theme.

The chapters—even the individual columns—stand on their own and need not be read in any particular sequence.

My approach can best be described as didactic. I take my readers on a journey, walking them through the same discovery process I traveled before them, imparting some knowledge—and hopefully a nugget or two of wisdom—along the way.

If you were to ask me what I hoped to accomplish by presenting these already-published columns in book form, along with expository writing to inform each chapter, it would be this: to help the reader see things in a different light; to inspire in him a sense of awe at the way a market economy magically delivers the goods and services consumers want at the prices they're willing to pay; and to encourage him to challenge conventional wisdom (there's a reason it's called "conventional"), even if a supposedly respected authority says it's so.

I leave it to you to decide whether I've succeeded.

1

Ye of Little Faith

N O INSTITUTION commands as much attention from financial market participants and the financial press as the Federal Reserve. Every word Fed officials utter, every nuance, inflection and choice of verb tense, is dissected and analyzed for its policy implications.

Expectations about Fed policy are immediately incorporated into market rates. The press reports what policy-makers say and how the markets react.

Traders read the stories, hoping for new information or insight from reporters with known access to the Fed chairman. Markets react again, and the whole cycle is repeated.

What's so curious, given our obsessive relationship with the Fed, is how little credit it gets for affecting economic outcomes. Just when the Fed has been most aggressive in its efforts to stimulate or curtail economic growth, faith in the power of interest rates seems to falter.

"It's not working this time," the cries go out.

The Fed affects aggregate demand, or the total demand for goods and services in the economy, by manipulating the benchmark overnight interest rate, known as the federal funds rate.

There are lots of theories about how this works. Economists trained decades ago generally have adopted the Keynesian view that the Fed lowers short-term rates solely to bring down long-term rates, which in turn reduces the cost of home mortgages and corporate borrowing for capital expenditures.

If that's the case, why do central banks around the world target a short-term rate? Rather than hoping market forces guide long-term rates to the desired level, wouldn't it be easier to buy and sell long-term bonds to influence the price?

And if low long-term rates were the panacea they're cracked up to be, how can we explain Japan's lost decade in the 1990s, with the yield on the 10-year Japanese government bond plummeting from 8.25 percent to 0.5 percent? (Hint: Sometimes low long-term rates are a symptom of a sick economy, not a cure.) The yield has been consistently below 2 percent since late 1997.

Many of the columns you'll read in this book, in this and other chapters, reflect my view of how interest rates work. For now, let's just say that interest rates change the incentive to spend and to save. When businesses and consumers aren't being paid to save—when bank deposits pay a barely discernible rate of interest, as they did in 2003 in the U.S.—they spend. (American consumers never seem to need much prodding.)

High real interest rates, on the other hand, encourage the public to defer consumption.

The thrust of Fed policy comes from the interaction between short- and long-term rates: The central bank sets the first; the market determines the second. The spread between the two is an excellent, real-time gauge of the stance of policy.

Don't expect to see this indicator widely advertised. Such a simple, accessible tool might compromise the livelihood of all those econometric modelers.

If the Market Can Do the Fed's Work, Who Needs the Fed?

————— April 23, 1999 —————

MILTON FRIEDMAN, Nobel laureate in economics, has long advocated getting rid of the Federal Reserve and replacing the central bank with a computer.

What Friedman means is that the economy would be best served by a steady rate of growth in the money supply. Since two Fed staffs in New

York and Washington doing reserve projections have been unable to hit the Fed's target (definition: something aimed or fired at) of 1 to 5 percent growth in the broad monetary aggregate M2 in almost two years, the odds are good that a computer could perform the function better than the Fed's marksmen.

While there is no talk of sacking Fed Chairman Alan Greenspan in favor of Microsoft's Bill Gates just yet, the Fed has already relinquished one of its roles—that of the economy's main driver—to the market, according to a May 3 *Business Week* article titled "The Fed's New Rule Book."

"In the face of all this uncertainty, FOMC members are now counting on the market to help regulate the economy for them by raising and lowering long-term rates to keep inflation in check," writes *Business Week*.

Business Week is just echoing the views expressed by the Federal Open Market Committee. With the exception of St. Louis Fed President William Poole, who understands the relationship between long and short rates, Fed officials were quick to cite the rise in long-term rates in February as a harbinger of slower economic growth.

ONE-WAY STREET

Isn't it curious that the Fed didn't rely on the market to do its work last fall? In a huge flight to quality into U.S. Treasuries after Russia's default in August, the yield on the 30-year bond plunged 100 basis points to an all-time low of 4.69 percent on Oct. 5. Yields on two-, five- and 10-year notes fell to 3.77 percent, 3.90 percent and 4.10 percent, respectively.

Yet the Fed felt compelled to do its own work, lowering interest rates three times, for a total of 75 basis points, on Sept. 29, Oct. 15 and Nov. 17. At the time of the Sept. 29 rate reduction, the 30-year bond yield was already 5¹/₈ percent.

Maybe the causality works only in one direction: Rising long rates slow the economy down, but falling long rates don't provide any stimulus!

That lopsided effect begs the real question of why we need a central bank if the market can do the job.

"If that notion were true, you have to ask yourself why some markets are so good at it and some are so bad," says Bob Laurent, professor of economics at Loyola University.

Citing the years of hyperinflation in Brazil, Laurent wonders what's wrong with the Brazilian market. "They never seem to get it right," he says.

Those who argue the market can do the Fed's heavy lifting base their case on the idea that rising long rates will sap demand for credit, including home mortgages and corporate borrowing. They never bother to ask themselves why interest rates (the price of credit) are rising: Is it the result of increased demand or reduced supply?

Think Beef

My first economics teacher (we're talking street economics here) used beef instead of credit to make the point. If all of a sudden people decide to consume more beef, assuming no change in the supply of beef, the price of beef will rise. In that case—represented by an outward shift in the demand curve—the higher price won't reduce demand because increased demand is the reason the price rose in the first place!

What if hoof-and-mouth disease pares the cattle herd in half? The price of beef will rise in that case, too. But the inward shift in the supply curve produces a higher price and a lower quantity demanded.

Now substitute credit for beef. If increased demand for credit pushes the price up, how can one argue that the higher price will cause demand to slow?

On the other hand, if the price rises because supply is being curtailed, then the higher price will crimp demand.

Simple Model

Calculating the supply and demand for credit at any given time is a Herculean effort. Guess what? You don't have to. All you need to know is two interest rates: one long, one short.

Think of the overnight federal funds rate as a proxy for supply. By adjusting the supply of reserves relative to the banking system's demand, the Fed can pretty much put the funds rate where it wants.

Think of the long rate as a proxy for demand. It ebbs and flows in response to the demand for credit and inflationary expectations. The spread between the two rates provides more information than all of Wall Street's proprietary models combined.

If the long rate is rising at the same time that the Fed is holding the short rate steady, you can be pretty sure that the rise in long rates is expansionary, not contractionary.

Every central bank in the world conducts monetary policy through a short-term interest rate. There is no reason why they can't use a long rate as their policy tool, buying and selling bonds to satisfy the banking system's reserve needs.

SHORT BEATS LONG

The fact is, they don't. If you ask economists to rank the two rates in terms of their economic importance, the ones who have bothered to test them will rate the short rate as number one, hands down.

"The shorter the maturity of the interest rate, the better predictor it is of future economic growth," says Ken Landon, senior currency strategist at Deutsche Bank in Tokyo. "The relationship between long rates and future growth is relatively weak and may merely be the result of the high positive correlation between short and long rates."

Long rates matter, but they don't matter nearly as much as everyone thinks. And if you want to know what effect the rise or fall in the long rate will have on demand, first take a look at what the short rate is doing.

POSTSCRIPT: Subsequently, during the deflation scare in June 2003, yields on Treasury notes and bonds fell to the lowest since the U.S. government began holding regular auctions in the 1970s. These lows—in some cases, the lowest since the late 1950s—are still in place: two-year note, 1.06 percent; five-year note, 2 percent; 10-year note, 3.07 percent; 30-year bond, 4.14 percent.

The Fed Gets So Much Attention Yet So Little Credit

————— July 10, 2000 —————

THEY DON'T call it "Bearron's" for nothing.

The weekly financial magazine's featured columnist, Alan Abelson, has been dissing the 1990s bull market in his "Up and Down Wall Street" column for, what, the last 5000 Dow points?

So it's not surprising to find *Barron's* once again in doubting mode. This time it's the notion that the Federal Reserve is well on its way to slowing economic growth to a sustainable, noninflationary pace, obviating the need for further rate increases. In the current issue, "Economic

Beat" columnist Gene Epstein claims that the second-quarter slowdown is a case of déjà vu all over again.

Epstein's not the only one to identify a pattern of weak second-quarter growth in the midst of an economic boom. That phenomenon was observable in 1998 and 1999 as well, with second-quarter real gross domestic product growth slipping to 2.2 percent and 1.9 percent, respectively, well below the 4.7 percent annual average in both years.

Analysts have come up with a variety of reasons to explain the Q2 washout, even though their hunches are relegated to the benefit of hindsight, not foresight. Among the usual suspects are: early tax refunds due to the popularity of electronic filing, which boosts spending in the first quarter at the expense of the second; unseasonably mild winter weather; and a big tax bite in April for those who don't like giving the government an interest-free loan for a year.

KEY DIFFERENCE

Spending is apt to rebound in the third quarter, Epstein maintains via his surrogate, economist Jason Benderly. Benderly expects GDP growth for the year to come in at 4.7 percent on a fourth-quarter-over-fourth-quarter basis, about the same as in 1998 and 1999.

Why do the Federal Reserve and Chairman Alan Greenspan get so much attention if, according to the Epstein/Benderly hypothesis, they are so irrelevant?

While there does seem to be a statistical quirk in the second-quarter data, there is every reason to believe that economic growth won't return to last year's blistering pace. The reason is that the overnight federal funds rate is 175 basis points higher than it was in June of last year, which is slowing the growth rate of the nation's money supply and lifting private borrowing rates.

The idea of explaining economic performance and inflation "ex-Fed" is endemic on Wall Street, where curiously a cottage industry is paid to discern every changing inflection in the Fed chairman's tone. Only on Wall Street is the Fed followed, feared and forecast—and quickly forgotten when it comes to the explanation of economic outcomes. Fed policy-makers are guilty as well, discussing inflation in terms of temporary effects from oil prices and the dollar.

DOWN GREENSPAN'S WAY

On Main Street, despite its lack of sophistication, things are much simpler. Folks are grateful for the extended period of prosperity and thank the Fed for good economic management. Alan Greenspan even "got a street in the suburbs," according to the *Chicago Sun-Times,* when Arlington Heights named one of its thoroughfares Alan Greenspan Way.

Benderly points to exports and government spending as two potential sources of economic growth in the second half, which seems sound given the shift in relative growth away from the U.S. and the expressed desire on the part of both the administration and Congress to find new uses for our tax dollars.

What makes less sense is Epstein's contention that rising wages and salaries—up an annualized 6.7 percent in the first half of this year compared to 6.5 percent in 1999—ensure increased spending since this is "the kind of income that tends to get spent."

SPENDING LEADS INCOME

Rising income is not necessarily a precondition for spending, just as falling income is not a precondition for a cutback. If that were the case, an expanding economy would never turn down since income is always rising until something makes it stop. Similarly, the economy would never emerge from recession if falling income were the determining criterion.

Clearly, something motivates consumer and business decisions to cut back on spending during good times and to increase spending when things look pretty glum. Usually it's the interest rate, or what they can earn if they forgo current consumption.

Nowhere in the *Barron's* article does it suggest that just maybe monetary policy might be a consideration in how the economy performs after what is expected to be a relatively soft second quarter.

Any discussion about the economy without reference to Fed policy is like bemoaning the shortage of available housing in New York City without any mention of rent control (which is exactly what the *New York Times* did yesterday).

DENIAL

The Fed may very well end up raising the federal funds rate another 50 basis points before it can call it quits. After all, a body in motion remains in motion until it is acted upon by a countervailing force. And a $9 trillion economy hurtling through space at a 6 percent rate in the three quarters ended in March doesn't lose half its momentum with a small nudge.

What's so interesting about the relationship with the Fed is that attitudes can run the full gamut in a short period of time yet always return to the same place.

In this cycle they've gone from denial last year (higher interest rates won't slow the New Economy) to acceptance after the Nasdaq lost one-third of its value in the spring (maybe they do matter) to grief (the Fed's overdone it) and back to denial (the Fed's done so let's get down and party).

POSTSCRIPT: *As it turned out, the second quarter of 2000 was the last hurrah for the U.S. economy. Even with inventory accumulation accounting for more than half the growth, real gross domestic product was hardly weak, rising an annualized 6.4 percent. It was the last strong quarter before a 0.5 percent decline in GDP in the third quarter and a recession in 2001.*

Is the Fed Irrelevant? Citizen Rubin Thinks So
——————— Aug. 9, 2000 ———————

IT WAS the best of times: Alan Greenspan at the helm of the Federal Reserve and Bob Rubin at Treasury. The relationship between the monetary and fiscal authorities was unusually warm and friendly.

The Rubin Treasury adopted a firm "no comment" policy on the Fed. The mood at the weekly breakfasts between the two most important economic policy-makers in Washington was described as open and amiable.

The fact that their 4½-year shared tenure coincided with the best economy in more than a generation probably contributed to the congeniality.

What a surprise it was, then, to learn that Rubin thinks the Fed's role in managing the economy is overrated.

In a June 27 interview with Charlie Rose, broadcast on PBS, Rubin said the following:

"There's an enormous tendency to overstate the role of the Fed in how our economic system works. If the Fed did absolutely nothing for the next two years, and if, in fact, inflationary forces started to assert themselves, then the bond markets would reflect that, and you would have the same constricting effect that you have if the Fed moves."

Every time I hear a comment like that, I have the same reaction: Why do we have a central bank? So that the U.S. can be part of the club, rubbing shoulders with other central bankers at the monthly Bank of International Settlements meetings? To provide a workplace for legions of academic economists?

VOODOO ECONOMICS

Earlier in the interview, Rubin told Rose that when he came to Washington in 1993, he found his previous experience on Wall Street—"an understanding of markets, some understanding of how economic matters worked"—relevant to his job as, first, the chairman of the president's National Economic Council, and then Treasury secretary from January 1995 to July 1999.

There is nothing in his assessment of the Fed's role to suggest he understands anything about how economic matters work.

"It's very hard to respond to that view," says Jim Glassman, senior economist at Chase Securities. "It's become folklore."

If the market is, as Rubin implies, its own central bank, "what's its agenda?" Glassman wonders. "What is it trying to achieve? Two percent inflation? Three percent inflation? The market's job is to price risk, not determine outcomes."

Rubin's assessment that short rates don't matter, that long-term interest rates equilibrate the economy on their own, is a holdover from the 1980s concept of the bond vigilantes. Any errant behavior on the part of the central bank and bond traders will hoist long-term interest rates and punish the economy accordingly.

EMPIRICAL EVIDENCE

Hasn't he done the analysis? If he did, he'd find that short-term rates beat long-term rates hands down, both in their correlation with economic activity and in their ability to influence it.

Ken Landon, senior currency strategist at Deutsche Bank in Tokyo, compared the two-year change in various interest rates with future growth in gross domestic product.

"The historical record clearly shows that rates at the short end of the yield curve have the closest correlation with the rate of economic growth," Landon says. "As you go out the curve, the correlation goes down." (Correlation describes the relationship between the movements in two series and does not imply causality.)

For example, the two-year change in the overnight federal funds rate has a negative 0.54 correlation with economic growth. That means 54 percent of the change in GDP growth can be explained by the change in the funds rate alone. The correlation is negative because a rise in rates has a depressant effect on GDP growth and vice versa. A perfect correlation is 1, in which case 100 percent of the movement in one series can be explained by the movement in the other.

Baa Minus

Moving out the yield curve, the correlation between future GDP growth and the change in 10-year and 30-year yields is –0.31 and –0.33, respectively.

Curiously, Landon found that the corporate bond rate has almost zero correlation with economic growth. For Aaa-rated corporates, the correlation is –0.19. For Baa-rated corporates, which Greenspan cites as a restraining or stimulating force on economic activity now that Treasury buybacks are distorting the sovereign yield curve, it's –0.09, which is close enough to zero for government work.

Regression analysis, which uses independent variables to explain a dependent variable (that is, establish causality), produces similar results.

"If all rates—long and short—are rising, it has a negative relationship to economic activity," says Bob Laurent, professor of economics and finance at the Illinois Institute of Technology's Stuart School of Business.

Most of the time, short and long rates move together. "But if you separate the two, if you hold the short rate constant and the long rate rises, it's actually positive for the economy," he said.

Executive Bob

How can higher long-term rates be positive? With any price—an interest rate is nothing more than the price of credit—there are different implications depending on whether the increase is coming from the supply side or the demand side.

Think about it. Let's say interest rates are rising along the entire yield curve with the exception of the federal funds rate. You can be pretty sure that the Fed is passively pumping out additional reserves—increasing the money supply—to meet the banking system's increased demand, which is how it works when the central bank targets an overnight rate.

In this case, monetary policy is expansionary. Mr. Greenspan used this sort of Wicksellian argument early in the year to justify raising rates, suggesting that holding the short rate down would be inflationary.

It's a good thing Trader Bob Rubin went to Citigroup and not to the Fed (his name still comes up as a possible candidate for Fed chairman under a Democratic administration). Everybody's favorite Treasury secretary, Rubin has been able to get away with such economic nonsense as claiming the U.S. contribution to the International Monetary Fund "doesn't cost the taxpayer a dime." (If there's no cost, why not contribute a lot more?)

At least we now know that he thinks the Fed is redundant. Hopefully he's pushing paper at Citigroup and leaving macroeconomic analysis to the research department.

The Bubble, or This Time
Really Is Different!

ASSET BUBBLES have been around since folks went gaga over tulip bulbs in 17th-century Holland.

While the nature of each bubble varies—it may be financial assets, real estate or some exotic item that the public will pay seemingly any price to own—they all have a few things in common.

First and foremost, they end badly. At some point, there's no greater fool to take an overpriced asset off the last buyer's hands. The game is up. Reality sets in. Prices collapse.

Second, because human nature doesn't change, the reaction to bubbles is pretty consistent over time. The whole process from onset of bubble to residue of bust is not unlike the five stages terminally ill patients go through—denial, anger, bargaining, depression, acceptance—as set out by the late psychiatrist Elisabeth Kübler-Ross in her 1969 book, *On Death and Dying*.

Bubbles borrow from the same lexicon. The language used to describe and deny the bubble in technology and Internet stocks in the late 1990s was no different than that heard in the late 1920s.

In fact, if you changed a few names and dates, and substituted "Nasdaq" for "Radio" (Radio Corporation of America, the speculative darling of the 1920s), John Kenneth Galbraith's *The Great Crash: 1929* would read like a history of the late '90s—complete with scandals that came to light after the bubble burst.

The first reaction to intimations a bubble may exist is denial. "This time is different," the believers intone.

In the 1990s, investors didn't care if a company had any "E" (earnings). The concept behind the business was enough to justify the "P" (price).

It's one thing to buy a stock because the price is going up; people do that every day. An entire industry of commodity-trading advisers uses black-box models specifically designed to buy "momentum."

It's another thing to convince yourself that momentum signifies value.

During the high-flying tech bubble, investors who never would have looked at food-retailing stocks decided that selling groceries (a low-margin business) on the Internet (a low-margin medium) was a brilliant idea.

Modern-day bubbles in economies with developed financial systems are fueled by excess money and credit creation. Yes, people act crazy. But without the complicity of the central bank, asset bubbles would be deprived of their needed fuel.

If too much money flows into goods and services and pushes up the price level, it's called inflation. When that same money chases financial assets or real estate, it should be a clue that monetary policy is too easy.

That puts central bankers in the uncomfortable position of having to determine whether asset prices are divorced from the fundamentals. There's no way a handful of folks setting the nation's monetary policy in Washington, D.C., have better information about asset prices than the thousands of risk-takers putting their money on the line every day in the market. And they admit it.

While former Supreme Court justice Potter Stewart's definition of pornography—"I know it when I see it"—may hold for asset bubbles as well, it provides no guidance for an ex-ante response.

Federal Reserve Chairman Alan Greenspan maintains that the best tactic is to respond aggressively when the bubble bursts.

European central bankers aren't so sure. For them, bubble prevention remains the most effective cure.

✺   ✺   ✺

D E N I A L

This Time Is Different—It's Always Different

———————— Dec. 28, 1999   ————————

IT HAPPENS in every business cycle. An asset or asset class gets over-valued—exactly which one varies—and the reaction is always the same.

Normally sane financial market professionals proclaim that "this time is different." Toss out the old rulebook; it's a brand New Era.

No less a seer than Federal Reserve Chairman Alan Greenspan often remarks that he has seen many so-called New Eras come and go (go being the operative verb here).

What's different this time around is the rationale for the share prices of start-up Internet companies that have no earnings, and in some cases no revenue, yet trade at ridiculous multiples.

Listen closely to the talking heads on the business news programs. They are starting to believe their own rhetoric.

"Interest rates don't matter."

"Interest rates are just a cost of doing business."

"Interest rates won't slow the New Economy down."

"Tech stocks are impervious to higher interest rates."

While interest rates may not matter when it comes to financing—venture capital is fighting to get in the door—they do matter when it comes to valuing future cash flows, better known as earnings.

Based on that dinosaur known as the dividend discount model, a company's value is nothing more than the present value of the expected future cash flows.

REALITY CHECK

"Unless you have permanently eliminated traditional valuation models from the equation, somewhere out there revenues are going to have to validate what's inherent in the stock price," says Bob Barbera, chief economist at Hoenig & Co. in Rye Brook, New York.

Barbera says that if you do a back-of-the-envelope calculation for many of the flying-high-without-earnings stocks and give the companies the benefit of the doubt (rosy assumptions about growth and margins), "there are going to be a great many disappointments. "There aren't enough FedEx trucks to deliver all the stuff they'd have to sell to justify the price."

Alas, sane voices, along with value investors, have been left in the dust. It's as if the enthusiasts got stuck in the first stage of psychiatrist Elisabeth Kübler-Ross's five stages of dying, introduced in her 1969 book, *On Death and Dying*.

Kübler-Ross found that people diagnosed with a terminal illness progress through a series of emotions to cope with the grief: denial, anger, bargaining, depression and acceptance.

It's one thing to buy momentum, to buy a stock price rather than a company (the opposite philosophy to the one espoused by legendary investor Warren Buffett). It's quite another thing to convince yourself that it's something other than what it is.

Sellers Vanquished

How is it that the Nasdaq has rallied almost 50 percent since mid-October, registered 59 record closes this year and produced an 86 percent return in 1999?

"We've completely destroyed the speculative seller," Barbera says. "He's gone bankrupt over the last four years."

The traditional seller, comprised of the public and institutional money managers, has been absent as well.

"More than 'In God We Trust,' the public swears by 'buy the dip,'" Barbera says. At the same time, "money managers have decided, if we go over the waterfall, we are going together. The last guy to say he was raising cash—Jeff Vinik—was dead in a year."

Denial on the part of investors. Fear on the part of sellers. The only thing missing is overly enthusiastic lending on the part of the banks.

Banks are renowned for over-extending credit, based on the theory that the underlying collateral can never go down. They did it with the oil and gas industry in the 1970s and 1980s, emerging markets (at least twice), real estate, junk bonds and hedge funds.

Eager Beavers

Now banks are using lending relationships with non-investment-grade companies to secure plum—and lucrative—underwriting deals. Last week it was reported that Chase Capital Partners, the venture capital arm of Chase Manhattan Bank, was aggressively targeting the equity business of non-investment-grade companies.

As long as the underlying collateral rises in price, everything is fine. Chase's start-up ventures accounted for 17 percent of its profit this year, according to Chief Executive William Harrison.

If some of these small companies were to go belly up, the macroeconomic effect would be small. It's when the loans go bad that things get dicey.

"As long as it's an equity-related phenomenon, it's fine," observes Paul DeRosa, a partner at Mt. Lucas Management Co. "If these companies have debt outstanding, when the stocks crash and several banks have exposure, that's where the real threat lies."

THEMES AND VARIATIONS

Bad loans and dysfunctional banks are what crippled the U.S. economy in the early 1990s and what have kept Japan depressed for the better part of a decade.

History repeats itself, not in exactly the same way each time but in a similar enough manner to make one pay attention to the cautionary signs.

Maybe this will turn out to be a New Era where companies' prospects are so bright as to justify even the most inflated expectations for revenues and earnings. On the other hand, maybe what we're seeing is momentum so strong that it has scared off all the sellers and offered up greater and greater fools that are always willing to pay a higher price.

Evaluating the Tech-Stock Interest-Rate Nonsense

———— March 15, 2000 ————

DAY AFTER DAY, some equity strategist goes on TV to declare that higher interest rates don't matter when it comes to technology stocks.

These cutting-edge start-ups have so much venture capital chasing after them, the thinking goes, that the idea of borrowing money has never even crossed these Young Turks' minds.

Borrowing costs are only one of the many direct and indirect channels through which interest rates affect a company's share price—probably the least important one.

Starting with the old model, a company's stock price is determined by earnings expectations plus a risk-free interest rate, which is used to discount future earnings streams, plus an adjusted risk premium.

In this so-called dividend discount model, the interest rate clearly matters but not because of the company's actual cost of borrowing.

"The idea that the value of future earnings streams are impervious to higher interest rates is a crock," says Steve Wieting, an economist at Salomon Smith Barney. "The effect of a change in interest rates on the cost of a firm is trivial compared to the idea that the value of those future earnings streams depends on alternative investments, opportunity costs and tolerance for risk."

Many technology companies have no earnings; smaller losses than the prior quarter's are considered a clean bill of health in the quarterly earnings report. By all rights, interest-rate increases should be more devastating to stocks whose profits are over the horizon.

LESS THAN ZERO

"For any given cash flow, a higher discount rate makes the present value of the cash flows worth less," says Tom McManus, portfolio strategist at Banc of America Securities. "In bond terms, the duration of the cash flows is longer. The effect of higher interest rates should be greater."

Should be, but isn't. Since the Federal Reserve started raising interest rates on June 30 of last year, the technology-heavy Nasdaq Composite Index has appreciated by 70.6 percent while the Dow Jones Industrial Average is down 7.7 percent, with losses pared after today's 3.3 percent rally. Dow cyclical stalwarts like International Paper Co. and DuPont are down 27 and 26 percent, respectively, in the last nine months.

There is one more channel, probably the most important one, through which interest rates affect a company's stock price: "the presumed sensitivity of demand for a company's product," McManus says. "No matter how good the management of a company, they have no control over demand as affected by interest rates."

NEW NEW THING

The fact that he said "presumed sensitivity of demand" suggests the perceived rules may be changing in this area, too.

"There's a feeling that tech companies are immunized to the increase in interest rates because tech has become an 'absolute must-have,' the corporate equivalent of spending on staples," he says.

In other words, the demand for technology is inelastic. Cheap or expensive, companies gotta have it. Gas, food and tech. A new "ex" category for the CPI.

At least that's a better argument than claiming interest rates don't matter because tech companies don't borrow.

Still, there's something wrong with the underlying assumption here, too.

"Do people really think that demand for technology is inelastic to income and to interest rates?" asks Susan Hering, chief economist at Carr Futures in Chicago. "The perfectly inelastic good is relatively rare."

History does not support the notion that technology companies ride through a slowdown unscathed.

'AT THE MARGIN'

"In every slowdown, the Nasdaq slipped along with the S&P 500," Hering says. That was true in the early 1980s, in the run-up to the 1990 recession, and even in 1994, when aggressive Fed tightening created the fear of slower growth (the reality of slower growth materialized for only a short spell in the first half of 1995).

"Maybe that logic is valid if a product is brand-new, and every company has to have it because if they don't the competition will get the edge," Hering says. "But budgets shrink in economic downturns."

What's more, business isn't the only source of high-tech demand. Mummy isn't going to buy Junior the latest Palm XXII when her hubby is pawning the Porsche to meet margin calls.

That old axiom—economics operates at the margin—keeps drifting through my mind. Every sector of the economy, every company, every source of demand doesn't have to slow in order for economic growth to slow. All it takes is some browning around the edges.

The tech bulls are not convinced. History won't convince them. Logic or reason won't. Guess they'll just have to witness it firsthand.

❖   ❖   ❖

A N G E R

This Time Is Different, Except It's the Same

———————— Dec. 4, 2000 ————————

THE NEW ECONOMY was supposed to have a new set of rules. Interest rates didn't matter. Technology spending was compulsory, not cyclical. The economy's top line was to have no impact on corporate America's bottom line.

Alas, it turns out that the New Economy doesn't dance to a different drummer after all. Instead, it rumbas and cha-chas to the same beat as the Old Economy, only at a different speed and intensity.

Where are all the New Economy prophets now? In the first quarter of 2000, when the Nasdaq Composite Index was trading in the rarified atmosphere above 5000, the tech gurus said higher interest rates would have no impact on start-up companies. Why? With so much venture capital in hot pursuit, the idea of borrowing money the old-fashioned way—paying a rate of interest for it—was strictly for wimps.

Internet CEOs paraded through the Bloomberg newsroom, waxing poetic about their business plans, touting a new metric, "ROV" (return on vision). A sock puppet was going to make pet-food sales on the Internet a lucrative proposition for Pets.com Inc., which closed up shop last month and went into voluntary receivership.

Vision? Yes. Return on it? Hardly.

THEORY OF RELATIVITY

"The grocery business is the lowest-margin business extant," says Bob Barbera, chief economist at Hoenig & Co. in Rye Brook, New York. "With dog food, if you double bag it you lose money."

Then there was Garden.com, which had the misfortune of being on the right side of the tulip trade some 360 years too late.

Don't forget Priceline.com, a name-your-own-price ticket seller, which at its peak had a market capitalization of $17.4 billion and is now valued at $374 million. "A reseller of plane tickets had a market cap three times that of American Airlines," Barbera says.

During the frenzied technology rally in the fourth quarter of 1999 and first quarter of this year, reason was tossed aside in favor of hype. The stable of technology analysts pooh-poohed the idea that higher interest rates mattered when by all rights they should matter even more for a company with no earnings. That's because the present value of any future earnings stream falls when the interest rate rises—especially when there is no stream and no earnings to discount.

STAGES OF GRIEVING

Denial begat anger begat bargaining. Okay, so maybe higher interest rates do matter when it comes to valuing a stock price, but tech spending would be untouched by higher interest rates. So important was productivity-enhancing information technology to a company's bottom line, in fact, that businesses would keep investing even when demand in the economy at large slowed.

According to this line of thinking, technology spending is as inelastic as gasoline and food purchases in the short run.

History doesn't support the premise that whatever the technology in vogue at the moment, it can rise above the vagaries of the business cycle. Rather, every slowdown has seen the technology-heavy Nasdaq slide and demand slow.

Only grudgingly did the grieving process move through denial to anger and bargaining. The economy could and would slow, along with sales, but companies would produce strong profits by cutting costs.

One by one, industry leaders in the area of computers, semiconductors, fiber optics, networking and telecommunications equipment reported or warned of slower revenue and profit growth in the second half of this year and into next year. Bargaining gave way to depression.

GURU-ITIS

Last summer, influential Morgan Stanley Internet analyst Mary Meeker conceded that most online companies were overvalued, but 13 of the 15 companies she follows are rated "outperform."

On April 28, Merrill Lynch's Internet wunderkind, Henry Blodget, predicted the share price of online retailer Amazon.com would rise 60 percent in 12 months. While there are still five months left to go, Amazon has fallen 50 percent since then.

Clearly acceptance is still a ways away.

Unlike some Old Economy companies like autos, technology is unique unto itself in that the relationship between the rise in stock prices and the rise in technology spending goes beyond correlation, Barbera says. There's causation.

"When auto stocks go down, it's a forecast of weaker sales, but the stock price doesn't influence a potential customer's purchase," he says. "With tech, lower stock prices aren't merely a forecast of slower spending but the cause of it."

With access to capital through initial public offerings or junk bond sales denied or the price too costly, technology companies have less to spend on—what else?—technology.

"They eat their own," Barbera says.

B A R G A I N I N G

Tech Gurus Were Just Products of Their Times
—————— March 21, 2001 ——————

IT'S BLAME-GAME TIME.

You may have noticed a slew of articles recently aimed at deconstructing the Nasdaq bubble—all with the benefit of hindsight (more than 3000 Nasdaq points of it). The same folks who dutifully reported the Internet gurus' every prognostication, documented every untenable new idea—selling potting soil or pet food on the Internet—have seen the light.

The Sunday *New York Times* devoted its entire business section, not to mention a front-page article, to the busted technology bubble and the latter-day prophets. All of a sudden the newfangled measures for valuing stocks, known as "metrics" in the trade, are under the microscope. Things like "Web-site traffic," "engaged shoppers" and "leading mind share" are now exposed for the hokum they always were.

On CNN, Robert Shiller (author of *Irrational Exuberance*) and James Glassman (author of *Dow 36,000*) accused each other of being irresponsible (not irrational). Henry Blodget, Merrill Lynch's wunderkind Internet analyst, was mentioned in 796 news stories in the first quarter of 2001 compared with 297 citations in the first quarter of 2000. Clearly reporters have come to bury Blodget, not to praise him.

Alas, Blodget and Mary Meeker, Morgan Stanley Dean Witter's "Queen of the Net," are coming under attack from all quarters. Which just goes to prove that markets—and reputations—go down faster than they go up.

Are the messengers really to blame? The Blodgets and Meekers of the world were just products of their time. If they didn't exist, we would have created them. Investors wanted encouragement. They wanted validation. They wanted to be told they could get as rich as Croesus by chasing dumb ideas and stocks of companies with no business plan and no viable way of ever earning a profit.

PERFECT COMPETITION

The Internet, with its low barriers to entry, was the great democratizing medium. Information was available to everyone. This was almost perfect competition as described in the textbooks.

At the same time, these companies were supposed to offer huge prospects for growth and profits. The business model mattered less than the dot-com domain name.

When the history of this era is written, one can only wonder what future generations of investors will think of some of today's great ideas, whose profit potential might have appeared limited in a more sober atmosphere:

• Pets.com, the defunct online pet-food retailer, learned the hard way that a gimmicky sock puppet was not the equivalent of a good business model. It blew through all its cash, only to learn that pointing and clicking for kibble was not a profitable business.

• TheGlobe.com, which describes itself as a "vibrant online community where millions of people around the world interact with each other around common interests and passions," saw its share price rise more than 600 percent, the biggest gain ever at the time, on the day after it went public in November 1998. If you build it—in this case, free home pages—they may very well come. But it doesn't ensure a profit.

• Webvan, the online grocer, tried to create a niche in a low-margin business in a low-margin medium (the Internet), only to see its shares lose 98 percent of their value since the high in December 1999. Webvan acquired HomeGrocer.com last year and has yet to discover any economies of scale in the Internet grocery business.

• Garden.com, an online gardening supply merchant, wanted to become the one-stop shopping center for the 67 million folks who get down on their hands and knees and dig in the dirt. The "attractive demographics," as described in a research report, did nothing for profitability. The company closed up shop in November 2000, a little more than a year after going public, and sold off its inventory, presumably including a bunch of worthless tulip bulbs.

• NetJ.com, a company that admitted it "has had no current business for some time" and "no day-to-day operations up to the present time" in a filing with the Securities and Exchange Commission, got out of the no-current-business business. Last year it acquired Global Tote Limited, which develops interactive horse racing and ancillary betting via satellite and the Internet. While it was finding itself, the stock fell 96 percent to 30 cents.

Whatever the tech gurus were saying about the growth and profit prospects for these and other companies, there was little caveat emptor on the part of the buyer. We live in a litigious society where if someone is harmed, someone has to pay. At a minimum, we demand our messengers perform their mea culpas.

The Public May Get More Than It Bargained For

——————— July 24, 2002   ———————

ENACT NEW LAWS. Write new regulations. Send Ken Lay to jail. Put the Rigases in the stockade. Drop Martha Stewart into a boiling pot of her homemade pot au feu. Sack Treasury Secretary Paul O'Neill. Bring back former Treasury Secretary Bob Rubin.

This is supposedly what the public is demanding to restore its faith in Corporate America and the stock market. Our elected and appointed officials are happy to oblige, competing with one another to see who can do more, rushing new legislation through Congress at a breakneck pace, with little regard for the long-term impact on the economy.

"The August recess is supposed to start next week, and Congress is fervently writing hundreds of pages of regulation this week that should result in sweeping changes in how corporations are regulated," says Jim Bianco, president of Bianco Research in Chicago. "Congress is more interested in scoring political points than solving problems."

The Bush administration—and its economic team in particular—is getting pilloried for its lack of leadership. The *Orlando Sentinel* called for Secretary O'Neill's resignation in a Tuesday editorial titled "Where's Paul?" criticizing the Treasury secretary for traveling to unpronounceable Eastern European countries when the markets were coming apart.

ET Phone Home

It's not clear exactly what O'Neill's presence on U.S. soil would have done to prevent individual investors from withdrawing their money from mutual funds or to encourage institutional investors to end their buyers' strike. What is clear is that appearances are more important than reality. The Treasury announced today that O'Neill would delay by one week his trip to Brazil, Uruguay and Argentina because Congress is close to completing legislation on corporate accountability, trade promotion authority, and homeland security, all important to the president's economic agenda.

There is a natural instinct in bad times to find someone to blame for the whole mess and to serve up a sacrificial lamb. But a carcass isn't the answer.

"This belongs in the slaughter-a-fatted-calf school of public policy," says Tom Gallagher, political economist for International Strategy & Investment in Washington, D.C. "Maybe at some primal level this works, but it's hard to take seriously."

Contrary to the general impression that strong policy-makers create strong markets, the truth is that "strong markets create the impression of strong policy-makers," Gallagher says. Sacking the Treasury secretary would only make the administration look as if it were panicking, he says, especially if the market continued to cascade lower following the resignation.

Who's on First?

Is this what the investing public really wants? The public may think it wants more rules and regulations, but that's just a smokescreen for its real desire: for the bleeding to stop.

Recent opinion polls offer contradictory findings on that subject. In the latest *Wall Street Journal*/NBC News poll conducted July 19–21, 63 percent of respondents said the president and Congress should not pass new laws but instead should focus on enforcing existing laws and investigating and prosecuting violators. Only 33 percent said new laws and regulations were needed.

In response to a similar question, 36 percent said regulators would go too far and impose restrictions on business that will hurt the economy, while 59 percent said they wouldn't go far enough. (Do I have this straight: A majority of Americans think we don't need new laws, and that regulators won't go far enough?)

Both Ways

During bad times—the major stock indexes are posting double-digit declines this month alone, some 2½ years into the bear market—the public wants the government to do something. On some level, Americans would like the government to guarantee our investments, deliver double-digit returns on our stock portfolios, even ensure that our 401(k) nest eggs are intact when we retire. We want the upside to be unlimited, and we want to be protected from losses. (In other words, the government should write a put on the Standard & Poor's 500 Index.)

We want limited government in good times and activist government in bad times. We want free capital markets except when they behave poorly. We want to be free to choose but not free to lose.

Maybe what we really want is for the government to intervene to boost the stock market, in the same way that the governments of Hong Kong and Taiwan do. (Some large hedge funds are convinced the Federal Reserve buys S&P futures when things get too dicey.)

Just one question: Does the public want the tax increases necessary to pay for all the protection it putatively wants?

✲ ✲ ✲

D E P R E S S I O N

Who's to Blame for the Stock Market Bubble?
———————— July 30, 2002 ————————

WITH CONTROL of both houses of Congress up for grabs in November's midterm election, Democrats and Republicans are trying to use the burgeoning corporate accounting scandals to score points with voters.

The Democrats are blaming the Republicans, long identified as the party of big business, for their hands-off approach to the economy. Someone should have been minding the store a bit better, the Dems say.

The Republicans are pointing their finger at the Democrats. After all, the shenanigans happened on former president Bill Clinton's watch. The crooks may have been exposed during Bush's term, but the incentives to lie and cheat were spawned by Big Bad Bill, according to GOP spinmeisters.

So who's the real culprit? Here's a brief summary of the blame-game candidates:

1. Blame George W. Bush. The president, with an MBA from Harvard and a good ol' boy's degree from the Institute of Texas Oilmen, was a pal of former Enron chairman and CEO Ken Lay, the poster boy for sleazy accounting. (Ken Lay was the biggest contributor to Bush's Texas gubernatorial campaign.)

Bush said he'd run the government like a corporation, staffing his administration with former CEOs of Fortune 500 companies. Managerial acumen may have been a strong selling point early in Bush's four-year term. In the wake of all the scandals, it's become something of an albatross, with business now synonymous with sleaze in the public's mind.

Unshackling business from excessive regulation may be a traditional Republican point of view, but the Telecommunications Act of 1996, which exposed local phone companies to competition, predated Bush. Besides, deregulation is not open season to commit fraud.

Bush didn't cause the corporate scandals any more than, well, his predecessor did. Which brings us to:

2. *Blame Bill Clinton.* The hanky-panky happened during his watch, the argument goes. This is almost as silly as blaming his successor for encouraging companies to bend or break accounting rules.

Conservatives like to intone about the moral climate of the Clinton White House, as if Enron's use of Special Purpose Entities had something to do with Clinton's use of a Special Purpose Intern.

Either corporate executives are moral people or they aren't. They didn't observe Clinton's personal behavior—lying under oath, for example —and decide to mimic it on a corporate level, fabricating phony revenue to inflate profits. If they did, they didn't know right from wrong in the first place.

Clinton is also accused of inadequate funding for the Securities and Exchange Commission, the securities market's watchdog. Appropriating money is Congress's job, so it's hard to blame lack-of-staffing issues on Clinton.

3. *Blame the public,* which bought into yet another get-rich-quick scheme. There's something to be said for this argument. Watching the stock price of technology companies with no earnings soar several hundred-fold, normally conservative investors abandoned their long-held principles of investing. Instead of diversifying, they moved their savings from balanced funds, which invest in stocks and bonds, into equity-only funds, into growth-company funds, and finally into technology-only funds.

"The public's to blame for suspending disbelief," says Paul Kasriel, director of economic research at the Northern Trust Corp. in Chicago.

Investors were just following analysts' recommendations....

4. *So blame the analysts,* whose loyalty in retrospect was with investment-banking clients, not with the customers/investors whom their research was intended to serve.

No one has any sympathy for analysts who told clients to buy a stock they were internally calling a dog. The Justice Department is investigating various analysts and their employers for possible fraud. Shooting the messenger appears justified.

On the other hand, the public heard what it wanted to hear, especially since it coincided with five consecutive years of double-digit stock market returns. No one cared about the accuracy of the message when the outcome was desirable.

So where does that leave us?

5. Blame the Federal Reserve. Now here's a criticism that holds significant merit. What many people fail to understand is that without the explicit or implicit cooperation of the central bank, the bubble couldn't have inflated.

True, a determination that a bubble exists is not something that can be made on one day by one person. At some point, however, the behavior of the market starts to lose touch with reality and mirrors past manias.

So why is the Fed in general and Chairman Alan Greenspan in particular to blame for the late 1990s stock market bubble? The Fed provided the tinder for the bubble, pumping out whatever reserves the banking system demanded to keep the overnight rate at its desired target.

Were there no central bank running a printing press, increased borrowing—by corporations to buy back their own stock, by individuals living high on the hog—would push up the cost of credit, or the interest rate. Certain investments would no longer be viable, and individuals would be induced to save more.

"They were never viable to begin with," argues Bob Barbera, chief economist at Hoenig & Co. in Rye Brook, New York, who thinks "we all worked hard to create the kind of bubble we had in the late 1990s. Animal spirits took us to excess."

That said, by the middle of 1997, the Fed made a decision to look the other way.

"Rather than regard the stock market as increasingly speculative, the Fed saw it as indicative of a change in the underlying dynamics of the economy," Barbera says. "It was not a growing bubble but a Brave New World."

Not everyone is as generous in accusing the Fed of partial complicity in the bubble.

"The bubble and the granting of stock options required cheap credit to sustain them," Kasriel says.

Because the exercise of stock options leads to the dilution of the shares, companies borrowed money to buy back their own stock, Kasriel explains. "Had the Fed not artificially held down the rate of interest, the higher rate that would have prevailed would have dissuaded further borrowing. The Fed aided and abetted the bubble, and now we are seeing the aftermath."

FULL CIRCLE

That aftermath includes the deflating of the bubble—the Nasdaq lost three-quarters of its value between March 2000 and early last week—new laws and regulations for businesses and accountants, and a lost hope for privatizing Social Security.

Economists of various persuasions "argue that the Fed played a key role in bringing on the Great Depression, which was the catalyst for the lurch toward socialism," Kasriel says. "Now the Fed is responsible for preventing the privatization of Social Security."

Two weeks ago in the Fed's semiannual monetary policy report to Congress, Greenspan discussed the "infectious greed" infusing the business community.

"It is not that humans have become any more greedy than in generations past," Greenspan said. "It is that the avenues to express greed had grown so enormously."

He made sure the boulevards remained inviting.

A C C E P T A N C E

Greenspan Admits Bubble, Ducks Responsibility

———— Aug. 30, 2002 ————

HE KNEW it was a bubble all along.

In the traditional kick-off speech at Fed Camp, otherwise known as the Kansas City Fed's annual Jackson Hole Conference, Federal Reserve Chairman Alan Greenspan admitted the late 1990s stock market boom was a bubble. Then he washed his hands of the whole thing.

"Bubbles are often precipitated by perceptions of real improvements in the productivity and underlying profitability of the corporate economy," Greenspan said. "Investors then too often exaggerate the extent of the improvement in economic fundamentals. Human psychology being what it is, bubbles tend to feed on themselves."

And where do they get the material to feed on, pray tell? Why, from the friendly central bank, which responds to increased credit demand by pumping out enough reserves to prevent interest rates from rising.

Greenspan seems to be responding to recent criticism—minor but growing—of his generally accepted exemplary stewardship of the U.S. economy.

After all, who wants to be remembered in the history books as the Fed chairman who presided over the biggest asset bubble in the country's history? Much better to have "Maestro" in front of one's name, and a long list of accomplishments—bailouts of speculators under the guise of avoiding systemic risk—after it.

IT'S A DUCK

"The speech shows he's panicking," said Bill Fleckenstein, president of Fleckenstein Capital in Seattle. "He's admitted we've gone from bubble to bust. Pretty soon, people will figure out that, based on the two previous asset bubbles that have burst—the 1920s and Japan—we're only one-fifth of the way through resolving the problem."

Fleckenstein believes that however bad the post-bubble hangover, Greenspan has made the adjustment process worse by printing more money, which has to go somewhere. Currently, housing looks to be the beneficiary.

Greenspan has clearly been working on bubbles, both in and out of the bathtub, for a long time. He finally put a concise collection of his thoughts down on paper to share with the luminaries gathered in the Grand Tetons to ponder the pressing issues of the day.

"We at the Federal Reserve considered a number of issues related to asset bubbles—that is, surges in prices of assets to unsustainable levels," Greenspan said. "As events evolved, we recognized that, despite our suspicions, it was very difficult to definitively identify a bubble until after the fact—that is, when its bursting confirmed its existence."

RAH-RAH, SIS-BOOM-BAH

With one exception in 1996, for which he was widely booed, the Fed chief kept his suspicions to himself. In fact, he quickly became the head cheerleader for the New Economy, touting equity analysts' long-term forecasts as a justification for the lofty levels of stock prices. (Greenspan's faith in earnings forecasts is even more ludicrous in retrospect, with many analysts exposed as go-getters for investment-banking business.)

After combing through the data, Greenspan concluded that "nothing short of a sharp increase in short-term rates that engenders a significant economic retrenchment is sufficient to check a nascent bubble. The notion that a well-timed incremental tightening could have been calibrated to prevent the late 1990s bubble is almost surely an illusion."

What about the little-used Fed tool of changing margin requirements, which is the amount an investor is required to deposit in his brokerage account? (The firm lends him the rest to buy stocks.) Margin requirements have been at 50 percent since 1974.

PREEMPTIVE STRIKE

No doubt anticipating he would be reminded of that option, Greenspan preempted the criticism with a footnote in his speech, claiming that "changes in margins are not an effective tool for reducing stock market volatility."

Funny, anyone who reads the transcripts of Fed meetings, released with a five-year lag, would find that statement disingenuous. In response to concerns about a stock market bubble raised by Fed governor Larry Lindsey at the Sept. 24, 1996, meeting, Greenspan acknowledged that "there is a stock market bubble problem at this point" and even conceded there were some reliable remedies.

"We do have the possibility of raising major concerns by increasing margin requirements," Greenspan said. "I guarantee that if you want to get rid of the bubble, whatever it is, that will do it. My concern is that I'm not sure what else it will do."

The only fitting response is the Fox News Channel's motto: "We report, you decide."

Bubble Babble Is Even Sillier Three Years Later
———— March 10, 2003 ————

WHAT BETTER WAY to memorialize the three-year anniversary of the bubble that burst than to take a stroll down memory lane and revisit what folks were saying back then?

It was March 10, 2000, when the Nasdaq Composite Index hit an intraday record high of 5132.52 and closed at 5048.62. Bloomberg

News' U.S. stocks outlook column on that day was titled "Computer Shares Cheaper Than They Look." The argument was that while Dell Computer Corp. might appear to be more expensive than Coca-Cola Co. based on the stocks' price-to-earnings ratios, Dell's greater projected growth potential made the computer company the better buy.

Using the same metric and logic, semiconductor stocks, which had risen 50 percent since the start of 2000, were actually cheaper than drug stocks, according to the story. A portfolio manager said technology stocks were the place to be for the short and long term.

He might have specified very, very short term. The Nasdaq started its descent the very next trading day and is now a quarter of its former self.

Projected growth turned out to be a poor predictor of both earnings growth and the stock price. Looking out a year from the peak, net income for semiconductor stocks in the Dow Jones Semiconductor Index fell 42 percent in the first quarter of 2001 compared with a year earlier, according to Thomson First Call. Pharmaceutical stocks in the comparable Dow Jones index saw profits rise 17 percent.

OLD/NEW ECONOMY

In the last three years, the Philadelphia Semiconductor Index has fallen 78 percent, while the Standard & Poor's Pharmaceutical Index is down a mere 9 percent.

The *Wall Street Journal's* "Heard on the Street" column on March 10, 2000, was wondering which sector would lead the way to Nasdaq 6000. Ruth Porat of Morgan Stanley Dean Witter was quoted as saying she expected Internet stocks to continue to lead (rather than lead the fall).

Friday, March 10, marked the end of the fourth losing week for the Dow Jones Industrial Average, which was down 13 percent year-to-date. The S&P 500 was down 5.1 percent while the Nasdaq was up 24 percent.

Analysts explained the divergence between old-line industrial stocks and new-era technology stocks as reflective of investor fears that higher interest rates would hurt the former. The Federal Reserve had raised the overnight interbank rate by 100 basis points between June 1999 and the Nasdaq peak on March 10, 2000. The Fed was to continue raising rates until May of that year, when the funds rate hit what was to be its cycle high of 6.5 percent.

Past Wasn't Prologue

In those heady times, equity strategists were touting the view that higher interest rates wouldn't hurt start-up companies because they didn't have to borrow. Venture capital was chasing every good and bad idea emanating from Silicon Valley.

The idea that interest rates play a role beyond the cost of borrowing —specifically, as a means of discounting future earnings to present value—got lost in the shuffle. And if you have no earnings, well, you do the math.

Despite all the disclaimers about past performance being no guarantee of future results, technology stocks' past became prologue during the bubble.

"As long as these areas are promising a growth rate superior to the industrial-type stocks, this trend will continue," Ned Riley, chief investment strategist at State Street Global Advisors, told Bloomberg News.

Tech Only

"Promising" would seem to be the operative word.

Then there's the hyperactive Jim Cramer, poster boy for technology stocks, hedge fund manager and journalist turned CNBC talk-show host. In a Feb. 29, 2000, keynote address to the 6th Annual Internet and Electronic Commerce Conference and Exposition, Cramer advocated buying 10 stocks, including Ariba Inc., Inktomi Corp., VeriSign Inc. and Veritas Software Corp., that were enhancing the "Web economy, the only economy that matters."

"Most of these companies don't even have earnings per share, so we won't have to be constrained by that methodology for quarters to come," said Cramer, who predicted another record year for the Nasdaq in 2000.

Why bother with those old-fashioned methods for analyzing companies, such as the ratio of the stock price to book value, or the net value of the underlying assets? Ten days from the peak of the biggest bubble in stock market history, Cramer was as entranced as the rest of them.

Even the Maestro

No discussion of the bubble would be complete, of course, without reference to someone who didn't just participate in it but had a hand in its creation. Fed chairman Alan Greenspan delivered a speech on March 6, 2000, extolling the revolution in information technology and predicting no end to the returns on investment.

"The fact that the capital spending boom is still going strong indicates that businesses continue to find a wide array of potential high-rate-of-return, productivity-enhancing investments," Greenspan said. "And I see nothing to suggest that these opportunities will peter out any time soon."

He wasn't alone. Three years later, investment is just beginning to recover, reinforcing the idea that the best cure for a bubble is prevention.

Do Asset Prices Belong in the Central Banker Toolkit?

—————— Nov. 13, 2003 ——————

WE CAN THANK better monetary policy for taking much of the volatility out of the business cycle over the past two decades. Recessions are fewer in number, shorter and shallower in nature, with Japan's lost decade of the 1990s the exception to the rule.

Central banks in developed countries have achieved price stability through either an implicit or explicit inflation target, obviating the need to slam on the brakes and cause a recession to "cure" inflation.

Reduced volatility in the real economy has gone hand in hand with increased volatility in asset markets. It's as if there's "a kind of moral hazard of economic policy-making: the more stable/predictable the economic environment, the more risk taking, investment, and innovation take place," writes Bob Keleher, chief economist at the Joint Economic Committee of Congress, in an April 2003 paper, "Monetary Policy and Asset Prices."

If financial imbalances and asset bubbles are occurring in low-inflation, stable economic environments, and if the size of asset markets relative to the economy has soared, then perhaps there is a role for asset prices in the conduct of monetary policy above and beyond their standard transmission mechanism function.

"From 1950 to 1982, housing was roughly equal to gross domestic product in the U.S.," says Joe Carson, head of global economic research at Alliance Capital Management. "Now it's 40 percent bigger than GDP. From 1965 to 1995, equity market capitalization was 50 percent of GDP. Now it equals GDP."

RECESSION DRIVERS

At the peak of the 1990s stock bubble in March 2000, the market value of U.S. stocks hit a high of 183 percent of GDP, according to Jim Bianco, president of Bianco Research.

The issue is not whether asset prices matter; they do. They create wealth for consumers and businesses and determine how capital is allocated.

The issue is whether central bankers should respond to perceived asset bubbles in the same way they react to inflation and other events that have the potential to destabilize the economy.

Consider that the last two recessions in the U.S. and the series of recessions in Japan in the 1990s were arguably the result of popped asset bubbles. In the U.S., the bubble was in real estate in the late 1980s/early 1990s and in the stock market in the late 1990s. Japan had a double whammy—overvalued real estate and equities—in the bubble economy of the 1980s.

MISALLOCATION OF CAPITAL

Residential real estate is booming in the U.S., and some analysts think stock prices have outrun the fundamentals yet again.

"Ignoring inflation in the asset markets and its potential influence on the allocation—and misallocation—of capital can have significant adverse macroeconomic consequences," Carson says.

Carson advocates using a broad price index, which includes a weighted average of real estate and stock prices in addition to consumer and producer prices, to assess the stance of monetary policy. Currently, the gap between the growth rate in his proprietary broad price index and the federal funds rate is the widest in 20 years.

One of the side effects of a rapid rise in asset prices is excessive debt accumulation—to finance even more asset accumulation, Carson says. "It is this misallocation of capital and rapid asset price inflation that's missed by the current analytical framework [for gauging inflation], creating the risk of another boom/bust cycle."

LACKING PRESCIENCE

In raising interest rates last week, both the Bank of England and the Reserve Bank of Australia noted a booming housing market and rapid credit growth.

All central bankers take asset prices into account, but only to the extent that they affect real output and inflation. They readily admit they don't have better information than the private sector does when it comes to diagnosing a bubble.

The main argument—and there are many—against responding to perceived asset bubbles is the most basic: Bubbles are difficult to identify in real time, except under the vaguest of doctrines established by the late Supreme Court justice Potter Stewart to define pornography ("I know it when I see it").

LOOSE DEFINITION

"Just because asset price misalignments are difficult to measure is no reason to ignore them," writes Steve Cecchetti, professor of international economics and finance at Brandeis University in Waltham, Massachusetts, and former research director at the New York Fed, in a May 9, 2002, *Financial Times* op-ed article. "If central bankers threw out all data that was poorly measured, there would be very little information left on which to base their decisions."

What about the squishy concept of the output gap, the difference between potential and actual GDP? The gap "is notoriously difficult to measure in real time, yet it remains an important input to central bank inflation forecasts," writes Kevin Lansing, senior economist at the San Francisco Fed in the bank's Nov. 14 *Economic Letter*, "Should the Fed React to the Stock Market?"

Another argument against a monetary policy response to asset prices is the lack of a "consistent relationship between changes in stock prices and changes in inflation," the JEC's Keleher writes.

CAVEAT EMPTOR

If the stock market has no reliable correlation to inflation, and low, stable inflation is what central banks care about as a means to the attainment of maximum sustainable growth, then maybe asset prices have no place in the central bankers' toolkit.

Where most economists agree is on the appropriateness of a monetary policy response once the asset bubble bursts.

"The biggest mistakes—in the case of Japan, for example—are what they did afterwards," says Frederic Mishkin, professor of banking and financial institutions at the Columbia Business School and a former New York Fed research director. "The focus should be on financial stability rather than the stock market."

Asset bubbles don't erupt involuntarily. In most cases, they are an outgrowth of excess credit creation, which originates with the central bank.

For example, the Fed lowered short-term rates by 75 basis points in the fall of 1998 to counteract the "seizing up" of financial markets. As it turned out, the seizing markets had zero effect on the economy. The Fed's largesse soothed the Nasdaq Composite Index to an 86 percent increase in 1999.

Maybe the issue isn't asset bubbles themselves but the policies and conditions that give rise to them. Those are the purview of the central bank.

Still Nonsense
After All These Years

NO TWO BUSINESS CYCLES are exactly alike. An expansion may benefit one region of the country or one sector of the economy more than another. A recession may differ in its depth and duration from the previous one.

Regardless of the dynamics, the same misguided economic analysis survives from one cycle to the next.

I've made an entire career out of exposing the nonsense that passes for economic analysis. Certain events trigger predictable responses from Wall Street's research departments, providing an equally predictable opportunity to recycle old columns, changing a few facts and figures to fit the specific circumstances. You'll see from the two columns in this chapter on "wage inflation," written four years apart, that some basic misconceptions never die; they just go into remission, only to flare up at a later date.

When readers ask me where I get ideas for my columns, I tell them I look and listen. I listen to the business news anchors and talking heads on TV. I read analysts' comments in the press. I keep an eye out for conventional wisdom wherever it exists.

I once got an idea for a presentation from a juicy piece of nonsense on TV. A business anchor said that the destruction wrought by Hurricane Andrew in 1992 would be great news for gross domestic product, as if destroying productive capacity makes any nation better off.

I'm pleased to report no evidence of destruction-is-good type analysis following the series of hurricanes that hit Florida in the fall of 2004 and the tsunami that devastated Southeast Asia a few months later.

Much of economics is common sense, especially if you get to the intuition behind the theory. Anyone with an inquisitive mind and a grasp of some basic concepts—supply and demand, for example—can see the flaws in what passes time and again for economic analysis.

Hurricane Sweeps Coast; Nonsense Sure to Follow

———————— Sept. 16, 1999 ————————

JUST AS SURE as Hurricane Floyd is sweeping the East Coast of the United States, a surge of nonsense on the economic and financial market impact of the storm is certain to follow.

Perhaps it's an appropriate time to preempt some of the forecasts of what a natural disaster means for the economy and the bond market.

While not all hurricanes are created equal—Floyd clocked in with 155-mile-an-hour winds but now looks to be packing far less punch than Hurricane Andrew did in 1992—the analysis will no doubt follow the tried-and-true formula.

The initial effect, economists will explain, is the loss of income, production and output. If a plant or factory is destroyed, employees can't very well report to work, perform their usual functions, turn out goods and get paid for their labor.

According to the economics textbooks, this qualifies as a supply shock, which is represented by a shift to the left in the supply curve and implies lower output and higher prices.

What's more, if regular distribution channels are disrupted, producers will have to pay more—and charge more—to ship merchandise less efficiently.

That's not how supply shocks are viewed by economists and traders, however. What they see is a loss of income, reduced spending, slower growth and, if things get bad enough, the potential for a dose of largesse from the Federal Reserve in the form of interest-rate cuts.

In other words, they see a demand shock where the initial and major impetus is a hit to supply. The Pavlovian response to acts of God is to buy short-term Treasuries.

This interpretation is not surprising, given Wall Street's preference for demand-side economics (driven by the models that have been predicting slower growth and higher inflation for the last three years).

TAX CUTS

Tax cuts inspire a similar reaction among bond traders. Just say "tax cut," and they think increased demand and higher inflation. The disinflationary benefits of tax cuts, which increase the incentives to work, invest and save, and elicit more output, fly by unnoticed.

By increasing the economy's productive potential—higher after-tax income entices more folks to enter the labor force, for example—tax cuts enable the economy to grow faster without generating inflationary pressures.

The same demand-side analysis is applied to a typical supply shock, whether it be a hurricane, earthquake or railroad strike. To be sure, those people in Florida and the Carolinas whose homes are destroyed by the hurricane may not splurge for a big family vacation to Vail at Christmastime. But in general they won't let their temporary hardship affect their overall spending.

That tendency to base spending decisions on an expectation of lifetime income rather than temporary income was articulated by the Nobel laureate in economics, Milton Friedman, as the permanent income hypothesis. The central idea is that people base their spending decisions on what they perceive to be their normal income. Increases and decreases in income that are viewed as temporary have little effect on their consumption, Friedman found.

BORROW

People attempt to maintain a fairly constant standard of living despite temporary setbacks and windfalls. Toward that end, if their regular source of income is disrupted, they will borrow. Increased borrowing means higher interest rates, all things equal.

While the short-term effect of Hurricane Floyd is open to dispute, there is general agreement on the longer-term effect. What was destroyed today will be rebuilt tomorrow. Any subtraction from gross domestic product growth in the third quarter will be added back in the fourth quarter and early next year.

But don't make the mistake of thinking that acts of God are good for the economy. I recall a comment by a business news anchor following Hurricane Andrew in 1992 that gave me the intro for a speech I was preparing. The anchor claimed that Andrew was "great news for GDP" going forward, given all the home building that was certain to take place.

DESTROY TO CREATE?

Great news? If it's such great news, why sit around waiting for natural disasters to strike? Why not bomb our own cities?

After a hurricane, housing starts will increase, but there won't be more net new homes.

After a hurricane, industrial output will increase, but it won't add to the nation's capital stock.

This is a rebuilding effort. We have to use scarce resources just to get back to square one—where we were before the hurricane struck.

So, please, the next time someone tells you a hurricane is a boon to GDP growth, please suggest that he torch his own home and business.

Those Looney Economic Theories Are Proliferating

——————— March 27, 2000 ———————

IT JUST isn't working. That old interest-rate medicine, delivered in a slow, intravenous drip, is not sedating the patient.

What's scary for anyone with even a soupçon of contrarian instinct in her is that everyone seems to have adopted this view after five 25-basis-point rate increases in the federal funds rate in nine months. Even the spontaneous-slowdown school has done a 180-degree wheelie. Not only is the Federal Reserve ineffective in slowing the U.S. economy but its gradualist approach may actually be fueling the boom.

Come again? This is like the one or two yahoos on the Bank of Japan's monetary policy board who vote for higher interest rates to increase the interest income of pensioners.

One suspects that the folks advocating the impotent-policy view learned somewhere along the line that monetary policy operates with a lag of anywhere from six to 18 months. I have no idea what empirical study produced that axiom, but it is repeated often enough by Fed officials that they must think it's accurate.

Economists have underestimated the strength of the U.S. economy for the last four years. It makes perfect sense that the degree of monetary restraint needed to derail the momentum will also be greater than people expected.

Patience. Why leap to the conclusion that interest rates don't/won't work? Remember all the warnings in the early 1990s that low interest rates weren't going to stimulate the economy? The federal funds rate was lowered from $9\frac{7}{8}$ percent to 3 percent in 24 separate moves. It stayed at 3 percent for 16 months from the end of 1992 to early 1994, to a chorus of cries that the Fed was "pushing on a string," which has something to do with that fallacious Keynesian notion of a liquidity trap. (Japan's malaise during the entire 1990s was similarly misdiagnosed as a liquidity trap when in reality it was a credit crunch, an inability of the banking system to lend.)

HALF-CROCKED THEORY

In fact, the 1990s boom may be more the doing of Alan Greenspan than of either Ronald Reagan or Bill Clinton.

Another loopy idea making the rounds is that the gradual, well-anticipated rate increases are giving the economy a chance to acclimate. Better to use surprise or the shock effect to achieve the desired results.

In this week's issue, the *Economist* magazine (the folks who brought you $5 oil right before prices took off) used the analogy of the frog and hot water.

"Pour boiling water on a frog and it will jump away; heat it up slowly in a pot of cold water, and it will die," the *Economist* writes.

The analogy is horribly misplaced. Expectations theory suggests that markets price in all available information immediately. If markets expect a rate increase in the future, they will adjust interest rates accordingly today. Investment decisions will be based on expectations about the future cost of credit. Lenders will demand a higher loan rate now if they expect their borrowing costs to be higher in the future.

THE SOONER THE BETTER

"It seems to me that if the rate increase is expected, it will operate sooner," says Bob Laurent, professor of economics and finance at the Stuart School of Business at the Illinois Institute of Technology. "If it's unexpected, it will delay the response."

Then there's the popular notion that the Treasury is working at cross-purposes to the Fed by paying down debt, thereby lowering market interest rates, especially those in the 30-year sector.

Whoa! One big credit customer steps back from the trough, and that's supposed to stimulate the overall economy? What's important is why rates are falling. The Treasury is borrowing less. It's a question of reduced demand for credit, at least from one entity.

WHY NOT EASE?

"If the government decides to spend more, everyone would agree that it's expansionary," Laurent explains. "Now the government is going to be borrowing and spending less, interest rates fall, and that's supposed to be stimulative? Ceteris paribus, it would have the effect of slowing the economy."

Is it just the economics profession that elects to make up such nonsense to explain something that doesn't appear to be working according to plan? Imagine if you went to a physician for elevated cholesterol levels, and the low-fat diet he prescribed didn't produce the desired result immediately. Would he recommend going back to a diet high in saturated fat?

Hey, maybe if raising rates isn't working, the Fed should think about lowering them.

'Wage Inflation' Should Just Die a Quiet Death

————— May 4, 2000 —————

WAGE INFLATION is one of those notions that financial market professionals toss around glibly all the time—even those who should know better.

There is no such beast as wage inflation. In fact, it's a misnomer. Inflation is defined as a general increase in the price level. Wages are the price of labor. Higher wages are higher wages. They're a symptom of inflation, not inflation.

Wages are just "another gauge of determining excess demand," says Jim Glassman, senior economist at Chase Securities. "There's this illusion—in the textbooks, in the economic profession—and this model that says labor costs drive inflation. That's because everything is viewed in terms of the NAIRU or Phillips Curve."

The NAIRU is the non-accelerating inflation rate of unemployment. It's an arbitrary level of unemployment below which inflation is supposed to accelerate. With every failure of inflation to accelerate when the unemployment rate dipped below 6 percent, 5.5 percent, 5 percent and 4.5 percent, the NAIRU-istas moved the goal posts rather than reexamine their theology.

The Phillips Curve is used to describe the perceived inverse relationship between the unemployment rate and wages. The fact that the Phillips Curve is now thought of as the relationship between unemployment and inflation suggests just how embedded the concept of wage inflation is.

PUSH-ME PULL-YOU

Wage-inflation aficionados subscribe to a "cost-push" model of inflation, which makes no sense even if you know no economics. The cost-push model argues that costs—specifically wages, which are the biggest input cost—rise, compelling firms to increase prices. It implies that businesses are dumb enough to hire someone and pay him more than his marginal revenue product, or the additional revenue earned.

"Why pay someone to reduce your profits?" asks John Ryding, senior economist at Bear, Stearns & Co. "It makes no sense."

The logic underlying the notion that changes in wages precede changes in prices is based on the Keynesian model, he says.

Students of the business cycle remain unconvinced. Wages aren't among the eight components in the Economic Cycle Research Institute's Future Inflation Gauge for the simple reason that they "aren't a good leading indicator of inflation," says Anirvan Banerji, director of research at the ECRI. "Wages lag."

The Keynesian model contrasts with Milton Friedman's description of how prices and wages interact. The way inflation works in Friedman's world is that an increase in the rate of money growth leads to an increase in spending, which encourages firms to increase output and employment. Selling prices adjust quickly. Ultimately, the worker realizes that all prices are rising and demands a higher wage.

ALWAYS AND EVERYWHERE

"Friedman used to say, labor by itself can't push up all prices," says Bob Laurent, a professor of economics and finance at the Stuart School of Business at the Illinois Institute of Technology in Chicago. "Prices are responding to an increase in demand, which is coming from the money stock change."

Laurent recalled a discussion during the 1973–1974 oil shock, when prices were going up because of a cutback in supply from the Middle East. Inflation, as measured by the consumer price index, rose from 3.4 percent at the end of 1972 to 12.1 percent at the end of 1974.

"Friedman wanted to know why the demand for other things hadn't gone down," Laurent says. "The central bank is the one that enables all prices to rise."

Friedman's contention that "inflation is always and everywhere a monetary phenomenon" is one of the few axioms economists agree on.

Anxiety over wage inflation was heightened following a report last week showing year-over-year compensation costs rising at their fastest pace in five years.

QUARTERLY NOISE

Today's report on productivity and unit labor costs did little to allay fears. News that non-farm business productivity rose a less-than-expected 2.4 percent in the first quarter was characterized as disappointing and given a thumbs-down by the bond market. The modest increase in output per hour worked hoisted unit labor costs by 1.8 percent in the first quarter following two quarterly declines.

These data are too volatile to view on a quarterly basis. For example, the last four quarters (starting with the first quarter of 2000 and working backward) saw non-farm productivity increase 2.4 percent, 6.9 percent, 5 percent and 0.5 percent.

Does anyone think the quarterly fluctuations reflect sudden structural changes in labor productivity?

Productivity has a strong cyclical component. It's no surprise that when real GDP growth dipped to 1.9 percent in the second quarter of 1999, productivity growth rose a dismal 0.5 percent.

The year-over-year results are impressive. Non-farm productivity growth rose 3.7 percent in the first quarter, matching the fourth quarter's pace, which was the fastest in seven years.

BAD FIT

Year-over-year unit labor costs—what it costs to produce one unit of output—rose 0.7 percent in the first quarter compared with a 0.6 percent increase in the fourth. In the four quarters ended with the first quarter of 1999, unit labor costs rose 2.4 percent.

"I'm not an inflation denier, but anyone taking you through the labor market to get there is barking up the wrong tree," says Ryding.

Even if one subscribes to the questionable cost-push model, with unit labor costs rising 0.7 percent and prices, as measured by the CPI, rising at 3.7 percent, there is absolutely no cost-push from wages to prices.

Still, economists will continue to debate the causality between wages and prices. Neither side will convince the other of the superiority of the argument. It's merely a question of preaching to the converted or being ignored by the faithful.

Costs Aren't the Cause of Higher Prices. Demand Is.

————————   June 4, 2004   ————————

NO ONE would argue with the idea that an economy can only produce what it has the capacity to produce, that output is circumscribed by land, labor and capital, the so-called factors of production.

It's also widely accepted that when the demand for goods and services exceeds the economy's ability to satisfy it, the result is higher prices (inflation).

So how did these rational constructs get translated into a theory like the NAIRU, or non-accelerating inflation rate of unemployment?

The idea behind the NAIRU is that there is some arbitrary rate of unemployment below which inflation will accelerate forever. It's based on the old Phillips Curve model of a trade-off between unemployment and wages. That the Phillips Curve somehow morphed into an expression of the inverse relationship between unemployment and inflation just goes to show the degree to which wages were viewed as the determinant of inflation.

The late 1990s, a period of fast economic growth and low unemployment and inflation, challenged the old assumptions about the level of the NAIRU: 6 percent, 5 percent, maybe 4 percent. It also called into question the concept itself.

As explained by former Federal Reserve governor Larry Meyer in his forthcoming book, *A Term at the Fed*, to be published July 6 by HarperBusiness, "If the unemployment rate falls below the NAIRU, there will be an 'excess demand' for workers. As a result, wages will start to rise more sharply. A faster pace of wage increases, in turn, will push up inflation."

ORDER OF THINGS

Meyer is an unabashed believer in the NAIRU—"a concept I'm attached to and that has attached itself to me"—despite its shortcomings.

"It's an imperfect proxy for excess demand" and "it's not useful if you don't know where it is and it changes," he says.

Yet the response to the NAIRU suggests it's about "as controversial as global warming," Meyer says.

One can understand why. Most discussions of the NAIRU (not necessarily Meyer's) make it sound as if producers, confronted with a tight labor market, passively pay up for labor, only to realize they can no longer sell their goods at a profit. So they raise their selling prices as a result.

That isn't how it works. Costs don't push prices up. Prices respond to an increase in demand, which is a response to an increase in the money supply.

PUSH-ME PULL-YOU

"Demand leads prices," says Jim Glassman, senior U.S. economist at J.P. Morgan Chase & Co. "Prices lead costs. Demand drives everything."

Profit-maximizing firms won't pay a worker more than his marginal revenue product, which is another way of saying he won't be paid more than his contribution to the business.

In the old days, when many industries were regulated and unions held more sway in the bargaining process, the idea was that higher costs pushed inflation up (hence, the designation "cost-push" inflation).

The thinking went something like this: Companies had to accept the wage demands of labor and marked up selling prices in response. That's "a misrepresentation of the process," Glassman says.

Workers in a global competitive marketplace understand their success is aligned with their companies' success.

A changing world doesn't change the role of wages. Wages are a price, specifically the price of labor. As such, they account for the lion's share of finished-goods prices.

KILL IT

Wages don't cause inflation any more than higher oil prices cause inflation. The central bank causes inflation by creating more money than the public wants to hold. Both wages and prices are manifestations of the inflation impulse.

Someone should put "wage inflation" out of its misery before it can strike again. Inflation is a general rise in the price level. While we can debate which measure best reflects the price level—a fixed basket of goods and services or the prices of the goods and services consumers buy in any given month, excluding the necessities of food and energy— labor costs are just another input in the equation.

Some of the old cost-push nonsense has crept back into today's thinking, thanks to a 1970s-like boom in commodity prices. Companies, confronted with higher raw-materials costs, are being forced to pass them along to their customers, or so the story goes.

NEW CHALLENGES

Commodity prices aren't levitating on their own. A synchronized rebound in global economic growth, combined with speculative demand for commodities such as oil because of fears of supply disruptions from the Middle East, has encouraged producers to raise prices. The rise in commodity prices is being fueled by the demand for finished goods.

Meyer, who is president of Meyer's Monetary Policy Insights, a division of St. Louis–based Macroeconomic Advisers, says his "beloved NAIRU" was widely challenged by his colleagues in his 5½ years at the Federal Reserve Board as inflation underperformed expectations based on an unemployment rate that dipped as low as 3.8 percent.

Now the tables have turned. Fed policy-makers are attempting to understand how inflation is accelerating with plenty of slack in the labor market and unit labor costs still falling on a year-over-year basis.

"All of a sudden, they're all believers in the Phillips Curve," Meyer says.

❉ ❉ ❉

Cockamamie Economics
Practiced the Daschle Way

————— Jan. 7, 2002 —————

ANYONE LISTENING to Democratic Senate Majority Leader Tom Daschle's speech on Friday came away with one of two impressions: 1) the speech was an opening volley in the 2002 congressional election —or in Daschle's own bid to unseat incumbent president George W. Bush in 2004; or 2) the guy is an idiot.

There was nothing about Daschle's economic analysis that made any sense. Flanked by the Democrats' icon of fiscal responsibility, former Clinton Treasury secretary Robert Rubin, Daschle said last year's 10-year, $1.35 trillion tax cut, with $75 billion of it coming in fiscal 2001, was "by far the largest factor" swallowing up the surplus.

First blunder. Let's move on.

"Not only did the tax cut fail to prevent a recession, as its supporters said it would, it probably made the recession worse," Daschle said.

The math on his first statement was a little fuzzy. His second notion was blurred beyond recognition. How a tax cut, a stimulus measure advocated by every branch of economics extant, can make a recession worse requires an explanation.

For that we go to Bob Rubin, the Dean of Upside-Down Economics. The cardinal principle of Rubinomics is that lowering the deficit is the key to economic growth, even if it means raising taxes. That theory is crazy enough to bring Lord Keynes back from the dead.

SHAKY FOUNDATION

The way things work in Rubin's world is that lower deficits lead to lower long-term interest rates, which stimulate investment and economic growth, further reducing the deficit.

Not to worry that he has things backwards. It's economic growth that reduced the deficit, not the other way around. The Clinton administration wasn't forecasting budget surpluses when it implemented its economic program in 1993. (Maybe the theory took several years to fully evolve.)

The surpluses came as a complete surprise. The federal budget went from a record $290 billion deficit in fiscal 1992 to a record $237 billion surplus in fiscal 2000 as tax receipts from five fruitful years of stock market gains poured into Treasury coffers.

Daschle said the dwindling surplus meant more government borrowing, "keeping long-term interest rates higher than they would have been," with adverse effects on consumer confidence, investment, spending and employment.

What High Rates?

That must be why the interest-rate-sensitive sectors of the economy are suffering! Housing plowed through the recession completely unfazed, helped by a decline in 30-year mortgage rates through early November. The Mortgage Bankers Association mortgage applications index for new home purchases hit an all-time high in late December. The refinancing index peaked in early November, just when interest rates turned up.

While December home sales haven't been reported yet, "2001 could turn out to be the best year in history for sales," says Michael Carliner, an economist at the National Association of Home Builders.

Economists are quick to remind us that there is no correlation between deficits and interest rates, a fact that seems to have eluded Daschle. What matters is the reason the deficit is widening or shrinking.

Inverse Correlation

The federal deficit widens in recession as the government increases transfer payments (unemployment compensation, welfare, food stamps, etc.) and tax receipts fall. Long-term interest rates tend to fall as the Federal Reserve lowers short-term rates to stimulate the economy. Long-term rates fell consistently from 1990 through 1993, the biggest deficit years.

The opposite is true in an expansion: Tax payments increase while government transfer payments fall. Rates tend to rise in periods of strong economic growth as the Fed reins in a booming economy.

"Japan has the world's lowest interest rates and the world's biggest budget deficit," said Alan Reynolds, a senior fellow at Washington's Cato Institute, a libertarian think tank.

As far as Daschle's accusations about the tax cut eating up the surplus are concerned, nothing could be farther from the truth.

"The slowdown in the economy is the single biggest factor in erasing the surplus," said Susan Hering, senior economist at UBS Warburg.

"There is no way you can pin the tax cut—$75 billion in 2001—on the move from a [projected] $313 billion surplus to a small deficit in 2002."

It's the Economy

Hering estimates economic effects—slower growth leading to lower tax receipts and higher government spending on unemployment compensation et al.—are responsible for $140 billion of the decline in this year's budget outlook from a $176 billion surplus (the Congressional Budget Office's projection in August) to a $10 billion deficit in 2002 (Hering's projection).

CBO is due to release updated budget projections later this month. Senate and House Budget Committee forecasts, reported yesterday in the *New York Times*, foresee something between a $15 billion deficit and a $1 billion surplus this year.

Anti-terrorist measures drained an additional $25 billion to $30 billion from this year's surplus, Hering says. Military spending is on track to rise 11 percent, the biggest jump since 1985.

Then there are the other assorted increases in discretionary spending happening in Daschle's own backyard. Congress has made avoiding the caps on discretionary spending an annual sport.

Spending Splurge

"Circumvention of spending caps, along with expenditures related to the events of Sept. 11, will push discretionary spending up a staggering $90 billion, or 14 percent, to $734 billion this year," said Chris Wiegand, an economist at Salomon Smith Barney. That would be the biggest increase since 1980.

If the spending caps put in place in 1997 and due to expire in 2002 had been adhered to, discretionary spending would total $549 billion in 2002, Wiegand said.

A direct casualty of the recession, tax revenues for the first three months of the new fiscal year are running $77 billion behind last year, adjusting for the deferral of the September corporate tax payment into October, Wiegand said.

After dissing the Bush tax cut, Daschle laid out an economic program of his own—including more tax cuts! His plan calls for a tax credit for companies that create new jobs and accelerated depreciation allowances for investment in plants and equipment, in addition to expanded unemployment and health-care benefits for the unemployed.

Given the vast gap between Daschle's statements about the vanishing surplus and the actual numbers, no wonder Brit Hume, managing editor at Fox News, had trouble containing himself during the panel discussion on "Fox News Sunday" yesterday.

"That speech that Senator Daschle made about the economy I hope was not circulated to high school economics students because it could cause a crisis in the confidence in the leadership in Congress if it did," Hume said. "I mean, he said things in there that were not only economically dubious, they're economically impossible."

If the Democrats are "going to run on nonsense economics this year, I think it can only help the Republicans," Hume added.

Taking a Look at Some of the Pent-Up Nonsense
———— March 4, 2002 ————

THE CONVENTIONAL WISDOM holds that the U.S. can't have a strong economic recovery because it didn't have a deep recession. Simply put, there is no pent-up consumer demand to impel spending.

No less an authority than Federal Reserve Chairman Alan Greenspan gave credence to that view when he presented the Fed's semiannual monetary policy report to Congress last Wednesday.

"Through much of last year's slowdown...spending by the household sector held up well and proved to be a major stabilizing force," Greenspan told the House Financial Services Committee. "As a consequence, although household spending should continue to trend up, the potential for significant acceleration in activity in this sector is likely to be more limited than in past cycles."

Most economists subscribe to the theory of a lack of pent-up demand, and there is something intuitively appealing about it. After all, if something doesn't go down, how can it bounce back?

In a Saturday *New York Times* story recapping the surprising 1.4 percent increase in fourth-quarter real gross domestic product (revised from a 0.2 percent gain) and 6 percent increase in consumer spending, Wells Capital Management senior economist James Paulsen was quoted as saying: "If nothing else, there soon won't be anyone left who needs anything."

FINITE UNIVERSE?

Is demand finite? With 94.4 percent of the labor force working, is consumer demand for restaurant meals, travel, entertainment, doctors, lawyers and insurance limited? What about the need or desire to trade in the five-year-old clunker for a shiny new SUV? Maybe it's time to upgrade the dishwasher, improve the sound quality of the stereo system and install one of those 50-inch TV sets.

"Estimates of demand are not a fixed number," says Joe Carson, an economist at Alliance Capital Management. "They tend to move up and down with changes in the economy, labor markets and financial markets. Whatever level of demand exists at the end of recession, it goes up from there."

Greenspan, Paulsen and the rest of the herd are focusing on the supercharged pace of auto sales in the fourth quarter. Driven by 0 percent financing, sales of motor vehicles and parts zoomed an annualized 81.3 percent in the fourth quarter.

As far as the Great American Dream is concerned, Greenspan et al. are arguing that because housing never weakened, it can't very well come back. New and existing home sales set a record in 2001 of 6.26 million units.

SMALL SLICE

Housing, or residential investment as it's called in the GDP accounts, is a very small portion of the total pie: 4.3 or 4.4 percent of GDP, according to Michael Carliner, an economist at the National Association of Home Builders. For that reason, even when housing's going gangbusters, its contribution to GDP growth tends to be quite small.

For example, going back to 1972 to capture the recoveries from four recessions, two of which (1973–1975 and 1981–1982) were long and deep, there are only 11 quarters out of 120 in which housing contributed more than 1 percentage point to GDP growth.

Four of those were in the aftermath of the 1981–1982 recession. Housing starts bottomed at 837,000 in November 1981, almost tripling to an all-time high of 2.26 million in February 1984. Yet the biggest quarterly contribution housing ever made to overall growth was 2.11 percentage points in the third quarter of 1983.

RESTRAINED SUPPLY

There are only three instances, in fact, in the past 30 years in which housing added upwards of 2 percentage points to real GDP growth. So residential construction, because of its small weight in the economy, isn't going to determine the recovery's fate.

The NAHB's Carliner is among those who say housing can't go much higher. Due to some fluky seasonal adjustment factors, total home sales hit a record 6.8 million annualized pace in January.

"We don't have any people who chose not to buy or were unable to buy the product," Carliner says.

On the supply side, there is no evidence that the late 1990s boom featured a speculative building binge like the one in the 1980s.

"There is no inventory overhang," Carliner says. "And there are a fair amount of unfilled orders, defined as a sales contract for a house that the builder hasn't conveyed yet."

EVIDENCE

As far as auto sales are concerned, the worst fears that October's 21.3 million annualized incentive-driven sales pace would lead to plummeting first-quarter sales aren't being realized. February's seasonally adjusted selling rate for cars and light trucks was 16.7 million, not far short of last year's 17.2 million pace, the second-best year on record.

Rather than robbing from this year's sales, all last year's sales seem to have done was steal from auto manufacturers' profits!

While there is some evidence that deep recessions are followed by strong recoveries and shallow slumps by weak initial rebounds, "any relationship between the severity of the slowdown in consumer spending and the strength of the subsequent rebound is hard to establish," says Peter Kretzmer, senior U.S. economist at Bank of America Securities.

Consumer spending generally declines during recession. Of the four post–World War II recessions where it never fell on a year-over-year basis, "two were followed by robust rebounds in consumer spending," Kretzmer says. "It's not at all clear that the stronger-than-average consumer spending during this recession points to weaker-than-average spending in the ensuing recovery."

The resilience of consumer spending and the U.S. economy has come as a surprise to most folks. They don't seem to understand that what the Fed prints (money) someone will spend.

If the magnitude of the decline were the sole determinant of the strength of the rebound, why isn't the pent-up demand crowd hawking a renaissance in capital spending following the collapse?

POSTSCRIPT: *The record pace of home sales in 2001 was eclipsed in 2002, in 2003, and again in 2004, when 7.98 million new and existing homes were sold.*

Field of Gloom Is Never Too Crowded for New Blood

——————— May 13, 2004 ———————

EVER SINCE the days of Thomas Malthus, economists have been worrying about man's ability to provide food and other necessities for a growing population.

Malthus, an English minister and political economist, wrote about these issues in 1798. World population has increased sixfold in the last 200 years, and living standards have risen. The number of deaths from famine and disease has been drastically reduced.

"Where did Malthus go wrong?" writes Greg Mankiw, chairman of the president's Council of Economic Advisers, in his best-selling text, *Principles of Economics.* "Growth in mankind's ingenuity has offset the effects of a larger population."

It takes fewer farmers to feed more people thanks to advances in technology and efficiency.

Biologist Paul Ehrlich picked up Malthus's mantle in 1968 with the publication of *The Population Bomb,* predicting famine and death on an unprecedented scale. Mandatory population control, if voluntary measures didn't work, was the only solution, according to Ehrlich.

The late economist Julian Simon challenged Ehrlich's prediction of massive shortages of natural resources. He offered Ehrlich a wager in 1980, based on the price of five metals of Ehrlich's choosing a decade hence.

If a quantity of copper, chrome, nickel, tin and tungsten that was worth $1,000 in 1980 was worth more than that in 1990 after adjusting for inflation, Ehrlich would win the bet.

LOSER

He lost. The prices of all five metals, adjusted for inflation, were down anywhere from 3.5 percent (nickel) to 72 percent (tin).

In the 1970s, a group of environmentalists known as the Club of Rome claimed the world would run out of oil by 1990 at the current rate of consumption. Supplies of other vital commodities—including natural gas, copper, aluminum and lead—would be depleted or exhausted within decades. The prices of basic agricultural and industrial commodities would soar to prohibitive heights.

Another doomsday scenario dashed.

While modern-day neo-Malthusians are still predicting some catastrophic supply shortage, more in vogue in this era of high productivity growth and excess capacity are predictions of the death of demand.

"America has more TVs than viewers, more phone numbers than talkers, more homes than households and more cars than drivers," trumpets the press release for a new book from Financial Times Prentice Hall, *The Death of Demand: Finding Growth in a Saturated Global Economy,* by Tom Osenton. "Consumers have gorged and are reaching their limit."

SATIATED CONSUMERS?

They are? Where are they hiding? I've never met anybody who said he or she has enough "stuff."

"I'd like to know someone who isn't running into income constraints," said Jim Glassman, senior U.S. economist at J.P. Morgan Chase & Co.

Osenton's thesis is that "innovation saturation" will lead to little or no growth in revenue for the next 10 to 20 years.

I was skeptical. So I called him.

Revenue of companies in the Dow Jones Industrial Average and Standard & Poor's 500 companies grew at an increasingly faster rate from World War II to the 1970s and at a declining growth rate since then, Osenton said.

Could some of that rise and fall in the growth rate of revenue, a nominal measure, have anything to do with inflation?

DATA MASSAGE

"Revenue as an earnings driver is losing steam," Osenton said in a phone interview. "That puts more pressure on productivity and cost cutting."

What's more, companies "continue to cut jobs and investment in innovation—a very bad combination for the long-term," the press release said.

Every book author risks appearing dated by changing circumstances. The revival in the labor market has been sharp and sudden, at least as reported in the official statistics. But to claim investment in innovation has been cut belies the uncharacteristically strong productivity growth during the recession and sluggish recovery.

"The rate of productivity growth has been declining since the 1950s," Osenton said, using decade comparisons.

Technically, he's correct. The year-over-year growth in non-farm business productivity peaked in the fourth quarter of 1950 at 7.2 percent.

However, following a slump from the mid-'70s to mid-'90s, when productivity growth averaged 1.4 percent, the growth rate has doubled. Someone else might look at the data and extrapolate a reversal of the 1950s to 1990s declining trend.

New New Thing

Using other measures of innovation, "there's been nothing but growth in patent applications, patent grants, and real and nominal research and development by industry and in aggregate," said Steve Wieting, senior economist at Citigroup Global Markets.

Even more troubling to Osenton is "the fact that there is no savior on the horizon to reinvigorate the economy and stimulate new growth," according to the press release.

That's the thing about entrepreneurship. Create the right incentives, and you never know where the next big idea or product will come from.

Even without innovation, demand isn't finite.

"That's one of the first premises of economics: scarcity," said Bob Laurent, professor of economics and finance at the Illinois Institute of Technology's Stuart School of Business. "People want more."

Pent-Up Nonsense

For most of history, innovation probably wasn't that rapid, Laurent said.

"Yet people went out and worked so they could buy something," he said. "Even if there's nothing new, they want more of something that is old, such as a bigger house."

A 24-inch TV screen used to be a big deal. Now folks want a 50-inch wall-mounted flat panel.

In every business cycle (some things never change), we hear about a lack of pent-up demand. The chorus was particularly loud and strident during the 2001 recession and sub-par recovery because sales of homes and autos never ebbed.

Real consumer spending rose 4.3 percent in the four quarters ended in the first quarter. Not bad for no pent-up demand.

Any discussion about the death of demand without reference to price is essentially meaningless. The demand curve—a pictorial representation of the quantity of goods and services demanded at any given price—is downward sloping. For most items, lowering the price increases the quantity demanded.

It's always worked that way. I suspect it always will. Both consumers and producers understand it.

I've never worried about a lack of human ingenuity. If I'm going to spend time worrying, it'll be about the sun going dark in 5 billion years, not the death of demand.

POSTSCRIPT: *At least three readers e-mailed after I wrote this column to tell me they had too much stuff. I stand corrected.*

Lump-of-Labor Fallacy Gets Gussied Up for a New Era

———— Sept. 16, 2003 ————

IF YOU'RE UNEMPLOYED and ready to pack it in because everything you read suggests strong productivity growth is the enemy, help is on the way.

Higher productivity growth, stronger corporate profits and stronger employment growth actually go hand in hand—sometimes with a long and variable lag, as this business cycle is proving. The acceleration in U.S. labor productivity, which rose 4.1 percent in the four quarters ended in the second quarter, is not about to upend the expansion either.

"Efficiency gains are fueling the recovery, not undermining it," says Jim Glassman, senior U.S. economist at J.P. Morgan Chase & Co.

Think about it this way: If businesses were to postpone efficiency- and profit-enhancing initiatives for the sake of the status quo (think Old

Europe), profits would suffer—and so would labor compensation.

"Real labor compensation tracks real productivity growth," Glassman says. "Real compensation gains are entirely consistent with rising profits."

In fact, the tip-off that productivity was accelerating in the mid-1990s—ignored or dismissed at the time—was the simultaneous rise in profit margins and real compensation, Glassman says.

PRODUCTIVITY PRIMER

How does productivity provide all things to all people? Let's start with the basics.

Labor productivity is defined as real output per worker hour. Productivity increases when companies produce the same amount, or more, with less. Since labor is the biggest input, even in goods production, companies achieve greater efficiency initially at the expense of labor.

That's how it always works. For the folks who get laid off in a cost-cutting sweep by business, life is tough. For the rest of us—and eventually for the unemployed who get retrained, recycled and rehired—productivity brings unqualified benefits.

Higher productivity translates into higher profits, higher wages and lower prices. In so doing, it provides a higher standard of living for all.

The benefits of increased productivity—often the result of investment in new technologies—first show up in companies' bottom line. That's what's been going on in the last few quarters. Businesses have restored pretax profits as a share of GDP to 8.4 percent (second quarter), above the historical average excluding the bubble years. Based on recent data, Glassman says third-quarter profits may have topped 9 percent.

COMPETITION

In a competitive, free-market system, companies can't hoard all the profits. Enhanced efficiency encourages some companies to cut prices to increase market share. The rest follow.

That's one way higher productivity yields higher real wages: Lower prices mean workers' wages buy more.

At the same time, if an employer doesn't raise the worker's pay to match the marginal value of her product, another company will. Either way, real wages rise. The consumer is the ultimate beneficiary of higher productivity.

Those who argue that stronger productivity growth is hampering hiring sufficiently to doom the expansion haven't looked at history. While no cycle is the same—the current investment-driven boom/bust cycle has little in common with the old-fashioned Fed-fighting-inflation postwar recessions—the expansions with the strongest rebound in productivity growth saw the strongest hiring. The recovery from the business cycle troughs in 1970, 1975 and 1982 all bear this out.

OLD SAW

The slew of recent articles on the deleterious effect of productivity suggests the "lump-of-labor" fallacy is due for a revival. This fallacy assumes there is a fixed amount of work to be done in an economy, to be divided up among the total supply of laborers. If machines do the work, there's less for people to do, resulting in higher unemployment.

No doubt this fallacy was behind France's romance with the 35-hour workweek. It also repeatedly fuels protectionist sentiment: the desire to protect domestic industries, via tariffs and quotas, from foreign competition.

If clothing manufacturing shifts to China, which it has, why, there will be nothing for U.S. workers to do! (These old chestnuts only resurface during bad times, not when the unemployment rate is 4 percent and companies are begging for workers.)

FIXED NONSENSE

The truth is, the amount of work is not fixed. New jobs and industries are created, just as old ones die off or move offshore. Structural changes in the economy—the transition from an agrarian to an industrial economy, from a goods-producing to a service-producing one—cause an evolution in the labor market.

The whole process is what the late Austrian economist Joseph Schumpeter called creative destruction.

In the short run, the closing of a factory and loss of a job is devastating to workers. In the long run, those workers get retrained, relocate or are absorbed by employers in search of a readily available labor pool.

For those who worry that a lack of job growth is jeopardizing the expansion, consider the alternative. Construction companies could get rid of their big earthmoving equipment and instead hire a lot of new workers and buy them all shovels.

Heck, why stop at shovels? Think of all the people you could employ if they all used spoons.

Help Wanted: First Handler for Bush's Pooches
—————— Feb. 13, 2004 ——————

JOBS ARE turning out to be as much of a hot-button issue for President George W. Bush in 2004 as they were for his father in 1992.

Everyone's read that Bush is the first president since Herbert Hoover to boast a record of net job losses during his term.

Everyone's seen the sunny projections of the Bush administration for 2.6 million new jobs this year, which translates to some 325,000 a month. (The forecast is based on full-year averages.) The average monthly increase since payrolls turned positive in September is 73,000.

And everyone's listened to the Democrats pound away at the president for his dismal job performance: his own and his inability to create new ones for everyone else.

Has anyone stopped to consider what the president's role should be in the area of job creation? The Oval Office isn't an employment agency, unless the White House is looking to hire.

"I didn't know we were asking the president to create jobs," said Jim Glassman, senior U.S. economist at J.P. Morgan Chase & Co. "I thought the president was supposed to put policies in place that encourage the private sector to create jobs."

OVAL OFFICE TEMPS?

Whether you think Bush's tax cuts were the right kind (across-the-board versus targeted), the right size or on the right income base (capital versus labor), it's hard to criticize the president for their failure to create jobs—unless, of course, you believe that raising taxes creates jobs.

The Democratic presidential candidates would have you believe Bush is to blame for the 2.3 million jobs lost since he took office in January 2001. On Monday, at a campaign stop in Roanoke, Virginia, Democratic presidential hopeful John Kerry said, "We need a president who will create jobs in America and put Americans back to work."

Kerry wasn't specific about what he would do to create jobs. And for good reason.

The only way a president can create jobs, or put people to work, is by hiring them himself (first handler for Barney and Spot?), pay someone else to hire them (extend tax credits to business), or dream up government-financed make-work projects that will employ them, which is what Franklin Delano Roosevelt did with the New Deal.

New Deal Revisited

The idea that the government can create demand by transferring resources from one entity to the next, courtesy of John Maynard Keynes, has undergone some serious reevaluation. You don't have to be a card-carrying supply-sider to subscribe to the idea that people respond to incentives, or that the goal of fiscal policy should be to increase the size of the pie, not redistribute income.

The orthodoxy that the New Deal pulled the U.S. economy out of the Great Depression is being challenged by economic historians. In *FDR's Folly: How Roosevelt and His New Deal Prolonged the Great Depression,* author Jim Powell argues that FDR's policies actually deepened the Depression. Taxes of all kinds—personal income taxes, corporate income taxes, inheritance taxes, "excess profits" taxes and excise taxes on everything from cigarettes and alcohol to cars, telephone calls, electricity and radios—went up.

"Yes, to hear FDR's 'Fireside Chats,' one had to pay FDR excise taxes for a radio and electricity," Powell wrote in a Dec. 29, 2003, daily commentary for the libertarian Cato Institute in Washington. "Consumers had less money to spend, and employers had less money for growth and jobs."

Politics, Not Policy

Social Security taxes on payrolls "made it more expensive for employers to hire people, which discouraged hiring," Powell said. And consumers had to pay higher prices too, thanks to crop destruction and the banning of discounting.

So how about all the people who were rescued from bread lines by a job with the WPA, TVA, REA or any other New Deal acronym? Every job created by the New Deal, financed by higher taxes, meant less money for consumers to spend on necessities, the demand for which would have encouraged private-sector job growth.

The White House stepped into a hornet's nest on Monday when Greg Mankiw, chairman of the president's Council of Economic Advisers, presented the annual *Economic Report of the President.* Mankiw said that outsourcing, which is "the latest manifestation of the gains from trade that economists have talked about at least since Adam Smith," is "probably a plus for the economy in the long run."

Poorly Put

The comment sounded uncaring—a criticism often leveled at the GOP—and created an immediate kerfuffle among Democrats and Republicans alike.

"They seem to want to turn a jobless recovery into a hopeless recovery," said Senate Minority Leader Tom Daschle, Democrat of South Dakota.

Telling an out-of-work machinist whose factory has closed and whose high-paying job was outsourced to China that his standard of living improved as a result doesn't sit well.

Following the linkage from outsourcing to cheaper goods for consumers to more money for consumers to spend on other things to increased demand for goods and services to new job opportunities may be too diffuse and difficult to follow.

Or it may be a preference for politics over policy in an election year.

Situation Wanted

There's another channel through which trade raises our standard of living.

"It allows companies to use their resources more efficiently, which means higher productivity, higher profits and higher pay for workers," Glassman said. "It's in a country's interest to subsidize those who lose their jobs because the net benefit is so much greater."

Mankiw addressed that issue as well, saying the public and private sector need to help displaced workers transition to new jobs "whether the dislocation comes from trade or whether it comes from technological progress." But the damage was already done.

It's "society's responsibility overall to provide an environment where people can find the new jobs, not to try to stop progress and keep people locked into the old jobs," he said.

That's what the president can do: not create jobs, but create the environment in which others will create them.

Just in case the president happens to be looking for someone personally, perhaps to care for the first pooches, I'll be happy to forward my résumé.

Postscript: By the end of Bush's first term in office, the number of people working in non-farm jobs was back to where it had been when he took office. Bush had outlived the comparison to Herbert Hoover.

4

Myths Under the Microscope

IF SOMETHING is repeated often enough, pretty soon people start to believe it, or so the saying goes.

Maybe that's why so many myths put down roots in the marketplace. Like the examples of unsound thinking in the previous chapter, some myths never die. Many of them aren't even challenged. They're just handed down from one business cycle to the next.

The U.S. is losing manufacturing jobs? Low-wage China must be stealing them. Never mind that U.S. manufacturing jobs have been declining since 1979 in absolute terms and since 1943 as a share of total employment. Productivity is reducing the need for factory workers worldwide.

Then there are the misconceptions about trade. Exports are good; imports are bad. Why it's desirable to use a country's scarce resources to produce goods for foreigners when it's more cost-effective to import them is never explained.

Tax cuts are another area where myths are deeply entrenched. Wealth transfers—putting money back in the pockets of people who will spend it—aren't tax cuts. Nor does the stimulus from an across-the-board cut in marginal rates and in capital gains rates fade. Lower tax rates act as an inducement to work, save and invest. They're the gift that keeps on giving.

The most widely misconstrued myths relate to oil, which is why I've included an entire chapter on it later in the book. Oil sure is one unique commodity because no matter what happens to the price, the effect is deflationary, according to the conventional wisdom. (It wasn't always so, either in concept or in practice.)

When the price of oil falls, it's viewed as deflationary (lack of demand). When the price rises, why, it's deflationary, too, because oil acts like a tax on the consumer.

As you'll see in the column from May 24, 2004, below, a demand-driven increase in oil prices is nothing like a tax. The response from producers to increased demand—additional supply—is the exact opposite of what happens when a tax is imposed.

Myths About Trade, or Thank God for the Deficit

———————— April 20, 1999 ————————

THE TRADE DEFICIT blew a gaping hole in the U.S. economy in February as imports exceeded exports by a record $19.4 billion.

What that means is, assuming no material improvement in March, the deterioration in the first-quarter trade deficit (the January–February average is $18.1 billion) from the fourth-quarter average of $14.4 billion will subtract as much as 2.5 percentage points from real gross domestic product growth.

And it's a good thing because without the trade drag, real GDP would post an increase on the order of 6 percent for the second quarter running.

To their credit, financial markets seem to have grasped the idea that what matters is domestic demand, which happens to be booming. Consumer spending, business fixed investment, housing and government spending will all make positive contributions to GDP growth in the first quarter. Inventories are expected to be neutral, which leaves trade as the sole negative.

The real significance of a widening U.S. trade deficit, GDP accounting notwithstanding, is the false fodder it provides for the protectionist element in Congress, which boasts members from both the Far Right and the Far Left.

"It gives Congress one more reason for not reducing trade barriers," says Dan Griswold, associate director of the Cato Institute's Center for Trade Policy Studies in Washington. "If anything, the falloff in exports in 1998—the first decline in 13 years—is a reason to redouble our efforts to stimulate trade."

FREE TO CHOOSE

Almost every warning about the trade deficit, every prediction about its deleterious effect on the U.S. economy, every doomsday scenario of bringing the country to its knees, is misguided. In what should be required reading for every government official, business executive, investor and student, Griswold goes about exposing those myths, one by one, in an April 1998 Cato policy analysis titled "America's Maligned and Misunderstood Trade Deficit."

"What matters to the economy is not the difference between imports and exports but the extent to which Americans are free to benefit from the efficiencies, opportunities, and consumer choice created in an economy open to world trade," Griswold writes.

Federal Reserve Board Chairman Alan Greenspan used the occasion of a speech in Dallas last Friday to warn of the dangers of protectionism and discourage all who would resort to those anti-competitive tactics.

Unfortunately, the entire trade debate is colored by the spurious notion that a trade deficit is bad and a surplus is good. Nothing could be further from the truth. Japan runs a huge trade surplus; the U.S., a huge deficit. You choose which model you want to adopt.

DRIVEN BY INVESTMENT

Contrary to popular belief, the trade deficit is not the result of unfair trade practices abroad, or a manifestation of U.S. companies' loss of competitiveness. It is not a net job killer and not a harbinger of industrial decline. In fact, "the trade deficit has virtually nothing to do with trade policy," Griswold explains.

Rather, the gap represents an excess of investment over savings. Since the U.S. invests more than it saves, it has to import capital from abroad—run a capital account surplus—to pay for it. In so doing, the U.S. can consume more than it produces, importing the difference via the current account deficit, which is the mirror image of the capital account surplus. (The current account includes trade in goods and services as well as investment flows.)

Because Japan as a nation saves more than it invests, Japan exports capital (runs a capital account deficit), which ultimately ends up going for the purchase of Japanese exports to the rest of the world (current account surplus).

It's about time that folks stopped passing judgment on the trade deficit. From an economic perspective, a trade deficit is neither bad nor good; it just is. Currently, the U.S. buys a lot more goods from the rest of the world than it sells because its economy is in better shape. The U.S. is in an enviable position. Our economy is healthy. We get to conserve our own natural resources while others deplete theirs.

DATA DISCONNECT

The U.S. bilateral trade deficit with relatively closed economies like Japan and China gets lots of media attention, especially in view of China's desire to join the World Trade Organization. But Griswold found "no relationship between bilateral trade balances and openness to U.S. exports."

The U.S. consistently runs a trade deficit with Canada and Mexico, two of the most open countries because of the North American Free Trade Agreement, and, even now, a surplus with Brazil, which is relatively closed.

Another myth ripe for debunking: The trade deficit is a signal of industrial decline in America.

"There is no connection between trade deficits and industrial decline," Griswold counters. Between 1992 and 1997, the trade deficit almost tripled, industrial production rose 24 percent and manufacturing output rose 27 percent, he notes.

GUARANTEED DEFICIT CUTTER

How about that giant sucking sound, heard by 1992 presidential aspirant Ross Perot?

Again, the statistics do not support the notion of job loss as a result of the trade deficit.

"Larger trade deficits correlate positively with falling unemployment," Griswold finds. "As an expanding economy creates jobs, it also creates demand for imports and for capital from abroad."

Just in case the trade deficit does become a real, rather than imagined problem, consider that the deficit did shrink during the 1990–1991 recession.

"If the trade deficit really is one of our nation's most pressing problems, the surest and swiftest way to tackle it would be to engineer a deep recession," Griswold offers.

POSTSCRIPT: *Six years later, the current account deficit is still with us. It's larger (a record 5.7 percent of GDP in 2004), louder (at least the folks warning of its dire consequences are) and still "unsustainable."*

Time for the Awful Truth About Debt Reduction
———— May 25, 2000 ————

ONE LEGACY of the Clinton administration—something Democrats can revel in—is the elimination of the U.S. budget deficit. That it's the Reagan deficits the traditional party of tax and spend has vanquished makes the victory that much sweeter.

In fact, so much money flowed into the Treasury's coffers in the late 1990s, the product of strong income growth and big capital gains, that the department began to buy back debt this year for the first time in 70 years.

Before historians start updating textbooks to incorporate the Clinton legacy, they might want to consider the truth about U.S. debt. It isn't going down; it's going up. If the statisticians are correct—and that's a big if—the federal debt will soar some 21 percent between now and 2013, the date targeted by the Clinton administration for the country to be debt-free at last.

How can that be?

The Clinton administration is committed to paying down the $3.5 trillion of marketable debt held by the public. That's the stuff we see: the regular Monday bill auctions, the monthly two-year note auctions, the quarterly refunding operations that used to make the front page of the business section before stocks became the national pastime.

Meanwhile, the debt held in the trust funds, including Social Security's, is galloping ahead. Currently Social Security taxes exceed benefit payments and get credited to the trust fund in the form of non-marketable Treasuries that earn interest.

LIMITED OPTIONS

Somewhere around 2013–2015, the inflows and outflows will be in balance. From that point on, the Treasury will need money to redeem the bonds to meet Social Security benefits in excess of Social Security taxes.

The government has three options: It can raise taxes, cut benefits or borrow. Which do you think is the most palatable solution when the public believes it is entitled to full benefits after years of paying in?

So why shut down the government bond market infrastructure if it's going to have to be resurrected almost immediately?

"It is the height of fiscal irresponsibility, at a time when the federal debt is actually increasing, to let the Treasury securities market wither away, knowing that it would have to be reinvented," said Francis Cavanaugh, an economist and 32-year veteran of the Treasury Department, including a stint as director of the Office of Government Finance and Market Analysis. "The transition would involve substantial costs to the taxpayer, as well as costly disruptions of private financial markets."

In a presentation at an American Enterprise Institute conference Tuesday, Cavanaugh presented some telling statistics from Clinton's 2001 budget and the quarterly *Treasury Bulletin*. Numbers for 2000 and 2013 are estimates.

	FY 1999	FY 2000E	FY 2013E
Gross Federal Debt	**$5.6 trillion**	**$5.7 trillion**	**$6.8 trillion**
Held by Government	2.0 trillion	2.2 trillion	6.8 trillion
Social Security	0.9	1.0	4.2
Other	1.1	1.2	2.6
Held by Public	3.6 trillion	3.5 trillion	0
Federal Reserve	0.5	0.5	0
Savings Bonds	0.4	0.4	0
Private	2.7	2.6	0
Domestic	1.5	1.3	0
Foreign	1.3	1.3	0

Since the Treasury market will have to be reborn sometime in the next decade, debt management under Treasury Secretary Larry Summers was either poorly thought out or politically motivated. Cavanaugh sees "no economic, financial or equity justification for shifting the ownership of the federal debt from the private market to, in effect, the private beneficiaries of the government trust funds. The shift will serve only the politics of the federal budget—to give the appearance of debt reduction when there is actually a substantial debt increase."

DETAILS

While some of the issues involved in functioning without a liquid, risk-free benchmark, including a potential deterrent for foreign central banks to hold dollar reserves, have been documented, Cavanaugh brought up a few only an old Treasury hand would be aware of. For example, the law establishing the Social Security Administration requires that the interest rate earned by the trust funds be calculated on the basis of current market yields on intermediate- and long-term

Treasuries. If there are no marketable Treasuries, there's no basket on which to calculate an interest rate, and the law will have to be amended.

The law will have to be amended as well, Cavanaugh said, if the interest savings from the marketable debt is to be credited to the trust fund as proposed by Clinton and presidential hopeful Al Gore.

What's more, to the extent that the winnowing of the Treasury market reduces Treasury yields across the board, the reduction in investment income increases the future strain on the Social Security system, which will be exhausted by 2037 without some kind of fix, according to Cavanaugh.

Two Birds, One Stone

And why, Cavanaugh wondered, is the government still issuing 30-year savings bonds if there won't be any more publicly held debt 13 years from now?

Cavanaugh sees a way out for the government to reduce its future financing burden, improve the trust funds' return and in the process throw a bone to government-sponsored enterprises, including Fannie Mae and Freddie Mac.

"If Congress really means to back up the GSEs, they should make the [government] guarantee explicit, reducing the cost to the GSEs, housing and the Treasury," he said. Then let the trust funds buy GSE debt, which they are currently authorized to do but which they don't do in practice.

The effect would be less nonmarketable debt and more marketable debt, as the Treasury is forced to borrow to make up for the lost revenue when the trust funds purchase GSE debt instead of Treasuries.

Talk about a legacy. Taming the Reagan deficits is child's play compared with saving Social Security and increasing demand for ballooning GSE debt. Now there's a duo that a lame-duck president like Bill Clinton could get excited about.

Postscript: *As it turned out, debt reduction wasn't worth the worry. Marketable debt didn't disappear; budget surpluses did. The $237 billion federal budget surplus in fiscal year 2000 turned out to be a record. It's been all downhill from there. The government's fiscal year 2004, which ended on Sept. 30, produced a record deficit of $413 billion.*

The Social Security trust funds eked out a few more years of solvency since the column was written. According to the Social Security

Administration Trustees' 2005 report, the benefits paid won't exceed the tax inflow until 2017. The funds will be exhausted in 2041.

The outlook for Medicare has deteriorated. The Hospital Insurance Fund, which pays hospital benefits, experienced an annual cash flow deficit in 2004, with the reserves expected to be exhausted in 2020. The enactment of a prescription drug benefit in 2003 has added to the long-term cost of Supplementary Medicare Insurance, which is partly funded by premium payments.

The total public debt outstanding as of March 31, 2005, was $7.8 trillion, more than what Cavanaugh estimated for 2013.

It's a Trap! An Economic Myth Stages a Revival
———————— May 27, 2003 ————————

JUST WHEN you thought deflation was the scariest thing on the horizon, along comes the phony specter of a new threat: a liquidity trap.

In case you're unfamiliar with this concept, its origin owes to the dead British economist John Maynard Keynes, who theorized about the inability of near-zero interest rates to revive the U.S. economy—restore it to full employment—during the Great Depression.

As explained by economist Paul Krugman in his *New York Times* op-ed column on Saturday, when interest rates fall close to zero, "additional cash pumped into the economy—added liquidity—sits idle, because there's no point in lending money out if you don't receive any reward," Krugman said. "And monetary policy loses its effectiveness."

Krugman, a frequent critic of the Bush administration, warned that the risks of falling into a liquidity-trap "quagmire" were high (the schadenfreude was palpable).

Perhaps Krugman should read the speeches of his former Princeton colleague, Fed governor Ben Bernanke. While it's true that nominal interest rates can't fall below zero, the thrust of monetary policy isn't defined by the level of the overnight rate, which is the chosen policy instrument for most central banks. Even when a central bank faces what the Federal Reserve refers to as the "zero-bound policy constraint," it still has an unlimited ability to print money.

NOT ZERO-BOUND

OK, you say. The Fed can print money, but the banks, which get deposits when the central bank buys Treasury securities in the open market, don't have anyone to lend it to. So there is no multiplier effect to energize the Fed's monetary stimulus.

Wrong. Even when the private sector has no demand for credit, which is hardly the situation today, there is one entity with a voracious appetite: the federal government. With the federal deficit likely to hit $400 billion this year, there's no lack of government bonds for the Fed to buy.

Nobel laureate Milton Friedman used to tell his students at the University of Chicago that as a theoretical argument, the liquidity trap didn't make much sense since the central bank can always expand the money stock. When the central bank puts out more money than the public wants to hold, at the margin someone will spend it.

As a practical matter—as an explanation for the Great Depression—Keynes's liquidity trap didn't cut it for Friedman either. The Fed allowed the money supply to contract by about a third, which for him was the cause of the protracted period of declining economic growth, wages and profits.

SOGGY STRING

The idea of a liquidity trap is often expressed by the metaphor of the central bank "pushing on a string." This diagnosis gets recycled whenever the economy isn't responding to low interest rates in the prescribed manner.

The liquidity-trap myth made a comeback in the early 1990s when the U.S., faced with a dysfunctional banking system, required an extended period of low interest rates first to heal banks' balance sheets and second to produce a response in the real economy.

Japan has provided a decade of delight for liquidity-trap theorists. Interest rates in Japan are near zero, economy-wide prices are falling (as opposed to some prices in the U.S.) and the economy is dead in the water.

Unfortunately, the diagnosis is incorrect.

"No country has ever been in a liquidity trap," says Allan Meltzer, professor of economics at Carnegie Mellon University and visiting scholar at the American Enterprise Institute. "Japan is not in one now. Neither is the U.S."

MISGUIDED POLICY

Falling prices and interest rates in Japan say more about mistaken monetary policy than anything else, Meltzer says. The Bank of Japan has the ability to buy more assets, which would increase money growth—Japan's broad money supply is up a scant 1.4 percent year over year—and end the deflation.

If the Japanese government ever got serious about cleaning up the banking system—forcing the banks to write off bad loans, forcing insolvent banks to close—the BOJ would get some help in its effort.

As far as the U.S. is concerned, Meltzer, who is the author of a new 848-page book, *A History of the Federal Reserve, Vol. 1: 1913–1951*, points to several periods when interest rates were at or close to zero, without any liquidity getting trapped.

"In 1954, interest rates were 0.5 percent or below, and we had no problem recovering," he says. "In 1948 to 1949, we had zero interest rates. Also in 1937 to 1938. We had no problem recovering."

PINK PARROTS

Meltzer is equally dismissive of the deflation threat.

"We just reported a GDP deflator of 2.5 percent" in the first quarter, Meltzer says. The implicit deflator measures price changes in the gross domestic product.

The highest reading in almost two years hasn't stopped a flood of talk and articles on the dreaded deflation ever since the Fed mentioned the risk of falling prices in the statement following its May 6 meeting.

"If Alan Greenspan said the grass is pink, Wall Street economists would see pink grass," Meltzer says. "I like Alan Greenspan, but they all speak as if he's the Oracle of Delphi."

The Fed chairman hasn't voiced any concerns about a liquidity trap just yet. To the contrary, like Bernanke (and unlike Krugman), he's talked about instituting "unconventional policy measures"—buying long-term bonds—should the overnight rate hit zero.

And if that doesn't work, I'll bet he has a few strings he could pull (or push).

❀   ❀   ❀

So Who's Stealing China's Manufacturing Jobs?
———————— Oct. 14, 2003 ————————

YOU KNOW all those U.S. manufacturing jobs that have been hightailing it to China? China sure is doing a lousy job of holding on to them.

China lost 16 million manufacturing jobs, a decline of 15 percent, between 1995 and 2002, according to a study of manufacturing jobs in the 20 largest economies by Joe Carson, director of economic research at Alliance Capital Management. In that same time, U.S. factory employment shrank by 2 million, or 11 percent.

In fact, in the seven years ended 2002, the number of China's manufacturing jobs fell at more than double the rate—15 percent versus 7 percent—of the other countries in the study. (Two of the top 20 economies, Mexico and Brazil, report manufacturing employment in index form, not as actual head count, and weren't incorporated into Carson's analysis. The payroll changes in that time period weren't large enough to alter the conclusions.)

Despite China's addition of nearly 2 million factory jobs in 2002, "the level of factory jobs [last year] was below 1998's and far below 1995's," Carson says.

So who's stealing China's manufacturing jobs?

It seems that China's advantage as a low-cost producer hasn't halted the insatiable drive worldwide to replace even dirt-cheap labor with productivity-enhancing equipment.

GLOBAL GLUT

Some 22 million manufacturing jobs were lost globally between 1995 and 2002 as industrial output soared 30 percent, Carson says. It seems that devilish productivity is wreaking havoc with jobs both at home and abroad.

Carson's investigation found that only five of the 20 countries increased manufacturing jobs between 1995 and 2002. Three of the five—Canada, Mexico and Spain—"seem to have benefited from regional trade pacts or currency agreements," he says.

The other two, Taiwan and the Philippines, showed a net 300,000 seven-year gain, large for those economies but small on a global scale.

Put in a global evolutionary context, the loss of 2.6 million manufacturing jobs in the U.S. since the start of 2001 looks far less ominous—at least to folks not seeking elective office. Facts about the extent of the decline in global manufacturing jobs would demolish the economic (not the political) argument for protectionist measures. Both houses of Congress have proposed legislation that would impose stiff tariffs on Chinese imports.

POKING HOLES

Facts about human capital's decreasing relevance in the manufacturing process would expose the silliness of appointing a manufacturing czar, an initiative announced recently by President George W. Bush. They would upend the misplaced notion that China's undervalued currency—the yuan has been pegged at 8.3 to the dollar for almost a decade—is giving the country's manufacturers a competitive edge and ballooning its trade surplus with the U.S. to $103 billion in 2002.

No reasonable degree of yuan appreciation can offset the labor-cost differential between the two countries. U.S. manufacturing workers make about 25 times what an average Chinese factory worker earns, according to statistical agencies in the U.S. and China.

The fact that China is losing factory jobs at a faster rate than the countries from which it is supposedly stealing them just might put to rest the notion of China as the job-thievery nation.

GOING WAY OF FARMER

The angst over the fate of U.S. production workers, whose numbers peaked in 1979, is not unlike the epitaph for farm workers in the early 20th century, says Steve Wieting, senior economist at Citigroup Inc.

"Real manufacturing output has risen 77 percent even though the number of manufacturing workers has fallen 22 percent since the 1979 peak," Wieting says.

Similarly, real farm output rose 96 percent since 1979 with 31 percent fewer agricultural workers.

Because output equals income, "something was earned with the gains in manufacturing and farm output during the last 25 years of falling employment in these industries," Wieting says.

A rising supply of food and consumer goods caused prices to rise more slowly than per-capita income, giving consumers more income to spend on other things—on services that didn't previously exist.

"While manufacturing and farm employment have fallen by 22 percent and 33 percent, respectively, since 1979, total U.S. employment still managed to grow 41 percent," Wieting says.

THEY WERE EXPENDABLE

Perhaps one day human beings will be redundant in manufacturing production. (Hey, that will free up more of them to man customer and technical support hotlines!) Hard as expendability is on workers themselves, increased productivity is the way progress is made.

The alternative isn't so appealing.

"Our studies suggest that hunter-gatherer societies offer full employment for all, simply providing the basic necessities of food and shelter," Wieting say.

Of course, with all of their resources devoted to providing food and shelter, they have little "income" left to consume anything else—made in China or otherwise.

Tax Cuts Evanesce in One-Off School of Economics

———————   Dec. 3, 2003   ———————

THE RECENT SLATE of economic news has sent the bears into hiding. It hasn't curtailed the flow of analyses and articles predicting the stimulus from tax cuts is about to fade (this from the same folks who said tax cuts wouldn't work in the first place).

If you believe what you read, tax cuts are a one-shot deal. They have no staying power, no behavior-changing incentives, no thrust past the initial first-round effect.

"Find me the theoretical construct that says tax cuts are a one-off," says Bob Barbera, chief economist at ITG/Hoenig in Rye Brook, New York. "It doesn't exist."

It's conceivable a taxpayer could get a $100 tax rebate and save the entire bundle. Or she could spend $90 of it, with the company whose goods she bought meeting the demand through increased productivity and using the profits to pay down debt, Barbera says. "Empirically, it never happens."

Research by Princeton University economics professor Jonathan Parker has found that consumers spend a substantial portion of tax cuts. By looking at the spending patterns of consumers who've hit the cap for Social Security taxes—$87,000 in 2003—and can't be considered poor, Parker was able to "tease out" the effect and see "spending start to rise."

ALMA MATER

Whatever your preferred school of economics, be it Keynesian, monetarist, supply-side or eclectic, tax cuts aren't a one-time event. Even if they're pure handouts, with no supply-side incentives—tax cuts that "put money in the pockets of the people who will spend it"—there's a multiplier effect. Spending becomes income becomes spending, and so on.

"We have the effects of the tax cuts extending out three years," says Bob DiClemente, chief U.S. economist at Citigroup Inc. "There are ripple effects, the classic multiplier."

DiClemente says it's important to differentiate between the demand-side and supply-side effects. On the demand side, "to say the effect is fleeting is to ignore the multiplier effect and get a failing grade," he says. "The supply-side effects, while not great, are continual to the extent they are perceived to be permanent."

The supply-side effects have to do with the tendency of certain tax cuts, such as cuts in marginal and capital gains tax rates, to increase the incentive to work, save and invest. In so doing, they raise the economy's potential growth rate.

For supply-siders, these are the only kind of tax cuts that matter. It's all about increasing the size of the pie, not apportioning the various slices.

SUPPLY-SIDERS

"Tax cuts work on incentives," says Don Luskin, chief investment officer at Trend Macrolytics LLC, an independent investment and research firm in Menlo Park, California. "If you put money in the pockets of people who didn't work for it and who don't act differently, there's no net stimulative effect. It's just a transfer of wealth."

Consider the effect of mailing a $1 check to 200 million people, Luskin says. The national debt goes up by $200 million, and no one behaves any differently.

"The check is truly a loan that somebody will eventually have to pay back, somehow—if only through inflation if the government prints its way out of debt," he says.

The whole point of cutting taxes is not to benefit A at the expense of B. It's to create incentives for both of them.

"You need to change incentives," Luskin says. "Encourage people to work longer hours, go back to school, take more risk, buy stocks instead of bonds."

MONETARISTS

The latest tax-cut package, passed in May, was essentially designed to create long-term incentives rather than provide short-term stimulus, although there was some of the latter in there, too (and the salesmen often got their talking points confused). The package accelerated the reduction in marginal tax rates, enacted in 2001, and made them retroactive to Jan. 1, 2003, and reduced taxes on dividends and capital gains to a maximum of 15 percent.

Monetarists view tax cuts in a different light—in terms of their effect on the money supply. Tax cuts increase the deficit, at least in the short run (whether supply-side tax cuts eventually pay for themselves is a proposition that exists on Art Laffer's cocktail napkin), causing the government to borrow more.

"If the central bank holds the overnight rate steady, it will lead to more rapid money growth," says Bob Laurent, professor of economics and finance at the Illinois Institute of Technology's Stuart School of Business. "To the extent that the government's demand for credit is supplied by banks, it means a permanent increase in money."

SCHOOL FOR SCANDAL

There isn't much evidence from these various schools of thought to support the idea that the effect of last year's tax cut will be fading anytime soon.

"The level of spending it created will remain even though the growth rate won't," Barbera says.

In the meantime, other forces have been set in motion. Increased spending has spilled over to profits, investment and hiring, which is the route to a self-sustaining expansion.

That's already happening. The Commerce Department's measure of profits from current production rose 30 percent in the third quarter from a year earlier. Business investment in equipment and software rose 18.4 percent last quarter, the biggest increase in almost five years. The economy added jobs for the third consecutive month in October, with leading indicators suggesting Friday's employment report could show even greater job growth.

It's not as if "we live in a static world, where the stimulus is fading and nothing else is going on," says Jim Glassman, senior U.S. economist at J.P. Morgan Chase & Co. "We managed to grow for the last 100 years and didn't always need a new tax cut."

The economy grew at an 8.2 percent annualized pace in the third quarter. More and more economists are reconsidering their forecast for a "slow" fourth quarter to something on the order of 5 percent. Readings of 62.8 on the Institute for Supply Management's November manufacturing index and 73.7 on the new orders index have typically been associated with multiquarter booms.

"At this point, we should hope the fiscal stimulus begins to fade," DiClemente says.

Higher Oil Prices Are Not Like a Tax. Really.

—————— May 24, 2004 ——————

IT'S AXIOMATIC that higher gas prices act like a tax on consumers.

It's also dead wrong. There is nothing about a demand-driven rise in oil prices that will discourage oil production and reduce the quantity supplied to the market, which is precisely the effect of a tax.

Tax something more, and you get less of it: Now there's an axiom you can hang your hat on. If the government imposes a tax on a good or service, the effect will be to shift the demand curve back (inward) or the supply curve upward, depending on whether the tax is levied on the consumer or producer. In both cases, the quantity supplied at the new equilibrium is lower than it was before.

Let's walk through an example before looking at why the analogy of oil prices as a tax is off-base. If the government levies a tax on widgets that the buyer is responsible to pay, the same widget a consumer paid $5.00 for previously now costs him $5.50.

The imposition of a tax, which raises the effective cost to buyers, makes widgets less attractive, reducing the demand for them at any given price. The effect is expressed as a shift inward, to the left, in the demand curve, reducing the quantity of the widgets sold.

SUPPLIERS BEWARE

Now let's suppose suppliers are responsible for forking over the widget tax to Uncle Sam. The seller now keeps only $4.50 of the $5.00 ticket price. Widget sales are less profitable at any given price, which induces sellers to supply fewer of them. The supply curve shifts inward, to the left, reducing the quantity supplied to the market.

Simply put, a tax on a good shrinks the market for that good. The tax "drives a wedge between the price the consumer pays and the price the supplier receives," says Bob Laurent, professor of economics and finance at the Illinois Institute of Technology's Stuart School of Business.

Is there anything about today's higher oil prices, driven by a combination of increased demand and speculation (speculation is expressed as a shift out in the demand curve) that vaguely resembles a tax? Are higher prices going to lead to reduced output? Hardly.

A demand-driven rise in oil prices acts as a signal to producers to pump more oil and capture more profit. Any oil producer with excess capacity is doing that in the face of $40 crude.

BORN TO PUMP

Members of the Organization of Petroleum Exporting Countries met in Amsterdam over the weekend to consider Saudi Arabia's request to raise the quota by 2 million barrels a day—an academic issue, since OPEC is producing 2 million barrels a day over its current quota of 23.5 million.

While OPEC members delayed a decision until their official meeting in Beirut on June 3, Saudi Arabia plans to boost output to 9 million barrels a day starting in June, up from 8.35 million in April.

Unlike the effect of a tax, there's no cutback in oil production, no inefficiency created by a wedge between buyers' and sellers' prices, and (heresy!) no clear depressing effect on economic growth.

Consumers have to allocate more household income to fill their gas tanks. Oil-consuming businesses do as well. Wealth is transferred from consumers to producers.

"The total amount spent doesn't change," Laurent says. "People are allocating more dollars for each gallon of gasoline. But the dollars don't get lost. It's not clear why this should have a dampening effect on economic activity, like a tax. There's no dead-weight loss."

CORRELATION ISN'T CAUSATION

Most commentators imbue oil with unique properties. When oil prices fall, they claim it's deflationary (lack of demand). When prices rise, it's deflationary, too, since higher prices sap demand.

The empirical evidence supporting this cockamamie theory is the observation that most recessions have been preceded by higher oil prices. No one ever mentions that the central bank's response to higher oil prices and inflation might have something to do with ensuing recession. And it matters whether higher oil prices are a result of increased demand (currently) or reduced supply (the 1970s).

What economic theory would view higher oil prices as contractionary? Presumably it has to do with the fact that the U.S. is a net importer of oil. The profits accrue overseas, not here.

Once again, the dollars don't disappear. The U.S. sends dollars overseas to purchase oil. Those dollars come back here as foreign direct investment or securities purchases.

NONSENSE

Try this for circular logic: Higher oil prices are the result of strong economic growth and the cause of weaker economic growth. It's just patent nonsense.

Everyone who thinks higher oil prices are the equivalent of a tax should buy a basic economics textbook and read the chapter on supply and demand. The resulting shift out in the demand curve for textbooks would be analogous to what's going on in the oil market right now.

And no, it's not a tax.

5

First Principles

A SEARCH FOR the etymological roots of the term "first principles" yields references to mathematics and metaphysics, Euclid and Aristotle, verification and falsification.

A first principle is one that cannot be deduced from any other. It is an irrefutable truth, a proposition that doesn't need to be proven. Some 20th-century philosophers have challenged the idea that we can know anything for certain—an avenue I have neither the qualifications nor the interest to pursue.

I use the term "first principles" in a generic sense to refer to basic tenets. The Founding Fathers were guided by first principles when they wrote the Declaration of Independence ("We hold these truths to be self-evident ..."). Mathematicians rely on a set of propositions that are consistent with one another—first principles.

The columns in this chapter get at what I consider to be some basic truths in economics. The concepts aren't complicated. You don't need an advanced degree to understand them. They can be appreciated without econometric testing or proof.

According to Aristotle, the reason first principles don't need to be proved is that they are self-evident. They are known to be true simply by understanding them.

The Greatness of the U.S. Is McDonald's and Microsoft

———— Aug. 23, 2000 ————

DEAR MR. ROBERT SAMUELSON:

I enjoyed the letter format you chose for today's op-ed column in the *Washington Post* ("Pay Attention, Kids"), where you implore your children to follow the political debate this election year.

While I agree that they should pay attention—free elections are what separate a democratic from an autocratic society—may I suggest a slightly different approach to spark their interest? Specifically, I refer to the passage in which you wrote:

"You've got to care more about the election, because it goes to the heart of who we are as a nation. The greatness of the United States is not McDonald's or Microsoft. It's our basic beliefs about how we should govern ourselves—including elections. Through the Declaration of Independence and the Constitution, we gave the modern world two wonderful ideas: liberty and democracy."

The greatness of the U.S., Mr. Samuelson, is precisely McDonald's and Microsoft. They are the product of how we govern ourselves. They are symbols of liberty and democracy.

GOLDEN OPPORTUNITY

If you tell that to your kids, they actually might come around. These companies represent the basis of the capitalist system, wherein companies identify a consumer need, conceive a product or service to satisfy it, and compete with other producers to deliver the best quality at the lowest price.

They represent the spirit of America as well: the idea that you can become anybody you want to be, that a geek with an idea can start a company, become a millionaire—no, a billionaire—in one-quarter of a lifetime.

You can become the standard for an entire industry that didn't exist when you had your idea.

No doubt your kids spend hours in their rooms surfing the Net or hanging out with their friends at McDonald's. If they could somehow be made to see that the Golden Arches represent not just a Big Mac but a Big Tent, that Windows represents opportunity, not just an operating system, you might actually find them sitting in front of the TV watching the evening news with Jim Lehrer.

You might want to start with some history. McDonald's started as a hamburger stand in San Bernardino, California, in 1948. In 1954, Ray Kroc, a Multimixer salesman from Oak Park, Illinois, visited Dick and Mac McDonald's drive-through restaurant, which ran eight Multimixers simultaneously, and signed on as franchising agent.

McMoscow

One year later, Kroc opened the first McDonald's in Des Plaines, Illinois, toting up $366.12 in first-day sales.

McDonald's went public on its 10-year anniversary in 1965 at $22.50 a share. Today, it's the world's largest restaurant chain, with a market capitalization of $41.6 billion. More than 43 million people a day in 119 countries eat under the Golden Arches.

The biggest and busiest McDonald's restaurant is in Pushkin Square in Moscow. Russians love McDonald's. Maybe it's the fast food that appeals to them, but I suspect McDonald's represents the antithesis of what was Russia for 75 long, dark years of communist rule.

In 1974, McDonald's decided it wanted to give something back to the community and started the Ronald McDonald House, which provides comfort and care to the families of seriously ill children receiving treatment at nearby hospitals. McDonald's Corp. pays 100 percent of the costs of administering the 206 Ronald McDonald Houses in 19 countries.

All American

Bill Gates's story is better known. Geek, computer nerd, visionary, genius, Gates dropped out of Harvard, where he was already developing programming language, to start Microsoft in 1975 with Paul Allen.

The rest, as they say, is history. Today Microsoft Corp. is the world's largest software company, with a market value of $373.3 billion. One hundred shares of Microsoft stock purchased at the initial public offering in 1986 for $21 each would be 14,400 shares today worth more than $1 million.

On any given day, depending on the vagaries of the stock market, Bill Gates is either the richest or second richest man in the world. (He's also under attack from the trustbusters at the Justice Department, but you might want to leave out that chapter of the story until you've hooked the kids on the concept.)

These two companies couldn't be the products of any other country. Just imagine the bureaucrats of the European Commission's competitiveness committee trying to ensure that an Egg McMuffin in Milan doesn't have a half-ounce more cheese than in Madrid.

I really think you could score points with the kids big-time, Mr. Samuelson, by bringing the election down to terms they can understand.

And if all else fails, you can ground them for a week, rescind their computer privileges and withhold their allowance for meals away from home. That should drive the point home.

Very truly yours,

Caroline A. Baum

POSTSCRIPT: *One hundred shares of Microsoft stock purchased at the initial public offering in 1986 for $21 each were 28,800 shares worth $769,536 as of Dec. 31, 2004. In the fourth quarter of 2004, Microsoft paid out a special one-time dividend of $3 a share, or $32.6 million. Bill Gates is still the richest person in the world, with a net worth of $46.5 billion, according to* Forbes *magazine's annual survey for 2005.*

McDonald's, which is celebrating its 50th anniversary this year, serves nearly 50 million people a day in more than 31,000 restaurants in 119 countries. After 12 stock splits, 100 shares purchased at the initial public offering price of $22.50 in 1955 had grown to 74,360 shares worth $2.4 million on Dec. 31, 2004.

Why the Minimum Wage Got the Maximum Shaft

——————   Aug. 30, 2000   ——————

THE MINIMUM WAGE is on the front page again. The economic arguments against raising it seem to have gotten lost in the editing process.

The statutory minimum wage has long been a hot-button political issue, a clear dividing line between Democrats (in favor of raising it) and Republicans (against it).

This time around, Republicans in the House of Representatives enthusiastically supported the Democratic initiative for a $1 increase in the minimum wage to $6.15 an hour, phased in over two years. The GOP dropped its insistence on tying the minimum wage bill to the repeal of the estate tax and overhaul of pension laws, both of which passed as separate bills.

House Speaker Dennis Hastert is insisting on $76 billion in tax cuts for small business to offset the cost of the minimum wage increase.

That's where the discussion of costs ended. Not one news story featured the economic argument against raising the minimum wage—primarily because no Republican was willing to make it.

Why is it that an issue that is used in every economics textbook to illustrate the unintended consequences of government-mandated price caps and floors is no longer challenged for the job killer that it is?

A few ideas come to mind, but first the economic theory behind the minimum wage.

Supply and Demand

The labor market is like any other product market. The equilibrium price is determined by the intersection of supply and demand.

Individuals elect to supply labor primarily to earn a wage. Firms demand labor for production. In a free market, there is one price at which supply (the amount consumers are willing to supply at any given price) and demand (the quantity firms demand at that price) intersect. That's the price at which the market "clears," or is in equilibrium.

Attempts by government to interfere with what Adam Smith called "the invisible hand" of the market have consequences that are, in most cases, the opposite of what was intended. Determining that a particular price is too high (the price of oil) or too low (the price of labor, or minimum wage) for moral acceptability, government officials sometimes set the price by decree.

"The market has proven itself a formidable foe that strongly resists attempts to circumvent its workings," write economists William Baumol and Alan Blinder in *Economics: Principles and Policy.*

Invisible, Unmovable Hand

When the government puts an artificial ceiling on prices, such as oil prices in the 1970s and apartment prices in New York City (rent control), the result is shortages, among other symptoms, as producers withhold supply from the market. Price floors, of which the minimum wage is the best example, lead to surpluses as supply (those willing to supply their labor to the market) exceeds demand (what firms are willing to pay).

"The effects of the minimum wage may be pronounced in the markets for unskilled labor—and presumably quite different from those that Congress intended," the textbook says.

It's unskilled labor, those at the bottom of the food chain, that's harmed by setting a minimum wage above what firms are willing to pay. McDonald's may be willing to pay a high school dropout $5.15 an hour to flip hamburgers, but at $6.15, the company will have the guy doing fries fill in.

To be sure, the unskilled workers who are lucky enough to retain their jobs are better off when the legal minimum wage is increased. It's those who are laid off or who won't be hired in the first place—because the number of people seeking jobs exceeds the demand at $6.15 an hour—that are harmed.

Yet not a peep was heard from staunch conservatives in protest of the proposed increase.

Bring Back Insecurity!

For one thing, the labor market is so damned tight that a little unemployment and worker insecurity seems like a good alternative to rudeness, at least as far as consumers are concerned.

No one can say that, however. Even Federal Reserve Chairman Alan Greenspan is careful when he warns about the tight labor market, couching his comments in the politically correct shrinking pool of available labor rather than the unemployment rate being too low.

The economic good times and scarcity of skilled labor have put fears of unemployment on the back burner.

The second reason for the silence is that the Democrats have seized the moral high ground and the Republicans are playing their game. After all, the Democrats are the party of the people, not the powerful. They provide succor and solace to the nation's poor, tired and hungry.

Whether they have achieved that end through all the social engineering and Great Society programs they've done is an open question (the failure of welfare suggests that the means to the end were misdirected).

Moral Wimps

What is clear is that "today's Democrats are buffered by a moral authority that Republicans simply don't have, an authority that comes in large part from their conspicuous alignment with the fight against inequality," said Shelby Steele, a research fellow at the Hoover Institution, in an Aug. 2 op-ed column in the *Wall Street Journal.* "Enemies of liberalism must conform to its ideological demands or be stigmatized as 'mean spirited' and therefore lacking the legitimacy to represent all Americans."

Conformity with liberalism spares people "life-altering stigmatization as racist, sexist or homophobic," Steele said.

Steele faults the conservatives for their failure to shape their principles of individual responsibility, merit, hard work, single standards, competition and initiative into "a countervailing vision of social decency" to compete with liberalism.

The "vision thing," as Bush *père* used to say, doesn't seem to exist circa 2000. If the Republicans aren't willing to seize the high ground in the minimum wage debate because they're afraid of being stigmatized, then creating an alternative to liberal dogma seems too much to ask.

Gephardt's Loopy Proposal Gets Lost in Debate
—————— Jan. 9, 2004 ——————

AS THE Democratic presidential candidates try to differentiate themselves from one another beyond the disclaimers—"I'm not George W. Bush," "I'm not Howard Dean"—all the attention has been focused on their plans to roll back some or all of the tax cuts enacted in the past three years.

That's too bad because there are some really loopy proposals out there. Take Dick Gephardt's idea for an international minimum wage. The congressional lifer and House minority leader from Missouri said that if elected, he would press the World Trade Organization to establish such a wage.

"The goal of the IMW will be to equalize a 'living wage' in each country to ensure the proper sustenance, health and welfare for that country's population," according to a position paper on Gephardt's Web site. "The IMW will vary based on a country's development level, and will seek to eliminate the proliferation of competition from slave, sweatshop and child labor around the world."

It's not enough for this self-described friend of labor to destroy job opportunities for entry-level workers at home. Now he wants to kill them abroad as well.

Imagine what would happen if a floor were imposed on wages in a country like China, where cheap labor is its comparative advantage, not to mention its ticket for emerging from a poor, developing nation to an industrialized one.

MISGUIDED

Jobs would come back to the U.S., that's for sure. Asia's engines of growth would sputter. The world economy could stall. American consumers would pay higher prices. Inflation would rise.

You can't fault Gephardt for his intentions. Raising living standards and wages for all workers is a noble goal—one most folks, regardless of their political persuasion, share.

It's his methodology that's misguided. Imposing a minimum wage in developing countries is tantamount to "sanctioning poor countries for the crime of being poor," says Dan Griswold, associate director for the Center for Trade Studies at the libertarian Cato Institute in Washington. "Wages are low because productivity is low, not because people there are lazy or dumb. They don't have the tools or the infrastructure or the education or the good governance to be productive."

The way to raise living standards and wages in these countries is not to do what Gephardt suggests and impose a price floor on labor. It's "to encourage market reforms and trade with them: buy their products and invest in their economies," Griswold says.

CAN'T FOOL MR. MARKET

Determining and implementing the IMW sounds like a bureaucratic nightmare, according to Gephardt's position paper.

"Phasing in a requirement for a development-based variable IMW could require compensation, under international trade law," the paper says. "Each country's needs and costs will be individually assessed, and a program of aid and development assistance will be tailored to its needs."

It's an awful lot of red tape for such an undesirable result: higher unemployment. That's what always happens when supply (of labor, in this case), attracted by a government-mandated above-market price, exceeds demand.

"If you set wages above productivity, it will create mass unemployment," Griswold says.

Any discussion of the minimum wage ultimately succumbs to emotion, not logic. When my economic thought processes were evolving, an economist friend of mine set me straight on the subject by asking me a few questions.

"Why raise the minimum wage to $7.50 an hour?" he asked. "Why not raise it to $100 an hour and make everybody rich?"

UNINTENDED CONSEQUENCES

Answer: Because there's a cost. The folks who hold on to their minimum-wage jobs are better off when the government imposes a floor. Employers, forced to pay a higher wage than the market will bear, cut back on their demand for labor (the demand curve is downward sloping) and lay people off.

If high-paid American workers really can't compete with Chinese workers earning 50 cents an hour, it's a well-kept secret: U.S. businesses employ more than 130 million workers.

China has an advantage in labor-intensive industries, such as apparel manufacturing. When it comes to high-paying jobs in information technology, however, "we can happily pay our workers many times more than what Chinese workers earn because they're more productive," Griswold says.

Gephardt clearly hasn't thought through the unintended consequences of his proposal for an international minimum wage.

"Does he think the world would be a safer, more secure and friendly place if we were the cause of massive unemployment?" Griswold asks. "The unemployed worker is a poor customer for U.S. goods. Does he want foreigners working for U.S. multinationals or for al-Qaeda?"

Food for Thought: Lessons from a Bird Feeder

———— Aug. 29, 2001 ————

I HAVE a new bird feeder. Or, more correctly, I have an entire bird-feeding facility, consisting of a large, squirrel-proof, multi-tube-and-perch feeder (all birds welcome) and a thistle bag for small birds.

I spend a lot of time staring out the window at my birds (the calming effect increases my productivity to no end), thinking about the laws of nature and economic theories as they apply to the avian kingdom.

My first tentative visitor, a yellow finch, showed up within an hour after I filled the feeder. Twenty-four hours later, I had a full house.

My first thought was that this was a clear case of Say's Law: supply creates its own demand. I introduce new supply to the market, and presto! An outpouring of demand.

What Jean-Baptiste Say, a late 18th-, early 19th-century French economist, meant when he described this phenomenon in 1803 was that total demand in an economy can't exceed or fall below total supply. In other words, demand is derived from what is produced. The money we receive from selling what we produce is used to purchase some other product.

WELFARE STATE

This premise of classical economics, replaced by John Maynard Keynes's idea that government could address that beast known as insufficient aggregate demand, is probably not the applicable principle. After all, I'm not producing anything. I'm a distributor, the middleman between someone else's production (the seed company) and hungry mouths.

What I must be doing is contributing to my birds' general welfare, making them better off by providing easy access to food. Since they no longer have to forage for food, they have more leisure to do whatever birds do when they aren't foraging.

Not so fast, says Paul Kasriel, head of economic research at the Northern Trust Corp. in Chicago. "You're creating a welfare system, creating dependency. They'll lose their foraging skills and become permanent wards of the Baum estate."

And here I set out to do something beneficial, forgetting about the law of unintended consequences.

And don't forget the social costs, says Chris Low, chief economist at First Tennessee Capital Markets.

"What if the birds get fat and have health problems?" Low says. "Bird consumption of insects will go down," upsetting the balance of nature. "The bird contribution to the economy falls."

SUPPLY AND DEMAND

Okay, forget macroeconomics. Maybe I'm operating in the world of microeconomics. What I'm really doing in providing food to these birds is shifting the supply curve out to the right, which lowers the equilibrium price and increases the equilibrium quantity demanded.

"You're giving them something at a pretty low price," says Bob Laurent, professor of economics and finance at the Illinois Institute of Technology's Stuart School of Business. "The search costs are minimal. The price to the birds falls."

As word gets out there's food around (granted it's imperfect information since not all birds have the same access to it), the demand curve probably shifts out as well, Laurent says. "That means the price goes up."

A higher price in the bird world might translate to a longer wait for location on the feeder or thistle bag. That's the same form inflation took in the Soviet Union. The government fixed prices, but consumers had to endure long lines to buy goods, not to mention encountering shortages and poor quality.

DISCRIMINATORY PRACTICES

A higher price might mean that small birds are discriminated against. (The thistle bag was an attempt to level the playing field.) To be fair, I confess to discriminatory buying practices: I buy seed without cracked corn because I don't want to attract the crows.

What were my birds doing, and where were they feeding, before I came along? Maybe what I'm witnessing is substitution effect: the switch to my birdseed instead of my neighbor's due to a change in the relative price.

In a bird's eyes, it's cheaper not to have to deal with intruders like squirrels. So my seed, even if it's exactly the same as the neighbor's, is a cheaper option.

Meanwhile, as I've been pondering the economic lessons from a bird feeder, I see my birds have eaten the entire quantity supplied. I'll have to go out and replenish the supply. I wonder what that's going to do to the price of birdseed and thistle. The initial price to the birds may have gone down, but if my price goes up I may have to reevaluate this whole economic model.

POSTSCRIPT: *I've expanded my avian facility to include shelter as well as food. I provide resting (sea-grass pockets) and nesting places (birdhouses). In addition to infrastructure, I supply home furnishing materials, including laundry lint, during the spring nesting season. And I've winterized the birdbath, courtesy of a floating de-icer.*

The Economy's Natural Tendency Is to Grow. Really.

—————— June 11, 2002 ——————

EVERY WIGGLE in economic activity, transmitted via a series of weekly, monthly and quarterly economic indicators, is dissected in an attempt to reach an ultimate conclusion. Is the U.S. economy back in gear, or is it still in the grip of a post-bubble correction, destined for months, maybe years, of underperformance?

The first quarter surprised to the upside, with economic growth of 5.6 percent exceeding the most optimistic forecasts. Yes, two-thirds of the growth in gross domestic product was due to inventories, which fell at a slower pace in the first quarter than they did in the fourth.

But that's the way it always works in recoveries. Deconstructing GDP growth and discounting inventories now that they're adding to growth after a record decline in the last half of 2001 isn't kosher.

First-quarter optimism quickly eroded into pessimism over second-quarter growth. Real consumer spending, up 0.2 percent in April, came in below expectations. Retail sales for May, to be reported on Thursday, are expected to show an outright decline and only a small increase excluding autos.

That will put consumer spending, the economy's mainstay, on a weaker trajectory than the first quarter's 3.2 percent growth.

BIG PICTURE

What gets lost in the analysis of these tenths-of-a-percent changes (the difference between a 0.2 percent and 0.3 percent increase is major for the markets yet a minor exercise in rounding for the statistical agencies) is the big picture. It is the natural state of the economy to grow. Left to its own devices, it will do just that. Inappropriate government policies can suppress that tendency or encourage it: right now, on balance, there's more of the latter than the former, especially on the monetary front.

True, the Federal Reserve can't make corporations invest in plant and equipment when they already have excess capacity. What the central bank can do is stimulate demand with a rock-bottom 1.75 percent federal funds rate so that ultimately demand will absorb the current supply.

"Everyone who studied macroeconomics in the 1970s—not at Chicago, but everywhere else—learned disequilibrium economics: why it is economies get stuck in a rut," says Jim Glassman, senior U.S. economist at J.P. Morgan Chase. "In an attempt to explain the 1930s, and also the stagflation of the 1970s, people cooked up all sorts of stories to explain why the economy could be chronically underemployed."

FREE TO ADJUST

The 1990s put the kibosh on the debate between classical and neo-Keynesian economists about the reasons for an extended period of sub-optimal economic performance. The economy's performance was no longer sub-optimal, so the focus shifted to what had changed.

Glassman says "significant reform of the U.S. economy" explains the economy's improved ability to weather storms.

"Deregulation, financial innovation, improved information technology and increased globalization all enhanced flexibility, accelerating the rebound from shocks that might once have led to long-term unemployment," Glassman says.

If the economy is free to adjust to a slowdown in demand—if employers, instead of being locked into long-term union contracts, can fire employees or rely on temporary workers for marginal changes in demand—the adjustment process will be short-lived.

"There's a reason why full employment acts as a gravitational pull on output," Glassman says. "A shortfall of aggregate demand relative to supply results in price adjustments that rebalance demand with supply."

FORCED LABOR

That's as true for labor as it is for goods. The rate of increase in the price of labor—wages—has slowed markedly in the last 18 months. The annual increase in average hourly earnings fell from a peak of 4.4 percent in December 2000 to a six-year low of 3.2 percent in May.

Then there's the discipline imposed by the capital markets themselves. With markets allocating capital to the sectors or companies that provide the best return on investment, it's no wonder financing for the beleaguered telecommunications industry has all but dried up.

"Market discipline is forcing severe cutbacks with painful repercussions," Glassman says. "The adjustment is occurring more rapidly than it might have in another era."

Say's Law Says It All

Maybe it's no surprise that recessions in the last 20 years have been shallower and shorter than the historical average. The U.S., hated and revered for its slash-and-burn style of capitalism, has absorbed multiple shocks to the system and carried on almost as if nothing had happened. The 1987 stock market crash, 1998's "100-year storm" (Russia's default and the near-collapse of hedge fund Long-Term Capital Management) and the terrorist attacks on the World Trade Center and Pentagon last September are three that come to mind.

Everyone thought the U.S. economy, already on the skids from a burst asset bubble, would be down for the count following the collapse of the Twin Towers. Yet the economy expanded in the fourth quarter, albeit modestly.

The Nasdaq Composite Index lost 72 percent of its value from March 2000 to September 2001. The broad stock market saw some $5.8 trillion of its value sheared in that same time period. Yet the U.S. economy has come back quicker and stronger than almost everyone expected.

Classical economists look to the theories of the late 18th-, early 19th-century political economist Jean-Baptiste Say to explain the tendency of an economy to expand. Say's Law, supply creates its own demand, states that an increase in the output of goods and services, through the revenue it generates, leads to an increase in demand. Unemployment is merely a temporary state.

"The incentive to produce is to profit," Glassman says. "Supply creates the dynamics that support demand."

So have faith. The economy wants to grow. Really it does.

Broken Windows Don't Generate Economic Growth

———— Jan. 6, 2003 ————

With President Bush set to announce the details of an economic stimulus plan tomorrow, and the Democrats distilling the plan to its essence—tax cuts for the rich—it's a good idea to look at the economic issues that separate the two parties.

Democrats want to redistribute income from the rich to the poor. They don't say that anymore; new Democrats realize Americans don't like class warfare, which hasn't stopped them from engaging in it. It's just that they do it more subtly nowadays.

The Democrats prefer tax rebates and tax holidays (specifically a payroll tax holiday) to reductions in marginal tax rates. They want to transfer money from one entity to another instead of increasing the size of the pie with incentives to work, produce and invest. The goal, as the Democrats see it, is "to put money into the pockets of the people who will spend it."

The debate starts and ends there. The rich will save the money; therefore, to stimulate the economy the government needs to transfer money to those who will spend it.

Where does the money come from? Does anyone explain the source of this government largesse?

The government has only two sources of revenue: it can tax, and it can borrow. (We'll leave printing money aside for now because that would require the complicity of the central bank, which is independent in the U.S.) To put money into the pockets of those who will spend it, the government has to take it from someone who would have saved it, spent it or spent part of it.

What Is Unseen

This transfer of spending power is not stimulus, as the 19th-century French political economist Frédéric Bastiat pointed out in his essay "What Is Seen and What Is Not Seen." Bastiat relates the tale of the broken window, wherein the owner of the shop whose window was broken by a hoodlum now has to pay the glazier to fix it, which puts money in the glazier's pocket to buy his kids shoes, which enables the shoemaker to ... and so on.

In other words, thank God for all the income generated by the broken window!

That's what's seen, Bastiat points out. What's unseen is what the shop owner would have done had he not needed to pay the glazier to repair his window. It's important to consider the unseen effects of any economic policy or action, Bastiat suggests—something many economists and policy-makers are unwilling or unable to do.

There is no real stimulus from transferring money from one person to another. These actions may appease our moral conscience as a nation and make us feel charitable as human beings, but it's a mistake to call this "economic stimulus."

Holiday on Ice

As Bastiat writes: "There is no benefit to industry in general or to national employment as a whole, whether windows are broken or not broken." (Today most central banks target an overnight interest rate. Any pressure on rates from increased government borrowing to finance transfer payments will be offset by the bank's purchases of securities. The actual stimulus comes from this monetization of the debt, which is not what the Democrats are talking about.)

The Democrats are promoting the idea of a payroll tax holiday. All workers have 6.2 percent of their paycheck deducted on the first $87,000 of income (effective in 2003). The employer chips in another 6.2 percent. Low-income families may not pay income tax, but they still owe payroll taxes.

Exempting a certain amount of income from the payroll tax, or providing a one-year tax holiday, would help low-income families, whose income never exceeds the cutoff point. Because employers would be exempt as well, it would lower the cost of hiring the marginal worker and stimulate employment, the Democrats claim.

Can of Worms

Employees may very well spend their holiday bonus, but employers probably won't run out to hire when they know the cost of those workers will go up at the end of the year.

According to Saturday's *Washington Post,* the Democrats have soured on the payroll-tax-holiday idea. House Minority Leader Nancy Pelosi was quoted as saying it "would drain funds from the Social Security trust fund."

Can you guess why she nixed the idea? It's a can of worms the Democrats would rather leave unopened. Any discussion about the Social Security trust fund would have to include the discomfiting fact that there is no Social Security trust fund. The trust fund is some IOUs the government writes to itself. The payroll taxes of today's workers pay current retirees' Social Security benefits. Nothing is saved or invested.

DON'T ASK, DON'T TELL

Introducing the Social Security trust fund into the debate leaves Democrats vulnerable on the subject of partial privatization of Social Security, wherein workers save for their own retirement rather than accept the meager returns offered by Social Security. A two-income couple making the average wage retiring today earns a real 2.3 percent from Social Security, according to the Social Security Administration— a return that will fall over time as fewer workers support more retirees.

What's more, advocating a payroll tax holiday would expose the contradictions in the Democrats' argument.

"The same people who say that allowing personal savings accounts would harm the system are saying we can take money out of the system, give it back to people and not harm the system," says Andrew Biggs, a Social Security analyst at the libertarian Cato Institute in Washington.

Once you realize that transferring money isn't stimulative per se and Americans' retirement funds aren't invested in anything, the basis for tax cuts for the rich becomes increasingly appealing, even for Democrats.

It Was a 'General Theory' for a Specific Time

———— Sept. 26, 2001 ————

FOR YEARS, monetary policy has been the only game in town, and Alan Greenspan the only gamesman running it.

All of a sudden the other head of the hydra—fiscal policy—is showing its, er, ugly head. The urge to splurge has begun.

After cautioning Congress against any rush to action in the wake of the World Trade Center terrorist attack, Federal Reserve Chairman Alan Greenspan and minister without portfolio Bob Rubin told the Senate Finance Committee in a closed-door meeting yesterday that any stimulus package should be "significant."

Don't spend, these gentlemen are saying, but if you do, do it with panache.

"They're invoking the Powell Doctrine," says Paul Kasriel, director of economic research at the Northern Trust Corp. in Chicago. Loosely translated, the doctrine—named after the current secretary of state and former chairman of the Joint Chiefs of Staff—holds that "if you are going to move militarily, do so with massive force and only if it is in the vital interest of the Republic," Kasriel says.

So how much is significant? In a $10 trillion economy, significant would be 1 percent of gross domestic product, or $100 billion, Dr. Greenspan said, according to senators at the hearing.

Late yesterday, the Fed's press office was forced to clarify Greenspan's Rx for fiscal stimulus, saying the $100 billion "includes the additional spending approved by Congress in the last two weeks" of about $45 billion.

Double Epiphany

Why the about-face from the Fed chairman, who did a flip-flop on the capital gains tax as well? (He used to think the appropriate capital gains tax rate was zero. Now he thinks now isn't the right time to be appropriate.)

"He's scared," says Kasriel. "He's not convinced that printing money alone will revive aggregate demand in the economy."

At a time when the Fed is pulling out the stops on the monetary front, Kasriel wonders if the Fed chief isn't "the least bit worried about the longer-run inflation implications of increased government spending financed with fiat money."

Given the lively debate about fiscal stimulus, I thought it was time to dust off my copy of Henry Hazlitt's *Economics in One Lesson*. The whole of economics "can be reduced to a single lesson, and that lesson can be reduced to a single sentence," Hazlitt wrote in 1946.

To wit: "The art of economics consists in looking not merely at the immediate but at the longer effects of any act or policy; it consists in tracing the consequences of that policy not merely for one group but for all groups."

Bastiat's Broken Window

Hazlitt pays a debt of gratitude to Frédéric Bastiat, the early 19th-century French political economist. (Bastiat seems to be enjoying something of a revival, cropping up in a speech by Dallas Fed president Bob McTeer and in the pages of *Barron's*.) Bastiat's famous essay, "What Is Seen and What Is Not Seen," tells a simple story of a hoodlum who heaves a brick through a shopkeeper's window, thereby providing income for the glazier who repairs the window.

That's what's seen. What's unseen is what the shopkeeper might have done with the money if he didn't have to repair the window—buy a new piece of equipment, for example, or a new suit of clothes.

It's not hard to figure out where Bastiat and Hazlitt are going with all of this. It was fashionable following the Great Depression and the publication of John Maynard Keynes's *General Theory of Employment, Interest, and Money* to think that the government could provide employment and income when the private sector was in a slump.

GENERALLY INCORRECT

"Keynes's *General Theory* was a general theory for a specific time," Kasriel says. The Great Depression "was a time when the private sector didn't want to spend at all. We're not there now."

Every job the government creates for a public project deprives the private sector of a job. Every dollar spent on a building or a bridge is a dollar less spent on plants or equipment.

When the government wants to spend, it has two choices: It can raise taxes or borrow (we'll leave the option of printing money, inflating, for another day). Someone else—the private sector—has to give up resources so that the government can spend.

In the short run, the GDP will probably get a boost if the government dumps $100 billion into the economy. After all, the government will be spending aggressively at a time when business and consumers are turning ultra-cautious.

In the long run, however, when the government commands an increased share of our limited savings and scarce resources, the result is a less efficient economy. Government spending doesn't add to the capital stock, it doesn't increase the economy's potential growth rate and it doesn't increase productivity.

Of course, one could argue that increased government spending on defense and security will add to our well-being. After all, if we're all dead as a result of a biological attack by terrorists, who cares about our productivity?

Keynes always said in the long run we're all dead. Maybe that's why he thought government spending could fix what ails us.

❖   ❖   ❖

What George Stephanopoulos
Didn't Ask Bob Graham

———————— April 28, 2003 ————————

YESTERDAY ON ABC's "This Week" with George Stephanopoulos, the host interviewed U.S. Senator Bob Graham of Florida, who has thrown his hat into the 2004 presidential race with a gaggle of other Democratic hopefuls.

Graham weighed in against President George W. Bush's tax cut. Instead of eliminating the double taxation of dividends, the keystone of the Bush proposal recently neutered by the Senate, Graham said we needed to "create demand" by "putting money in the pockets of people who will spend it."

Boy, I wish I had been sitting in Stephanopoulos's seat. Then again, it's much more fun to fantasize about what I would have asked Graham—and what he would have said in response.

CB: Would you explain to me, Senator, how you create demand by transferring purchasing power from one entity, in this case the government, whose sources of income are limited to taxing or borrowing from the public, to another?

BG: Higher-income people save more. Lower-income people spend more of what they earn. Giving tax cuts to the wealthiest Americans is unfair. If we are going to help our economy, we must quickly put money into the pockets of those Americans who will spend the money as soon as possible.

CB: Alan Greenspan told us the rich benefited most from the stock market bubble and were similarly hurt the most—their spending declined more—by the bubble bursting.

BG: I don't know anything about that.

CB: That's all right. Neither does he. Go ahead.

BG: What we need is a tax cut that gives Americans the confidence they need right now to begin pumping their hard-earned dollars back into the economy.

IN THE BEGINNING

CB: Where exactly does the government get the money to provide the tax cuts that will give Americans the confidence to begin pumping their hard-earned dollars back into the economy? It has three options: It can tax, it can borrow, it can inflate. We'll leave bachelor No. 3 for another time.

If you raise taxes on one group and redistribute the income to another group, there's no net stimulus. A spends instead of B. Yes, the poor do have a higher marginal propensity to consume. But that's not stimulus. It's a transfer of the ability to spend from one party to the next.

Helping the needy is a noble goal, but let's not confuse charity with stimulus. Stimulus means growing the pie. Redistributing income is what it says: robbing Peter to pay Paul. While those in receipt of the government's largesse may be better off, we aren't better off as a nation.

REDEFINING HELP

Besides, handouts don't necessarily help at all. The welfare system was a classic case of well-intentioned help becoming a huge hindrance by creating incentives to have more children and stay on the dole.

As far as deficit financing is concerned, if the Federal Reserve accommodates increased government borrowing by printing money (to prevent the overnight rate from rising), it can increase demand in the short run. Eventually, the money illusion fades and we are left with higher inflation, not faster real growth.

BG: Well, faster real growth is what I'm talking about. We need to get this economy moving again. There are probably many arguments to be made about the elimination of the dividend tax or some of the other tax cuts proposed in the president's budget, but there is not one to be made that these cuts provide an economic stimulus, certainly in the short term.

SHORT-RUN ILLUSION

CB: Did you ever consider that short-term economic stimulus is another misnomer? If it's only good in the short term, it isn't good at all. We waste too much time—and you folks in Congress waste too much of your political capital—crafting schemes to pump up spending for the election cycle and not enough focusing on long-run policies that create incentives to work, save and invest for the future.

I don't know whether the elimination of the double taxation of dividends and retained earnings will lift the stock market by 5 percent, 10 percent or not at all. And a forecast shouldn't be a prerequisite for tax reform. Corporations' preference for financing with debt, which is deductible, rather than equity, which is not, encourages borrowing. It would have been cleaner to eliminate the double taxation at the corporate level, but I suspect the Bush administration didn't want to fight the PR battle that it would create by giving those evil corporations a tax break.

It's About Incentives

BG: The federal government is facing several tough challenges, including the need to strengthen and reform Social Security, modernize Medicare and provide a prescription drug benefit to its participants, and fund the ongoing war against terrorism. Additional tax cuts will rob us of the resources necessary to meet these challenges.

CB: All I can say is those challenges are less onerous with an economy growing at 4 percent than at 2 percent. And if you want to raise the growth rate, you have to encourage entrepreneurship, give someone the incentive to create the next big idea. To do that, you have to increase the potential reward, or profit, for taking the risk.

It's not about how much money someone is willing to give up to buy a good or a service. It's about how much work some individual is willing to do: the profitability of going to work.

BG: It was a lot easier with Stephanopoulos sitting in that chair.

Pilgrims' Progress, or the Story of Thanksgiving

——————— Nov. 26, 2003 ———————

It is the tradition of this column every year at this time to relate the story of Thanksgiving. For source material, I am grateful to the accounts of William Bradford, governor of the Plymouth Bay Colony beginning in 1621 (Bradford's history, *Of Plimoth Plantation*).

Most Americans think of Thanksgiving as a day off from work, a time to gather with friends and family and celebrate with a huge feast. If children know anything about the origins of this national holiday, declared each year by presidential proclamation, it's that the Pilgrims were grateful for a good harvest in their new land and set aside this day to give thanks.

What they and many adults don't know is that things weren't always good for the Pilgrims, a group of English Separatists who came to the

New World to escape religious persecution. Their first winters after they landed at Plymouth Rock in 1620 and established the Plymouth Bay Colony were harsh. The weather and crop yields were poor.

Half the Pilgrims died or returned to England in the first year. Those who remained went hungry. Despite their deep religious convictions, the Pilgrims took to stealing from one another.

Finally, in the spring of 1623, Governor Bradford and the others "begane to thinke how they might raise as much corne as they could, and obtaine a better crop than they had done, that they might not still thus languish in misery," according to Bradford's history.

OLD-WORLD BAGGAGE

One of the traditions the Pilgrims had brought with them from England was a practice known as "farming in common." Everything they produced was put into a common pool, and the harvest was rationed among them according to need.

They had thought "that the taking away of property, and bringing in community into a common wealth, would make them happy and flourishing," Bradford recounts.

They were wrong. "For this community (so far as it was) was found to breed much confusion and discontent, and retard much imployment that would have been to their benefite and comforte," Bradford writes.

Young, able-bodied men resented working for others without compensation. Incentives were lacking.

After the Pilgrims had endured near-starvation for three winters, Bradford decided to experiment when it came time to plant in the spring of 1623. He set aside a plot of land for each family, that "they should set corne every man for his owne particular, and in that regard trust to themselves."

A NEW WAY

The results were nothing short of miraculous.

Bradford writes: "This had very good success; for it made all hands very industrious, so as much more corne was planted than other ways would have been by any means the Govr or any other could use, and saved him a great deall of trouble, and gave far better content."

The women now went willingly into the field, carrying their young children on their backs. Those who previously claimed they were too old or ill to work embraced the idea of private property and enjoyed the fruits of their labor, eventually producing enough to trade their excess corn for furs and other desired commodities.

Given appropriate incentives, the Pilgrims produced and enjoyed a bountiful harvest in the fall of 1623 and set aside "a day of thanksgiving" to thank God for their good fortune.

"Any generall wante or famine hath not been amongst them since to this day," Bradford writes in an entry from 1647, the last year covered by his history.

With the benefit of hindsight, we know that the Pilgrims' good fortune was not a matter of luck. In 1623, they were responding to the same incentives that have been adopted almost universally four centuries later.

6

Understanding the
Yield Curve

E CONOMISTS CALL IT the term structure of interest rates. Traders call it the yield curve.

Either way, it's the pictorial representation of the yields on various U.S. Treasury securities, or other sovereign debt, maturing in 0 to 30 years.

The Treasury yield curve is anchored and influenced by the federal funds rate. This overnight, uncollateralized rate at which banks lend to one another is set by the Federal Reserve and holds sway over a whole host of short-term rates, from Libor (London Interbank Offered Rate, the rate at which dollars are lent among banks overseas) to certificates of deposit to commercial paper to short-term Treasury notes.

The funds rate is also the Fed's policy tool. The Fed raises or lowers the funds rate to influence aggregate demand.

The long rate, in theory, is the sum of the current and future expected short-term rates. As a practical matter, the yield on long-term Treasuries incorporates the real cost of borrowing and expectations for inflation over that maturity spectrum. Long rates also reflect the degree of confidence in a country's fiscal policies (including its ability to repay its debts), its currency and its system of government.

The informational content in the yield curve derives from the fact that the shortest rate is set by the central bank and the longest rate by the market. It is the relationship between these two rates, rather than their absolute levels, that suggests whether monetary policy is tight or loose.

There's a reason the spread between the funds rate and the 10-year note rate was added to the Conference Board's Index of Leading Economic Indicators in 1996: It's one of the best predictors of the business cycle. It's also widely misunderstood.

Given the advantages of the spread—it's free, it's available in real time and it's never revised—it manages to be one of the best-kept secrets around.

Alan Greenspan Shows His True Wicksellian Colors

———————— April 10, 2000 ————————

WHEN ALAN GREENSPAN speaks nowadays, financial market professionals focus almost exclusively on the question of is he or isn't he—targeting stock prices, that is.

Such myopia caused most folks to overlook a brand new indicator in the Federal Reserve chairman's toolkit last week. In speeches at both a White House conference on Wednesday and a technology forum in St. Louis on Friday, Greenspan invoked the ideas of Swedish economist Knut Wicksell (1851–1926) on something called the "natural rate."

The natural rate, as Wicksell described it, is the interest-rate level that keeps an economy operating at full employment with stable prices. Think of it as the equilibrium rate for noninflationary growth. The rate is not constant over time but fluctuates with economic conditions.

By definition, the natural rate is unobservable, which should increase its appeal among central bankers.

If the central bank rate (Wicksell called it the market rate) is below the unobservable natural rate, it has inflationary consequences as businesses see opportunities for profitable investment and consumers keep spending apace.

If, on the other hand, the natural rate is below the market rate, consumers will be induced to increase their saving (reduce their spending) and businesses to curtail investment, both of which have deflationary consequences.

UNUSUAL CITATION

While Alan Greenspan has clearly read Knut Wicksell—he tossed out the natural-rate concept at his semiannual Humphrey–Hawkins testimony many years back—Wicksell is not someone who appears frequently in the Greenspan oeuvre.

But there he was in two speeches last week.

"The Federal Reserve has responded to the balance of market forces by gradually raising the federal funds rate over the past year," Greenspan said. "Certainly, to have done otherwise—to have held the federal funds rate at last year's level even as credit demands and market interest rates rose—would have required an inappropriately inflationary expansion of liquidity."

What Greenspan is saying, in effect, is that if credit demand is pushing up intermediate- and long-term rates and the overnight rate is being held steady, the central bank must be running an expansionary policy.

How can he know that, simply by observing the relationship, or spread, between two interest rates?

SO SIMPLE IT'S HARD

Simple. An interest-rate spread between a short-term rate and a long-term rate contains a world of information. The same demand for credit that pushes up long-term rates would lift the overnight rate, too, if the Fed didn't do something to prevent it. What the central bank does when it targets an overnight rate is passively supply the reserves the banking system demands in order to keep the rate from rising. And bank reserves are the raw material for an expansion in the money supply.

The spread is such a simple economic model that most Ph.D. economists don't get it. They see a rise in the long rate and cry, "slowdown," no matter what the central bank is doing with the short rate.

Greenspan explained why a rise in long rates need not be contractionary. After all, the price of something can rise because of an increase in demand or a cutback in supply—with very different implications.

This is something of a radical departure for the Fed chief, who has backed himself into a corner with his wacky theorizing on the available pool of labor and productivity-induced excess demand. There is nothing in the minutes from Fed meetings to suggest that policy-makers pay attention to the spread. In fact, Fed officials talk as if long rates operate independently of what the central bank does.

Unobservable Observations

While the long rate is not the equivalent of Wicksell's natural rate, it does provide useful information.

"We still can't observe the natural rate, but we know where we are relative to it by observing a rate that is farthest away [from the central bank rate] on the curve," says Bob Laurent, professor of economics and finance at the Illinois Institute of Technology's Stuart School of Business.

Laurent, who did some of the seminal research on the spread, explains it this way:

"If you think of setting price in the credit market, if you set it too low, there will be too much demand and the central bank will have to create more money to accommodate it," he says. "If the rate is too high, the public will be induced to save and the central bank will have to absorb credit."

Greenspan's Wicksellian detour did not go unnoticed by John Ryding, senior economist at Bear, Stearns & Co.

"Greenspan is saying that because the rate of return on capital is higher—which is why capital spending as a share of GDP has risen to 14 percent—leaving the federal funds rate at 4.75 percent would have been inflationary," Ryding says. "By allowing rates to drift higher, the Fed has followed the natural rate of interest higher."

Strange Timing

Greenspan may simply have been playing good defense, given that his venue was the White House, says Bob Barbera, chief economist at Hoenig & Co. in Rye Brook, New York. Anything that gets in the way of Al Gore's succession to the presidency is apt to be regarded unfavorably.

Greenspan's reliance on Wicksellian theory comes at a curious time, given the plunge in 30-year bond yields at a time when the Fed is raising short-term rates.

Private long-term rates haven't mirrored the fall in Treasury yields, which are being driven by a reduction in issuance, debt buybacks and increasingly rosy assumptions about the budget surplus. So the inversion between the 6 percent federal funds rate and the 5.68 percent 30-year Treasury rate may not be sending an accurate message that the bank rate is too high.

But the yield-curve inversion is certainly not expansionary, as some analysts contend. The long-term rate is falling because of the federal government's reduced credit demand, present and future. Assuming no increase in credit demand anyplace else, it doesn't take a long-dead Swedish economist to explain the implications.

The Only Thing Stubborn About Long Rates Is the Analysis

————— Oct. 1, 2001 —————

NORMALLY ON the day before a Federal Reserve meeting, this column would devote itself to the outlook for and implications of monetary policy.

With the federal funds rate trading below 1 percent two weeks ago following the terrorist attack on the World Trade Center and Pentagon, and the M2 money supply exploding by a record $164.5 billion in the week ended Sept. 17, it's hard to get excited about a cut in the target overnight rate, even if it's to a 40-year low of 2.5 percent from its current 3 percent, which is widely expected.

Another 50-basis-point rate cut would bring the cumulative stimulus since January to 400 basis points. Yet everyone, including the Fed, is grousing about long rates being stubbornly high.

Have you ever stopped to think why every central bank in the world targets short rates if it's long rates that move the economy?

"If the long rate is the rate that matters, why not go into the market and set that rate directly?" asks Bob Laurent, professor of economics and finance at the Illinois Institute of Technology's Stuart School of Business. "The Fed can easily buy 30-year bonds."

What's more, there are ample instances to upend the theory that long rates move the economy, a view shared by 99.9 percent of the economics community.

FALLING ROCKS

According to that logic, "the fall in 10- and 30-year rates last year should have been stimulative to the economy," says Paul Kasriel, director of economic research at the Northern Trust Corp. in Chicago.

Instead, the economy went straight down the tubes with long yields.

Just maybe the economy's performance had something to do with what's going on at the short end of the yield curve, where the Fed reigns supreme, and the interaction between the two rates.

The Fed, of course, was jacking up the overnight rate from mid-1999 to mid-2000 to slow economic growth before inflation could accelerate. The fact that long rates were falling spontaneously should have been a red flag.

"To say that long rates are too high makes no sense," says Jim Glassman, senior economist at J.P. Morgan Chase. "If you were talking about a rate some institution sets, it would be one thing. But a market rate? That rate represents the balance of credit demand and supply."

MISUNDERSTOOD

Long-term rates are the most misunderstood phenomenon in finance. If it's long-term rates that move the economy, Japan should have been booming this past decade instead of being mired in a slump.

When folks talk about long-term rates being stubbornly high, exactly which long rates are they talking about? The Treasury's 10- and 30-year rates? They yield 4.54 percent and 5.38 percent, respectively. In an absolute sense, these yields are historically low, not high. Over the last two decades, the average 10- and 30-year yield has been 8 percent and 8.4 percent, respectively.

Relative to short-term rates, such as the 3 percent federal funds rate or the 2.81 percent two-year note rate, long-term rates are high.

That's a good thing. When the Conference Board revamped its Index of Leading Economic Indicators a few years back to improve its prognosticating ability, it saw fit to include an interest-rate spread; specifically the spread between the funds rate and 10-year note rate.

The spread enters the LEI with a plus sign if it's widening. Would long-rate aficionados be happier if the long rate was below the short rate at 2.5 percent? Probably not. On some level they recognize an inverted yield curve does not represent the epitome of economic health.

CAUSE OR EFFECT?

So where should long rates be? How about 4 percent? Lower than 4 percent? Higher than 4 percent but lower than 5 percent? What rate is neither stubbornly high nor too low? Do you see how silly this discussion is?

"If all of a sudden people decided to spend more today and save less for tomorrow, it would push up rates," Kasriel says. "The Federal

Reserve prints enough money to keep the short rate steady. So a rising long rate is expansionary."

Long rates can't be looked at in isolation: Why the rate is high—a result of reduced credit supply (cause) or increased credit demand (result)—is more important than the rate itself. If long rates rise because more people want to borrow and spend at any given price, how can that be contractionary?

Perhaps it's the rates on long-term investment-grade or high-yield corporate bonds that are stubbornly high. The average yield on bonds rated Baa by Moody's is 8 percent while the Merrill Lynch High-Yield Index yields 14.18 percent.

The high-grade yield is more than 2 percentage points below the 20-year Baa average rate. And it's down almost 100 basis points from 9 percent in May 2000, when the Fed was concluding a year of interest-rate increases.

PHONE HOME

There's a reason high-yield bonds have high yields. It's called risk. During an economic slowdown that seems destined to turn into a recession, the market has to price in increased default risk.

So, long Treasury yields and investment-grade corporate bond yields aren't high. Junk yields are high for a reason. The only stubbornly high element is long rates relative to short rates, which is beneficial.

If you're one of the folks who are stubbornly calling long rates stubbornly high, I'd appreciate some enlightenment on the subject.

More on the Misguided Thinking About Long Rates

———   Oct. 4, 2001   ———

EVERYONE FROM Alan Greenspan to Robert Rubin to Paul O'Neill to George W. Bush to Jon Corzine has weighed in on the need for a package to stimulate the U.S. economy. There is one caveat, however: It can't raise long-term interest rates.

They can't all be that stupid, can they? The implication is that they want to accommodate an increase in the demand for credit without an increase in the price.

"If you could figure out a way to increase spending and prevent rates from going up, now that would really be expansionary," says Paul Kasriel, director of economic research at the Northern Trust Corp. in Chicago.

Kasriel hasn't figured out how to do it just yet.

For some theory, let's turn to the field of microeconomics, which focuses on the behavior of individual decision-making units (consumers, businesses). From microeconomics comes the important concept of the law of supply and demand.

Supply and demand aren't fixed. Instead there's a schedule, or curve, that plots the supply and demand for an item at any given price.

The demand curve is downward sloping (there are some exceptions which aren't relevant to this discussion). That means that as the price of an item rises, the quantity demanded falls, and vice versa.

Shifting Curves

Buyers aren't the only ones motivated by price. Producers (businesses) respond to price signals as well. When the price of corn rises relative to soybeans, farmers are apt to devote more acreage to planting corn. The supply curve, in other words, is upward sloping.

It's this automatic response to price signals on the part of consumers and producers that makes free-marketeers wince at any attempt by government to interfere with what Adam Smith called the "invisible hand." Supply and demand strive to be in harmony: The point where the supply of an item equals the demand is called equilibrium.

Things come along to shift both the supply and demand curves, which means finding a new equilibrium. Let's say medical science finds some new anti-cancer agent in beef, and consumers decide to buy more beef at any given price than they did before. The demand curve for beef shifts out, implying a higher price and higher quantity demanded.

Is the higher price a harbinger of reduced demand for beef? Of course not. We just demonstrated that the reason for the rise in price was increased demand.

Fuzzy Thinking

Most folks can grasp a concrete example. When it comes to interest rates, specifically long-term rates, their thinking gets fuzzy. If an entity (in this case, the government) demands more credit at a given price than it did before, both the price of credit (the interest rate) and the quantity demanded will rise.

How on earth do Greenspan, Rubin, O'Neill, Bush and Corzine expect to craft a fiscal stimulus package that doesn't push long rates up, all things equal?

Federal Reserve Chairman Alan Greenspan has always had a bugaboo about the federal deficit, withholding his seal of approval on tax cuts until George W. Bush took office in January.

"Greenspan operates on the premise that the government deficit is the major determination of interest rates when, in reality, private credit demand swamps public," says Sandy Batten, senior analyst at CDC Investment Corp.

Greenspan also seems to think that government spending is inflationary per se, when the only thing inflationary about it is the central bank's willingness to accommodate it.

EXPECTATIONS HYPOTHESIS

If the government is going to spend $75 billion in addition to the $55 billion already approved by Congress (that includes $10 billion of loan guarantees for the airlines), it should hope long-term rates go up, says Bob Laurent, professor of economics and finance at the Illinois Institute of Technology's Stuart School of Business. "Otherwise it means the [stimulus] program isn't successful."

Since long rates are the sum of current and expected future short-term rates, if long rates tumbled as fast as short rates, it would mean "the market expects short-term rates to be lower in the future, which would not be a vote of confidence in the stimulus program," Laurent says. "To say a rise in long rates is bad is a misreading of what's going on."

Greenspan is also worried about the "crowding out" effect, by which government spending pushes long rates up and makes borrowing more expensive for private companies, whose productivity-enhancing capital investment is crucial to keep the New Era from meeting its maker. (By convention the government's productivity is considered to be zero. No comment.)

HUH?

The reason the government is initiating a stimulus package is precisely because the private sector is not willing or eager to spend. So the choice is: reduced borrowing and falling long rates, or increased government borrowing and higher long rates.

With all the grousing over stubbornly high long-term rates, the Treasury's surprise sale today of $6 billion of the benchmark 10-year notes seems counterproductive, to say the least.

Following the Sept. 11 terrorist attack on the World Trade Center and Pentagon, the demand for high-quality, safe Treasuries soared, causing a shortage of active issues in the repo market, where dealers finance inventories using securities as collateral.

"Why did the Treasury issue long-term securities today?" wonders Northern Trust's Kasriel. "If there's increased demand why provide more supply if long rates are what they care about?"

Cause and Effect Matter
When It Comes to Rates

—————— July 29, 2003 ——————

IT IS AXIOMATIC that when the economy improves, market interest rates start to rise.

They have to. Interest rates are the price of credit. And when the demand for credit picks up, so does the price. To the best of my knowledge, no one has figured out how to supersede the law of supply and demand.

Of course, not every wiggle in yields is a reflection of a contemporaneous shift in credit demand. Sometimes the move in rates is anticipatory. If actual demand doesn't meet that expectation, rates won't stay at the elevated level. They'll fall back, so the damage to the economy is effectively nil.

As predictable and unavoidable as the cyclical rise in interest rates is the reaction: Higher rates are going to nip the nascent recovery in the bud. Thursday's *Wall Street Journal* featured a front-page story to that effect, suggesting the rise in rates in response to signs of an improving economy was threatening to snuff out those same hopeful signs. The story went on to say that higher rates on Treasuries would draw money out of the stock market, which would bring rates down.

In other words, higher rates cause lower rates. Lower rates, in turn, cause higher rates.

Huh? How do we ever get out of this closed loop? And somehow the central bank, the ultimate supplier of credit, got left out in the cold.

LOOP-THE-LOOP

"Higher rates do not mean lower rates," says John Silvia, chief economist at Wachovia Corp. in Charlotte, North Carolina. "Such circular reasoning is unacceptable even for undergraduates."

It may be unacceptable for undergraduates, but it passes for analysis in the hallowed halls of some of Wall Street's research departments, whose economists can't seem to differentiate between cause and effect.

Forget all the econometric models for a minute and focus on the logic. If rates rise because more people are demanding more credit, how does that translate into reduced demand for credit and lower interest rates? Higher rates are the effect of a stronger economy, not a cause of a weaker one. Anyone who thinks they are a cause needs to reread the chapter on the law of supply and demand in every basic economics text.

A rise in price can be the result of increased demand or reduced supply. The implications for quantity demanded—Q is on the horizontal axis while P, or price, is on the vertical axis—are very different.

BASIC MICROECONOMICS

"If consumers want to buy more at any given price than they wanted previously, the demand curve shifts to the right (or outward)," it says on page 58 of the fifth edition of *Economics: Principles and Policy,* by William J. Baumol and Alan S. Blinder. "Any factor that causes the demand curve to shift outward to the right, and does not affect the supply curve, will raise the equilibrium price and the equilibrium quantity."

If it was increased demand for credit that caused the price to rise, you can't very well segue to the conclusion that the higher price will be the cause of weaker demand in the future. If it were, how would the economy ever get out of the interest-rate loop-the-loop and produce a sustained expansion?

The problem with this analysis is it fails to recognize that "price is an endogenous variable: Something caused it to happen," says Sandy Batten, senior economist at Bear, Stearns & Co. "People take it as an exogenous variable and ask how the economy will respond."

Individual agents (producers and consumers) respond to price: Price is a cause in microeconomics. The actions of all these individuals "become price determining," Batten says.

FORGETTING SOMEONE

A change in market interest rates can't be viewed in a vacuum. It's the source of the change that's crucial in determining the impact.

The entire discussion about the impact of long-term rates on the economy omits the most important economic agent in this equation: the ultimate supplier of credit, known as the central bank.

What if the higher price (interest rates) is coming from the supply side? Is there any evidence the Fed is constricting the supply of credit to force the price up? Not that I'm aware of. And there's an easy way to check.

The overnight federal funds rate stands at 1 percent, where the Fed promises to hold it for the "foreseeable future," whatever that is. Money supply growth is soaring. The spread between short and long rates is historically wide. Credit spreads have been narrowing.

WHY, NOT WHAT

Alas, there is no evidence that the higher price of credit is the result of any supply constraint on the part of the Fed.

"There is a distinction between the central bank policy rate and market rates," says Ram Bhagavatula, chief economist at Royal Bank of Scotland Financial Markets. "The central bank can make policy easy or tight in relation to market rates."

That's why all these financial-conditions indexes with a long-term interest rate as a variable without an interest-rate spread to determine whether the change in the rate is supply- or demand-driven are fatally flawed.

Undergraduates might be forgiven for making that kind of a mistake. Ph.D. economists shouldn't be.

7

The "Political" Economy

P RINCIPLED POLITICIANS" is something of an oxymoron. Most candidates run for office on a platform of noble ideas. Once elected, at the first sign of discontent from a favored constituency, they forget they ever *had* principles and start trading favors for votes.

Elected officials wheel out the goody cart, which may take the form of targeted tax benefits, support for legislation they would have derided as candidates, or protectionist trade measures, which help the few at the expense of the many.

When the visible hand of government intrudes on the invisible hand of the market, the outcome isn't pretty. That never stops politicians from trying to secure short-term gains (read: votes) at the expense of sound long-run policies. No one said good politics is good policy.

Everyone was surprised when President George W. Bush, an avowed free-trader, slapped tariffs on steel imports early in his administration to help an industry plagued by chronic overcapacity and inefficiency.

The reason for the discrepancy between words and deeds was politics: The steel-producing states of Ohio, Pennsylvania and West Virginia were considered key to Bush's 2004 reelection effort.

Then there's the monstrosity known as the tax code, which has become a behavior-modification tool instead of a source of revenue for the limited functions of the federal government prescribed in the Constitution. "Tax reform" measures invariably end up adding hundreds of pages to the tax code, a sure sign that true reform got lost somewhere between conception and enactment.

Just imagine if the estimated $200 billion Americans spend each year complying with the federal tax code were put to more productive use.

Alas, the idea of tax reform—encompassing a flatter tax, fewer deductions and a broader base—will remain a pipe dream as long as there are so many vested interests with the muscle to protect their tax-preferred status.

The Tax Code Shouldn't Be a Government Pez Dispenser

———— Sept. 4, 2002 ————

IN CASE anyone had any doubts, the government regards the tax code as a way to encourage people to behave in a specific manner, discourage behavior it deems undesirable and hand out goodies to favored constituencies.

For example, taxes on tobacco and alcohol—"sin taxes"—are designed to discourage smoking and drinking, activities that are bad for our health, make us unproductive citizens and cause early death, which means there will be fewer working stiffs contributing to Social Security to support a growing number of retirees.

Then there are a whole host of tax benefits for engaging in what is deemed to be "good" behavior. Home ownership, for example, is made more affordable by the deductibility of mortgage interest. Charitable contributions are also deductible, creating an incentive to share one's wealth with those less fortunate.

The administration and Congress now have put the investor class in their sights. With the stock market headed for a third consecutive year of losses—a misfortune last experienced in 1939, 1940 and 1941—the government wants to demonstrate that it feels our pain and is toying with the idea of allowing taxpayers to deduct up to $20,000 of capital losses against ordinary income. Currently, the maximum deduction against ordinary income is $3,000.

LOSE/LOSE

As a taxpayer and an investor, I'm all for any break the government gives me. As a principled person, I wonder why no one is proposing that losses always be fully deductible in the year in which they occur (they can be carried forward).

"It's a two-faced policy," says Pete Sepp, vice president for communications at the National Taxpayers Union in Washington. "You're penalized when you make money. You're penalized when you lose it."

Throwing investors a bone in a bad year—a bad election year, coincidentally—flies in the face of having a simple, fair, flat tax code that encourages economic growth and provides a stream of revenue for the government to perform its legitimate functions. And it gets around the real problem, which is "we shouldn't be taxing capital gains at all," says Dan Mitchell, senior fellow in political economy at Washington's Heritage Foundation.

To the extent that deducting losses "mitigates the adverse economic impact of bad policy," it's better than nothing, Mitchell says. It would be far better to "do the right thing: Lower the capital gains tax, which punishes savings and investment, and remove the double tax on dividends."

MORAL HAZARD

The "philosophical inconsistency" regarding capital gains and losses isn't evident in other places in the tax code, according to the NTU's Sepp. Casualty and theft losses, for example, can be written off. So can bad loans on the part of small businesses, "which is a close parallel to taking the kind of risk" that results in capital losses, which can't be written off, Sepp says.

The government has already created a moral hazard for institutional investors: When losses are too great, the government comes to their rescue with a bailout in the name of averting systemic risk. Now individual investors will be lulled into complacency.

"Investors need to appreciate risk," says Jim Glassman, senior U.S. economist at J.P. Morgan Chase. "There has to be some symmetry."

TAX THE RICH

The real crux of the problem may be the constituency affected by the tax treatment of capital gains and losses.

"The only people you can fashionably discriminate against are the rich," says Stephen Moore, president of the Club for Growth in Washington.

Now that half of all American households own stock, either directly or through mutual funds, Congress has apparently decided that the investor class is a constituency to be ignored at its own peril.

There's always some special-interest group that needs assistance, and Congress is generally too happy to oblige. It's not the purpose of the tax code to minister to one group one year and another group the next year.

The tax code should be simple enough so that returns can be completed without professional help, flat enough to discourage tax avoidance and fair enough so taxpayers see the playing field as level. If the poor really think taxing (punishing) the rich is sound policy, it can only mean they reject the American Dream of rags to riches in one generation.

Using the tax code to curry favor with a particular constituency and win votes may actually backfire. Coddling investors with a bigger deduction for capital losses this year may end up hurting the stock market, which is the opposite of policy-makers' intent, Moore says.

"Instead of helping the stock market, it may actually encourage investors to sell stocks now and book the losses," he says.

A bigger deduction this year won't help investors if they're confronted with bigger paper losses next year.

How About Some Tax Reform
Along with Tax Relief?

———————— April 12, 2002 ————————

MONDAY IS April 15, the deadline for filing income tax returns to the federal and state governments.

Don't breathe a sigh of relief just yet. Americans have to work until April 27 this year—Tax Freedom Day—before they can begin to keep the fruits of their labor.

Every year the Tax Foundation calculates the day when Americans will have earned enough money to cover their tax liability to federal, state and local governments. Using historical data, the Tax Foundation has calculated Tax Freedom Day back to 1900, when it was Jan. 20. At mid-century, it fell on March 29, with the total effective tax rate (federal, state and local taxes) mushrooming to 24.2 percent from 5.7 percent at the turn of the century.

The total effective tax rate peaked at 33.3 percent in 2000, when Tax Freedom Day fell in May for the first time ever. With the tax relief of

2001 and 2002, Tax Freedom Day fell four days earlier this year than it did in 2000.

We work one-third of the year for the government and two-thirds of the year for ourselves.

Don't confuse tax relief with tax reform. Both the Tax Reform Act of 1997 and the Economic Growth and Tax Reform Reconciliation Act of 2001 increased tax complexity even as they reduced capital gains and marginal tax rates.

BIG BURDEN

Consider the following stats for this year, compiled by the IRS, the National Taxpayers Union and the Tax Foundation:

• The estimated cost of complying with the federal tax code is $194 billion, about 2 percent of gross domestic product.

• The average taxpayer will spend more than 28 hours on tax forms and related activities this year, a total of 6 billion hours.

• 60 percent of taxpayers will use a professional to prepare their taxes because the system is so complicated.

• The IRS tax code is 9,471 pages. Tax code regulations consume 91,824 pages of print. The total, 101,295, is 70 times longer than *War and Peace*.

There's got to be a better way.

There is: the flat tax or the fair tax, both of which exempt the poor and set a low flat rate for everyone else.

The fathers of the flat tax are economists Robert Hall and Alvin Rabushka. Hall, a professor of economics at Stanford University and senior fellow at the Hoover Institution, is better known these days as chairman of the National Bureau of Economic Research's Business Cycle Dating Committee. In fact, he was taken aback when I called him this week to discuss the flat tax.

STONE COLD

"I haven't had a journalist call me on the flat tax in years," Hall said. "I thought it was an ice-cold issue."

Not quite. The House of Representatives is once again considering a tax code replacement act, which would set a date of Dec. 31, 2005, to scrap the current tax code and require Congress to enact something to replace it.

This Republican initiative, while noble in intent, is bucking up against the political establishment, which uses tax favors to curry support with special-interest groups.

Steve Forbes made the flat tax the signature issue of his unsuccessful runs for the Republican presidential nomination in 1996 and 2000. His proposal for a 15 percent flat tax—the poor pay nothing—with the return filled out on a postcard-size form gathered some momentum in 1996. By the time the 2000 campaign rolled around, the stock market boom had everyone so punch-drunk that the idea of any kind of change was dead on arrival.

POSTCARD RETURN

The flat tax as proposed by Hall and Rabushka would work like this: A low rate—19 percent—would harness a broad tax base and produce the same revenue as the current tax system. (That revenue estimate is from the 1995 revision to their book, *The Flat Tax*, based on 1993 IRS data.)

"Our system rests on a basic administrative principle: income should be taxed exactly once as close as possible to its source," Hall and Rabushka wrote.

Workers pay tax on what they earn (wages, salaries and pensions), with no deductions. To make the system progressive, only earnings above a per-family allowance would be taxed.

Under the Hall–Rabushka system, filing an individual tax return would entail adding up wages, salaries and pensions, subtracting the family allowance, multiplying by 19 percent and subtracting the amount withheld from the employer. That's it.

Businesses would pay taxes on all income outside of wages, salaries and pensions—but only once. No deductions, but no double taxation either.

SAVE THE TREES

"Not a single form 1099 would be needed under a flat tax with business income taxed at the source," Hall and Rabushka wrote.

The lack of paperwork—tax forms, filing instructions—would save a few hundred thousand trees a year, according to the authors, which should rally the environmentalists behind the flat tax.

A close relative of the flat tax is the fair tax, under which Americans would keep their entire paycheck and pay a 23 percent tax on what they consume. A monthly rebate would cover necessities for everyone below the poverty level.

It seems that a simpler flatter tax system is a no-brainer, but clearly it's not.

The cost of direct compliance with the tax code is only one egregious example of the inefficiency of the current system. A simple flat tax would improve incentives to work and invest, raising economic output while lowering interest rates and inflation. Individuals and businesses would make decisions for economic reasons, not for the purpose of tax avoidance. Tax evasion would become a less profitable pursuit. The army of paper pushers—tax lawyers and accountants—could do something productive with their time. Corporations could save billions of dollars on lobbying fees (lobbyists would have to find gainful employment).

When one considers that a country like Russia, where tax evasion was sport, went to a 13 percent flat tax and saw 2001 revenue soar 47 percent, one has to wonder what the U.S. is doing with a backwater swamp of a tax code.

POSTSCRIPT: *Any nascent interest in the flat tax inevitably runs headfirst into the American Dream. With a record 69.2 percent of households owning their own home in the fourth quarter of 2004, the constituency aligned against the elimination of the mortgage deduction is so large as to nip any reform effort in the bud. No wonder President Bush stipulated early in his second term that any simplification of the tax code—lower rates, broader base—would retain the deductions for mortgage interest and charitable giving.*

Keep Uncle Sam Out of the Investment Business
———— Jan. 19, 1999 ————

FOR A BRIEF TIME this evening, attention will shift away from exchange rates in Brazil, policy pronouncements from Japan and the impeachment trial of the president of the U.S. Instead, all eyes will be glued to President Bill Clinton as he delivers his annual State of the Union address to Congress and the American people.

Not that the country is crying out for new policies. The president can look his audience in the eye and say, with complete honesty, that the state of the union is good (no wagging finger necessary). The stock market has blessed Americans, individually or through retirement accounts, with gains in excess of 20 percent for the last four years running. Consumer confidence is high. By and large, consumers approve of the job President Clinton is doing and would prefer that the first priority of government be to do no harm.

But the president is determined to claim his place in history, over and above the legacy of being only the second president to be impeached by the House of Representatives.

Clinton can already claim to be the president—a Democrat, no less—who reined in the Reagan deficits, turning a record fiscal deficit of $290 billion in 1992 into the first surplus—$70 billion—in almost three decades in 1998. The Office of Management and Budget is forecasting a budget surplus of $76 billion in the current fiscal year.

What a plum it would be for a scandal-plagued president who governs on the basis of public opinion polls to be able to tell Americans that their retirement savings system is on sound footing.

WHO DOES IT?

Until today, the White House had been closemouthed about the president's specific proposals for Social Security reform. Today, however, presidential spokesman Joe Lockhart said that the president plans to propose that Congress transfer 62 percent of the projected budget surplus over the next 15 years—$2.7 trillion—to the Social Security trust funds to keep them afloat through 2055.

The president will propose investing $675 billion of that money in stock and bond markets to increase the trust funds' returns. Currently the trust funds are invested in U.S. Treasury securities. (In reality, the surplus in the trust funds—more money coming in from payroll taxes than going out to retirees—is an accounting entry. The money goes into the general fund and pays for everything from B-52 bombers to government salaries to welfare payments.)

There is no disagreement on the need for Social Security reform. Without it, the system will be insolvent by 2012, with the benefits paid out exceeding the taxes collected.

"The only real issue is who should have control over the investing and who should own the investment," says Stephen Moore, director of fiscal policy studies at the Cato Institute.

CONFLICT OF INTEREST

Allowing the government to invest the surplus in the stock market —an attempt to boost the fund's return while maintaining its current pay-as-you-go structure—is one of the worst ideas to come down the pike in a long time.

"You want to empower people, not empower the government," Moore says. "That would be privatization in reverse. The government should be divesting its ownership. Instead the government would become the largest shareholder of most of the Fortune 500 companies in 10 years' time."

Consider the potential pitfalls: Politically correct crusaders would put pressure on Congress not to invest in tobacco or chemical companies, companies that have a glass ceiling or companies that don't have a racial quota, Moore offers. Money would be directed instead toward companies that are doing what the government considers socially desirable projects.

"Every aspect of every investment decision would tend to be based on political rather than economic factors," notes Carolyn Weaver, resident scholar at the American Enterprise Institute.

As a majority shareholder, the government would be in a position to select board members and influence corporate decisions. At the same time, the government legislates, regulates, taxes and enacts policies that favor some industries over the others. Talk about a conflict of interest.

GREENSPAN VOTES NO

"Who votes the proxies?" Jim Bianco, president of Bianco Research, wants to know. "If the government starts appointing politically correct boards to vote the proxies, we're not going to get the compounded 10 percent rate of return we've gotten in the stock market for the last 70 years. If we blur the line between public and private entities, we'll wind up with the return we could have gotten off government investments like T-bills."

No less an authority than Federal Reserve Chairman Alan Greenspan cautioned against allowing the federal government into the investment business. In the question-and-answer session following his Humphrey–Hawkins testimony last July, Greenspan said that he knew of no way to "essentially insulate government decision-makers from having access to what will amount to very large investments in American private industry." Allowing the government to hold stock and vote claims on management would have "very far-reaching potential dangers for a free American economy and a free American society," Greenspan added.

IMPOSSIBLE INSULATION

The proponents of government-directed investment realize that some kind of Chinese wall would have to be erected to ensure neutrality in investments and matters of corporate governance. For example, designated professional money managers (How would they be chosen? On the basis of their contributions to a political party?) could be authorized to invest only in index funds, which means passive investment that mimics an index, such as the Standard & Poor's 500 Index.

What about smaller companies that aren't in the S&P 500, the AEI's Weaver wonders. "Any decision the government makes will alter the distribution of wealth and ownership in the economy."

With billions of dollars pouring into companies that might be polluting the environment, using child labor, moving jobs overseas, selling weapons to Iraq or being sued by the federal government, Congress would be under enormous pressure to adjust the index accordingly.

"Pulling even one stock from an index, let alone multiple stocks, would transform a passive investment strategy into an active strategy and would politicize investment decisions," Weaver adds.

PRIVATIZE

Privatizing Social Security means allowing private individuals to invest the money that they pay in the form of a payroll tax in a private savings account to save for their future. It does not mean giving the government a new entitlement and the power to direct huge sums of money to corporations in the individual's stead.

It really doesn't matter if the government does the investing or appoints an outside board to do the investing. The view that government-directed investment can be insulated from the political process is "just not credible and possible," Greenspan said last July.

Hopefully the administration and Congress will listen.

✻   ✻   ✻

Gore's Social Security Fix Isn't a Fix or Secure
———————— May 19, 2000 ————————

THE ISSUE of Social Security privatization has finally hit the front pages. With any luck, the public will come to understand that individual choice is not synonymous with "risky scheme."

That's what Vice President Al Gore would have you believe. He called the idea of allowing individuals to invest 2 percent of the 12.4 percent payroll tax in private retirement accounts—part of a plan put forth by Republican presidential candidate George W. Bush—a "catastrophe" that would put individuals at the mercy of a volatile stock market.

Who said anything about the stock market? For years, employees have had the option of investing their 401(k) plans in a variety of mutual funds, many of which have nothing to do with stocks. Choices run the gamut from no-risk Treasury securities to low-risk money market funds to riskier bond and stock index funds to risky growth stocks for those with a good stomach.

Alas, that's just one of the scare tactics being used to derail a much-needed discussion on the future of Social Security. When one considers the source of the fear-mongering is the same Al Gore who, as part of the Clinton–Gore team, supported the idea of the government investing some of the Social Security trust fund in the stock market, the degree of dissembling takes one's breath away.

Gore, like his boss Bill Clinton, parades as a fiscal conservative. If elected, his chosen fix for Social Security would be to continue the Clinton administration's commitment to pay down the $3.5 trillion of marketable debt by 2013.

DIRTY LITTLE SECRET

What's more, Gore proposes to credit the interest saved by retiring marketable debt—some $230 billion—to the Social Security trust fund in the form of IOUs, which actually has the effect of increasing the non-marketable debt. (The Treasury has about $2.2 trillion in nonmarketable debt, most of which is "held" in the Social Security trust funds or sold to state and local government authorities.)

The dirty little secret of the Gore plan is that it doesn't fix anything. In 2015, the trust funds' receipts will equal their expenditures. The

Gore plan will extend the solvency until 2021, but that's a fine point that will resonate primarily with actuaries.

"The president's proposal to transfer general revenues to the Social Security trust funds would extend the funds' solvency from an accounting point of view but would not alter the underlying long-run imbalance between total federal revenues and spending," said Dan Crippen, director of the Congressional Budget Office, in testimony last November.

Earlier this year, the Government Accounting Office agreed, saying that the administration proposal "does not represent a reform plan."

It's something of a mystery why every working person isn't 100 percent behind the idea of privatizing Social Security, with its $21 trillion in unfunded liabilities, or promises to pay in excess of what it takes in.

UPENDING MARX

Opinion polls suggest that workers overwhelmingly would prefer to invest their own Social Security taxes instead of the government. Yet labor unions, ostensibly in the interest of protecting their rank and file, are as opposed to privatizing Social Security—even carving out a small piece for personal retirement accounts—as they are to granting permanent normal trade relations to China.

"By giving workers access to capital, it would turn Marx upside down," says José Piñera, president of the International Center for Pension Reform.

There was something of a to-do a year ago when it became known that some large labor unions wrote a letter to the chief executives of nine big financial firms, including mutual fund giant Fidelity Investments, J.P. Morgan & Co., Merrill Lynch & Co. and mega-pension-fund manager State Street Global Advisors, asking for their positions on the privatization issue. The press reports suggested that the unions were using their not-inconsiderable financial muscle to influence public policy.

UNION INFLUENCE

"There were a bunch of news stories claiming that various Wall Street investment houses were promoting privatization and funding third parties to promote the effort," said Stephen Regenstreif, director of retirees for the American Federation of State, County and Municipal Employees. "There were no threats. We just asked what their position was."

The unions oppose privatization on the grounds that Social Security is supposed to be the "foundation of retirement security" and "risk free," Regenstreif said.

Of course, the Supreme Court, in two important cases—*Helvering v. Davis* (1937) and *Flemming v. Nestor* (1960)—said that there is no legal right to Social Security. Instead, a worker's retirement security is "entirely dependent on the political decisions of the president and Congress," writes Charles E. Rounds Jr., professor of law at Suffolk University in Boston, in *Property Rights: The Hidden Issue of Social Security Reform,* published by the Cato Project on Social Security Privatization. "Paying Social Security taxes does not give rise to any contractual right to Social Security benefits."

CHILEAN MODEL

Benefits are not a worker's property. They do not devolve to his heirs. When one considers that there is nothing in the Social Security trust funds except a bunch of IOUs, and what they owe you is $21 trillion and what they pay you is an average 2 percent return, it's a wonder that the public isn't jumping at the opportunity to opt out of the system, even in a small way.

That's exactly what they did in Chile in the early 1980s. As Minister of Labor and Social Security from 1978 to 1989, Piñera was the architect of Chile's private pension system.

Given the opportunity to remain in the state system or opt out, most Chileans headed for the exit. Initially, 10 percent of a worker's monthly wages were automatically deposited in a private savings account (PSA) of the individual's choosing, selected from among a group of government approved and supervised companies. Competition among the investment companies—on returns, costs and customer service—made the market more efficient.

POWER TO THE PEOPLE

Each Chilean worker has a PSA passbook and receives a quarterly statement. He can access his account from computer terminals so that at any given moment he knows the exact status of his retirement money.

"Chile had a semi-socialist economy and we were able to bring a free-market revolution" to the pension system, Piñera said. "No matter what government is in power, the pension system is secure."

Average annual returns exceeded the most optimistic estimates while the influx of long-term investment capital boosted productivity and economic growth. The poverty rate fell.

Argentina, Peru, Colombia, Bolivia, El Salvador and Mexico have adopted similar reforms, empowering workers through private ownership of retirement benefits.

The U.S., so enlightened in so many ways, is still in the Dark Ages when it comes to pension reform. Bipartisan congressional bills propose everything from a small carve-out for private retirement plans to a full-scale privatization plan proposed by Senator Rod Grams, Republican of Minnesota.

Al Gore will have none of it. This week, he told a gathering of the American Association of Retired Persons that Bush's plan "would take the security out of Social Security. We could see the end of Social Security as we know it."

What we know, and what he ain't saying, is that the only way the government will be able to meet its future obligations is to increase the payroll tax to at least 50 percent of total income or cut benefits by one-third.

Rather than scaring seniors, ending Social Security as we know it should be the rallying cry for workers of the world to unite.

POSTSCRIPT: *President Bush made Social Security reform the top priority for his second term. The Democrats made blocking it an even bigger priority. The debate, if you can call it that, never advanced much beyond name-calling and scare tactics. No wonder public support was waning as this book went to press.*

As for the existing program, Social Security benefits will exceed taxes in 2017, according to the 2005 annual report of the trustees of the Social Security and Medicare trust funds. At that point, the trust funds will have to use "interest payments" to meet obligations before redeeming "assets" in 2027. Since there are no real assets in the trust funds, only promissory notes, the government will have to raise money (tax, borrow) or cut benefits to cover the costs. The Social Security trust funds are projected to be exhausted by 2041.

❈   ❈   ❈

How Microsoft Harmed Me, a Personal Saga
April 4, 2000

EVER SINCE Judge Thomas Penfield Jackson issued his finding of facts in November, determining that Microsoft Inc. had monopoly power and used it to stifle competition, thereby harming consumers, I've been thinking about the nature of my personal injury.

The harm to consumers is only part of the judge's findings of law, handed down yesterday, that Microsoft repeatedly violated antitrust laws and abused its monopoly power. I'm going to leave the question of Microsoft's exercise of monopoly power and antitrust violations to the legal experts, but as an ordinary consumer who uses a computer and Microsoft software in my daily life, both at work and at home, I'm as competent as the next gal to discuss the personal harm inflicted by the software giant.

1. DOS, darn those windows!

In the beginning there was MS-DOS, or Microsoft's disk operating system. It was pure hell learning that "C-colon-backslash" nonsense. I was forever slashing the wrong way. I never knew when to leave a space between commands and when not. And that black and white screen was deadly dull.

But learn I did. Enter Windows.

After struggling with DOS, I was not thrilled at the prospect of tackling yet another incomprehensible operating system, which was understood primarily by techies. Somehow I kept closing all the windows. I didn't even see the benefit of having multiple windows open at the same time—especially since all of mine kept closing.

I hold Bill Gates personally responsible for the mental pain and suffering incurred as a direct result of my software initiation experience.

2. Something for nothing, more for less.

In the old days, when Netscape controlled some 90 percent of the Internet browser market, I had to pay for the software if I wanted all the documentation (the software itself could be downloaded for free). Now both Microsoft and Netscape give their browsers away free, complete with all the bells and whistles.

Who wants something that the company producing it values at nothing? You get what you pay for, right?

"It's hard to imagine that the consumer was harmed by paying for a monopoly product formerly and now getting it for free," says Robert Levy, senior fellow in constitutional studies at Washington's Cato Institute.

Then there's the price of Windows itself. In 1993, the retail price of the complete Windows operating system was $230. Today it's $209.

What that means is that I overpaid in 1993.

A PC user can upgrade his software to Windows 98, the current consumer standard (Windows 2000 is still a business product) for $109, which is Microsoft's suggested retail price. Street prices for upgrades, available at various outlet stores, average $88.

And, to use Labor Department lingo, there's been considerable "quality improvement" in the product. You get more for your money, including a uniform plug-in for all peripherals (speakers, mouse, etc.), complete integration with the Internet and support for CD-ROMs and DVDs.

"Users pay less than one-fifth for Windows today than they were paying in 1990 when it had far fewer features," Levy points out. "If price gouging is the mark of a monopolist, then Microsoft doesn't qualify."

3. Green with euro-envy.

Europeans are lucky! They'd never find themselves in a situation where the government, in the interest of social harmony, has to take action against companies that "trammeled the competitive process" (Judge Jackson's words for Microsoft). Those kinds of companies are stillborn in Europe.

Then again, if the continent had more fiercely competitive companies, European productivity growth might not lag that of the U.S. According to Chris Iggo, chief economist at Barclays Capital Group in London, the gap is about 1.5 percentage points. It is through productivity growth that a country's standard of living improves.

Data on pan-European productivity are hard to come by, so Iggo constructed a synthetic series, comparing real output to the number of employees for both the Euro zone and the U.S. Iggo's calculations suggest that Euro-zone productivity growth was zero in 1999.

"They got growth by hiring more people, not by becoming more productive," he says.

It's a small price to pay for living in a world where the government puts social policy first and aims to protect its citizens from predatory practices.

4. Too many choices.

The technology industry in the U.S., including computers, software, telecommunications and the Internet, is probably the most competitive industry in the world. So much so that potential profits of some of these highfliers are being called into question in the wake of the government's ruling against Microsoft with a stunning, two-day 9.25 percent dive in the Nasdaq Composite.

But oh, the headaches for the consumer! We are offered a huge assortment of innovative products, introduced at a blistering pace, for ever cheaper prices. It's positively mind-boggling! Just think of the time it takes to sort through all the options and make an informed decision.

Judge Jackson seems to think that Microsoft stifles innovation and thwarts competition. In this area, I have to disagree. There are too many products on the market, not too few. The government ought to think about nabbing some of those other scoundrels in the technology industry that have made my life just plain miserable.

Rubin's Choice Seat Is a Reminder and an Omen

———— Aug. 3, 2004 ————

JUST IN CASE you missed the message of the Democratic National Convention last week that happy days can be here again if we elect John Kerry, the Kerry campaign used subliminal signals to supplement the speeches.

Sitting in the seat of honor to the right of Teresa Heinz Kerry during her husband's acceptance speech Thursday night was none other than Robert Rubin, the Democratic party's éminence grise.

Rubin was the first chairman of President Bill Clinton's National Economic Council, an utterly useless post that should have been eliminated if the Bush administration were serious about smaller government. Instead, it tried to install a Rubin clone—one Stephen Friedman, another former chairman of Goldman, Sachs & Co.—in a job that, as best as I can tell, exists solely to coordinate among the president's economic advisers. (If they can't talk to one another without an intermediary, hiring a staff psychologist would seem to be a better use of the taxpayers' money.)

So there was Rubin, looking as solemn at Teresa's side as Federal Reserve Chairman Alan Greenspan was uncomfortable perched next to Hillary Rodham Clinton at her hubby's first State of the Union address in 1993.

What's more, Rubin and his wife Judith were among the select guests invited to join the Kerry and Edwards families at a party following Kerry's Thursday night speech.

RUBINOMICS

Observant TV viewers, which may not be the same subset as undecided voters, would be tempted to draw two conclusions from the Bob-and-Teresa photo-op: 1) Kerry is serious about deficit reduction, which is high on the list of voters' priorities; and 2) Rubin is serious about another stint in government—Fed chairman, perhaps—in a Kerry administration.

Let's start with No. 1. Rubin is the poster boy for deficit reduction. Early in the Clinton administration, Rubin persuaded the new president to forgo middle-class tax cuts and new government "investment" to "grow the economy" in favor of a tax increase and spending curbs.

Thus was born Rubinomics. This dubious economic theory holds that raising taxes reduces the deficit, brings long-term interest rates down and stimulates investment and economic growth. The fact that Rubin had the causality wrong—economic growth reduced the deficit; reducing the deficit didn't produce economic growth—is just an inconvenient detail.

UNPAID ADVERTISING

The turnaround in the federal budget during the Clinton years from a record deficit of $290 billion in 1992 to a record surplus of $239 billion in 2000 owes largely to the increase in productivity, which raised the economy's potential noninflationary growth rate, and the stock market bubble, which produced a windfall in revenue from capital gains taxes and options-related income for the Treasury.

The post-Clinton Democrats adopted fiscal discipline as their own, which isn't that hard a sell given the profligate spending of the Bush administration.

While Kerry's most visible economic advisers are Gene Sperling, Rubin's deputy at the NEC who was elevated to chairman in 1997; Roger Altman, another Clinton Treasury hand; and Alan Blinder, a Princeton

University economics professor, it's Rubin who provides the gravitas, who participates in key economic policy discussions, who signs off on all of the big issues.

Putting Rubin in the seat of honor next to Heinz Kerry was an unspoken endorsement of Kerry's economic plan, which features new spending on health care and education and middle-class tax cuts, to be paid for with the revenue from rolling back the tax cuts for those making over $200,000 a year.

IN PLAY

The fact that the nonpartisan Tax Policy Center says the tax rollback won't pay for the new initiatives is less important than Rubin's implicit imprimatur on Kerry's plan, touted as a means to cut the deficit in half by 2008.

The second subliminal message from the seating selection at Thursday's conclusion of the convention is more interesting: Rubin is considering, and being considered for, a high-level economic post in a Kerry administration.

Rubin's name has been bandied about as a possible candidate for Fed chairman. When Rubin left the Treasury in 1999—he is currently chairman of Citigroup Inc.'s executive committee—he was adamant about not wanting another Washington post that would take him away from his family.

THE RUBIN FED?

"I don't see him coming back to Washington unless it was to be Fed chairman," says Greg Valliere, chief political strategist for Charles Schwab's Research Group. "But he's the odds-on favorite [in a Kerry administration] if Greenspan steps down in 2006."

From the Kerry campaign's point of view, it doesn't really matter whether Rubin would consider going back to Washington or was merely willing to convey that impression to bolster the candidate's economic credentials.

The seating "was a convenient and potent prop," Valliere says. "It was good politics—and good for the markets."

Still, it's not idle speculation to consider how Rubin would be as Fed chairman. For starters, he's a lawyer, not an economist. Second, his grasp of economics appears slim, confined to buzzwords and mantras rather than a command of how the various parts of the economy interact.

Treasury secretaries will forever be indebted to Rubin for the legacy of the "strong-dollar policy." No matter how nonsensical the concept, his successors must utter that meaningless mantra or else be censured by the foreign exchange market.

QUESTIONABLE STIMULUS

As Fed chairman, Rubin would have to demonstrate that he understands the difference between Treasury's strong dollar policy (a posture) and the Fed's money-creation monopoly (a process), which is the real determinant of the currency's value.

Where Rubin might add value to the Fed is in the communications department. He's so smooth, he might actually help the Fed sharpen its communication skills and increase its transparency.

When it comes to the implementation of monetary policy, just the idea of a Rubin Fed would keep me up at night. Someone who thinks raising taxes stimulates the economy is apt to think raising interest rates will produce the same result.

8

Sir Alan

MY CAREER as a financial journalist coincides almost exactly with Alan Greenspan's tenure as chairman of the Federal Reserve. I started my job in May 1987; he started his in August.

We are both still gainfully employed in our respective lines of work. He's still Fed chairman. I'm still a journalist, albeit with a different news organization.

There are other similarities between us. Greenspan knew Ayn Rand (he was part of her inner circle); I read Ayn Rand.

You could say we were made for each other. You could also say I was meant to keep him honest.

Because the Fed holds sway over the economy and financial markets, Alan Greenspan is rarely far from my thoughts. The idea for the first column in this chapter—a comparison of Greenspan to the late film director Alfred Hitchcock—was sloshing around in my head for about five years before I finally committed it to paper.

I have read everything Greenspan has said over the past 18 years. (Given his penchant for repetition, it feels as if I've read everything several times.) Many of his more popular phrases and bons mots are ingrained in my memory.

I penned my first article on "Glasnost at the Fed" in 1989 when I was at Dow Jones. The secrecy surrounding the Fed's operations never made any sense to me, even as a cub reporter learning about Fed policy on the job.

The central bank changes policy because it wants people to change behavior. Interest-rate adjustments should be announced by the chairman with a bullhorn, not through puffs of white smoke that have to be interpreted by a cottage industry of "Fed watchers," most of whom are graduates of the Federal Reserve system.

Each week this group would dutifully project the banking system's demand for reserves and compare the estimates to the Fed's provision of reserves (the amounts weren't always announced) to determine if the Fed was adjusting the federal funds rate. Even the choice of open market operation on a particular day of the week had significance.

Is this any way to conduct monetary policy? You bet it was—until 1994, when the Fed started announcing interest rate changes in real time.

Back then, a number of Fed watchers predicted the demise of Western civilization if the Fed were to give away such state secrets. My answer was always the same: The Fed is the lender of last resort, not the employer of last resort. (I'm happy to report that most Fed watchers have taken up etymology now that the Fed is more transparent.)

In the old days, few analysts and journalists were willing to criticize or challenge Greenspan. Following the stock market bubble and bust, it became almost fashionable.

While I've taken issue with the conduct of monetary policy over the years—the decisions themselves, the way they're communicated, the justification for them—my real beef with Greenspan is his persona. He's cultivated the image of an all-knowing, all-seeing personality whose sphinxlike pronouncements reverberate around the globe.

Congress seeks Greenspan's counsel on almost everything, and Greenspan is happy to oblige. Some of the topics on which he's testified or spoken in the last five years are: fiscal policy, the federal budget, education, energy policy, trade policy, corporate governance and accounting practices, banking, bank regulation and supervision, deposit insurance, government-sponsored enterprises (Fannie Mae and Freddie Mac), derivatives, the aging global population, Social Security and Medicare, the mortgage market, household debt, globalization, risk management, technological innovation, productivity, the stock market, stock options, financial literacy, structural change in the economy and transparency.

The only thing Greenspan is unwilling to comment on is the U.S. dollar, which is ironic since the Fed actually has some control over the supply of dollars in circulation, and hence the value.

Even former Fed economists who admire Greenspan say he has pursued the cult of personality at the expense of the institution, arguing against adopting a policy rule, such as an inflation target, in favor of an ad hoc approach.

Greenspan claims any rule would hamper the Fed's flexibility when, in fact, it would give the central bank greater leeway to implement short-term stabilization policy.

The only flexibility a rule-based policy would seem to hamper is Greenspan's.

More and more Fed officials are talking about greater transparency and an inflation target. Greenspan talks about transparency but moves grudgingly to lift the veil of secrecy.

He doesn't hold press conferences or submit to media questions, opting instead for off-the-record chats with selected reporters from the print press, who dutifully disseminate the nuggets of information he shares with them in the next day's paper. He controls leaks from his policy-setting committee, even as he releases material, nonpublic information to his "signal corps," as former Fed governor Larry Meyer calls the chosen reporters.

Greenspan's name never appears in these stories as the "Fed source."

Monetary policy may be his game, but Greenspan has always played for bigger stakes.

Greenspan Directs the Fed with a Touch of Hitchcock

———— Feb. 12, 2001 ————

FILMMAKER ALFRED HITCHCOCK, the master of suspense, has long been an idol for would-be directors.

One of his trademarks was using an inconsequential plot device to set his narratives in motion. Whether it's the uranium in the wine bottles in *Notorious*, the secret formula (in Mr. Memory's brain) in *The Thirty-Nine Steps*, the secret treaty in *Foreign Correspondent* or the little tune in *The Lady Vanishes*, the audience soon forgets why this particular item is of such vital importance to the characters.

Which is exactly the point. Hitch needed to involve his audience, take us from one place to the next, without calling attention to the device. As if to underscore how inconsequential it was, he gave it a nonsense name: the "MacGuffin."

Alan Greenspan, chairman of the Federal Reserve for more than 13 years, is not unlike Alfred Hitchcock in this respect. Greenspan knows where he has to take monetary policy and concocts a plot device, or MacGuffin, to get us from point A to point B, after which it matters very little what the rationale was. And when the device is no longer a means to an end, Pffff! It retires gracefully to the great bathtub of "Greenspan-watches-it" indicators—to float endlessly, never to sink.

Cast of Characters

Many of Greenspan's MacGuffins were introduced on the occasion of his semiannual monetary report to Congress, formerly known as the Humphrey–Hawkins testimony. Who can forget such luminaries as P*, the credit crunch, the natural rate, the real rate, policy neutrality, lead times, vendor deliveries, the gold price, the employment cost index, worker insecurity, the quit rate, the pool of available workers and, most recently, the claim that productivity increases aggregate demand rather than aggregate supply?

"Greenspan pulls some of these things off the shelves of economic obscurity and infuses them with an importance disproportionate to their actual significance," says John Ryding, senior economist at Bear, Stearns & Co.

The one thing you will never hear the Greenspan Fed accept responsibility for, according to Ryding, is inflation. In the Fed's view, "inflation is a product of private-sector imbalances," he says. "The Fed's role as regulator-in-chief is to guide the economy through these imbalances."

Screenplay

Greenspan's MacGuffins serve the purpose of creating a theoretical framework for policy actions.

"He wants to have a theory behind what he does that's familiar," says Neal Soss, chief economist at Credit Suisse First Boston. "He's willing to say that the theory fits the circumstances in one month and not the next."

Often they're euphemisms for something that is politically unpalatable. For example, in November 1999, Greenspan used the shrinking pool of available workers to justify a 25-basis-point increase in the federal funds rate. The labor pool consists of the army of unemployed plus those folks who aren't in the labor force but would like a job.

If you graph the unemployment rate and the available labor pool, you'll find they are indistinguishable from one another. No surprise since the unemployment rate is the largest component of the available pool, Ryding points out. "The pool is a refined version of Phillips Curve thinking."

It's not politically correct for a Fed chairman to tell Congress he's raising interest rates because too many people are working. Better to wade into the pool than suffer death by drowning.

STARRING ROLE

I suspect that the reason so many of Greenspan's MacGuffins make their debut at the Humphrey–Hawkins testimony is that it gives the Fed chief a clear edge. The Fed Board staff spends weeks preparing the testimony, drawing on the latest research (directed by the chairman, of course, who is looking for empirical evidence to support his hunches) by a legion of Fed economists.

Greenspan may be in the hot seat on Capitol Hill—fielding questions, deciding just how much to reveal and how much to obfuscate—but he holds the trump card.

Imagine the House Banking Committee staff's reaction when Greenspan introduced P* (P-star) in February 1989, a monetary-based model of expected inflation based on the relationship between the current and long-run price level.

Not wanting to appear stupid, the congressmen nod knowingly and quickly reconsider any line of questioning they were about to embark on.

DIALOGUE

The Senate Banking Committee is not so easily duped. In February 2000, the Fed had already embarked on a tightening cycle and anticipated the need for additional rate increases. Greenspan hauled out a concept he'd tested a month before—successfully, he must have thought—at an Economic Club of New York dinner. To wit, Greenspan argued that the increase in productivity was being incorporated into higher stock prices, boosting aggregate demand more than potential supply. What he was saying, in essence, was that productivity growth, long his New Economy mantra, was inflationary.

The senators weren't buying.

"Now all of a sudden we have this theory, well, you know, you're getting this run-up in the equity assets, that creates a wealth effect. That's going to stimulate a demand without a supply to respond to it, so now we've got to curtail the economy?" inquired Senator Paul Sarbanes, a Maryland Democrat, struggling to understand the concept.

It was not Greenspan's finest hour.

EDITING PROCESS

Back in 1994, the U.S. economy was finally gaining some traction after a short recession and an extended period of sluggish growth with paltry job creation. The overnight federal funds rate had been at 3 percent—zero percent adjusted for inflation—for 19 months when the Fed started to nudge it higher on Feb. 4, 1994.

Greenspan knew the funds rate would have to rise significantly; he needed the cover to do it.

Enter policy neutrality, a perfect construct for a central banker because it can't be observed and isn't constant. To encourage the economy to grow at its maximum potential over time, "we must move toward a posture of policy neutrality—that is, a level of real short-term rates consistent with sustained economic growth at the economy's potential," Greenspan said at his Feb. 22, 1994, Humphrey–Hawkins testimony. "That level, of course, is difficult to discern and, obviously, is not a fixed number but moves with the developments within the economy and financial markets."

Greenspan goes up to Capitol Hill again on Tuesday to deliver the Fed's monetary policy report to the Senate Banking Committee. There's already a prime MacGuffin candidate, hinted at by Greenspan last month in testimony before the Senate Budget Committee on the fiscal challenges of federal budget surpluses: consumer confidence.

CLOSE-UP

Under questioning from Senator Sarbanes again, the Fed chief conceded that economic growth was "very close to zero," partly as a result of inventory liquidation.

"The crucial question, Senator, is whether that marked decline breaches consumer confidence, because there is something different about a recession from other times in the economy; it is not a continuum from slow growth into negative growth; something happens," Greenspan said.

He's going to try to prevent that "not-a-continuum" something from happening by lowering interest rates, hopefully stabilizing both the stock market and the economy in the process. At the moment, nothing else matters.

If confidence should rebound and Greenspan still wants to lower interest rates aggressively, why, he'll just pluck something else out of his central banker's toolbox to justify it. The end comes first; then he finds the means to achieve it.

If it takes uranium in wine bottles, so be it.

Greenspan and Marx, United in Proletariat Views

————— Nov. 17, 1999 —————

AFTER DECLARING WAR on the army of the employed yesterday, raising interest rates because of the diminishing pool of available labor, Fed Chairman Alan Greenspan should clarify for the markets—not to mention the American public—exactly what his strategy is.

"Where does the endgame in interest rates end?" asks John Ryding, senior economist at Bear, Stearns & Co. "The Phillips Curve endgame strategy is not just to prevent the unemployment rate from falling. It's to engineer an increase in the unemployment rate. How much will they have to slow growth to accomplish that?"

Searching for an historical model for the Fed's rate rationalization, Ryding dusted off his copy of Karl Marx's *Das Kapital* last night.

"There is not much difference between Marx's 'reserve army of unemployed' and Greenspan's 'available pool of labor,'" he says.

Marx wrote in his famous 19th-century treatise that in order to be profitable, capitalists needed a pool of unemployed workers to exploit. Only by paying labor less than their marginal revenue product—the additional revenue earned from the sale of the product produced by that worker—could capitalists extract a profit, Marx wrote.

In most respects, Alan Greenspan, a devotee of the free-market philosophy of Ayn Rand—at least until he became a public servant—is about as far away from Karl Marx as it gets. So what was he thinking about when he crafted the statement following the Fed's announcement yesterday, justifying the rate increase in terms of the dwindling available pool of workers?

CAPITALIST CLASS

"Greenspan is searching for a mandate," says Neal Soss, chief economist at Credit Suisse First Boston. "Perhaps he's spitting in the eye of the people on the committee who forced him to tighten. He may be testing what is the nature of the Fed's mandate."

In the 1980s, that mandate was crystal clear. "It was to whip inflation even if it was at some cost," Soss says.

The 1990s has been a decade of prosperity. Minorities, individuals with only a high school diploma, and handicapped workers have benefited from the economic boom and strong demand for labor, which has pushed the unemployment rate to a 30-year low of 4.1 percent.

The public approved of economic prosperity, and Greenspan, reading the mandate correctly, had the prescience to allow strong growth to persist longer than a Fed chairman with a more rigid ideology would, according to Soss.

"Now he's testing the limits," he adds. "Is the Fed's public mandate to tell Americans they can't have jobs when they have no problem getting them?"

LABOR POWER

It seems something of a stretch to assume that Greenspan is knowingly provoking Congress, which has oversight responsibility for the Fed, to come down on him for his action, at least for the stated rationale. On the surface, it seems that Greenspan is relying on a Phillips Curve model, which he is known to disavow and which has significant implications for monetary policy.

The pool of available workers is not going to get noticeably deeper after yesterday's 25-basis-point increase. Enough quarter-point increases, and it will. That may be why the bond market, expecting an all-clear from either a third rate increase or a pass from the Fed, can't muster any enthusiasm.

Of course, many of Greenspan's comments about the overvaluation in the stock market—initiated against the better judgment of his staff—have been criticized. Any money manager who heeded his warnings, first uttered at Dow 6400 in December 1996, would be out of business by now.

PROLETARIAT REVOLUTION

While it may have been an institutional mistake for the chairman of the Federal Reserve to comment on the level of stock prices, it was clearly a political mistake for Greenspan to link the Fed's rate increase to the shrinking supply of available workers. Curiously, there has been little hue and cry from Congress just yet.

"I'm afraid Greenspan's walk-on-water reputation will prompt them to assume that if he raises rates, it must be necessary," Soss says.

Congress is preoccupied with trying to wrap up the budget negotiations and get out of town. The media mostly ignored the implications of the Fed's statement.

I'll bet that if and when the economy starts to look less perky, our elected representatives will find it in themselves to take to the soapbox to protest the harm to the ordinary working man, who just happens to be going to the polls next November.

At that time, Greenspan is going to take some heat for being too much like Karl and not enough like Groucho.

The Emperor's New Clothes Are Threadbare

———— Feb. 17, 2000 ————

Look at the Emperor's new clothes. They're beautiful! What a marvelous train! And the colors! The colors of that beautiful fabric! I have never seen anything like it in my life.

—HANS CHRISTIAN ANDERSEN

ALAN GREENSPAN, chairman extraordinaire of the Federal Reserve Board, delivered his semiannual monetary report to Congress today.

To the financial markets, he delivered a clear message: Interest rates are going to rise until the economy slows.

To legislators, he delivered a warning: Keep your hands off the budget surplus.

To the stock market, he delivered a challenge: Put a lid on it, or I'm gonna do it for you.

Greenspan came out swinging from the first sentence. In short order he defined the debate:

1. There is little evidence that the U.S. economy is slowing.

2. Labor and current account imbalances are developing that, unless checked, will derail the expansion.

3. The misalignment carries a greater inflationary risk today than it did before.

While productivity growth continues to accelerate and technological innovation is not likely to slow anytime soon, the Fed chief isn't taking any chances. The reduction in the available workers for hire and the gaping current account deficit—two "safety valves" for the U.S. economy —are reaching extremes.

"These safety valves that have been supplying goods and services to meet the recent increments to purchasing power largely generated by capital gains cannot be expected to absorb an excess of demand over supply indefinitely," Greenspan said.

DUMB AND DUMBER

The Fed chairman reiterated a point that he made in his Jan. 13 speech to the Economic Club of New York. (It sounded flaky then and it sounds even flakier in rerun.)

"Accelerating productivity entails a matching acceleration in the potential output of goods and services and a corresponding rise in real incomes available to purchase the new output," he said.

In other words, productivity growth boosts aggregate demand faster than it boosts aggregate supply.

Wait a minute! For years, Greenspan has been waxing poetic about the increase in trend productivity growth, about the synergies among technologies that allowed the U.S. economy to expand at a stunning 4 percent rate without generating inflationary pressures. Now faster productivity growth is the villain?

"The logic of Greenspan's position implies that the Fed's job would be easier if productivity growth were only, say, 1.5 percent," says John Ryding, senior economist at Bear, Stearns & Co. "This is nonsense."

HE'S NAKED!

None of the solemn-faced members of Congress dared to question the chairman's logic. The emperor may have no clothes, but he's still the emperor!

"Here's a guy who wants to get rates up and he's using whatever resources he can to dream up ways to justify it yet keep the pressure off himself," says Paul DeRosa, a partner at Mt. Lucas Management Co. "It's a bit of a strain."

Greenspan claims that the wealth effect—capital gains from five years of double-digit increases in the U.S. stock market—has boosted domestic demand by a full percentage point. The excess demand has been satisfied by importing goods and services from abroad and inducing idle labor into the work force (the safety valves). Because the chairman sees both these trends as unsustainable, domestic demand has to slow.

What he doesn't do is address the issue of why the economy has been growing "too fast" in the first place.

"Either we're discounting future productivity gains or else monetary policy has been too loose," DeRosa says. "If you were running the central bank, which would you choose?"

SUPPLY AND DEMAND

The issue of margin requirements came up again in the Q&A following the testimony, along with income inequality, bailouts, oil prices, budget surpluses and debt reduction. When asked about the sharp rise in margin debt—the amount of money borrowed from New York Stock Exchange member firms for stock purchases—and the possibility of raising the margin requirements, Greenspan demurred.

"The evidence suggests that it has very little impact on the price structure, on the market or anything else," he said.

What evidence? Initial margin requirements are set by the Fed and have been at 50 percent since 1974.

As with most things, if you raise the price of speculation (via higher margin requirements), the result will be less speculation demanded. Unless, of course, the law of supply and demand has been repealed.

Brokerage firms aren't the only source of securities loans, of course. Banks are actively engaged in securities lending.

"The Fed is a bank regulator. Why doesn't the Fed browbeat the banks for their securities lending?" wonders Jim Bianco, president of Bianco Research in Barrington, Illinois.

GOOD OR BAD?

Especially if the Fed thinks that stock-market-driven wealth is the source of the problem, the Fed has several ways to set an example.

Greenspan is relying on the rise in real intermediate- and long-term interest rates to perform a balancing act between supply and demand.

While this process was thought to be "well advanced" in recent speeches, now he's not so sure. Interest-sensitive spending has remained robust, Greenspan said, and the Fed "will have to stay alert for signs that real interest rates have not yet risen enough to bring the growth of demand into line with that of potential supply, even should the acceleration of productivity continue."

It sure sounds as if productivity is a good thing—a buffer—once again.

"Even in the bad economics textbooks, productivity is a good thing," Ryding says.

Want Fiscal Advice? Ask the Monetary Authority

——————— Jan. 23, 2001 ———————

THE MOST IMPORTANT market event this week is neither an economic statistic nor a quarterly earnings report. It's the appearance of Federal Reserve Chairman Alan Greenspan before the Senate Budget Committee on Thursday.

With tax cuts high on President George W. Bush's agenda—much to the consternation of liberals who think a close election means the new leader must appease his left flank—the senators will want to know from Greenspan what he thinks about Bush's proposed $1.6 trillion tax cut.

The Budget Committee is charged with writing a budget resolution, a blueprint that will incorporate Bush's tax cut, centered around across-the-board reductions in marginal rates, into the larger budget framework. The official subject for Thursday's hearing is "evolving fiscal challenges."

Greenspan's challenge, should he choose to accept it, is to sanction, or advise against, tax cuts at a time of budget surpluses. The Democrats have used Greenspan's previous priority list as the basis for their opposition to tax cuts. In the past, the Fed chief advocated paying down the debt first and tax cuts second. A distant third was spending the surplus on new fiscal initiatives.

REDUNDANT CAPS

Some Beltway insiders are predicting that political-animal Greenspan will come out in favor of lower taxes. After all, he's an old friend of Vice President Dick Cheney and Treasury Secretary Paul O'Neill, as well as a lifelong Republican. As a devout follower of Ayn Rand, he's philosophically opposed to the expansion of government, and presumably would support giving taxpayers a refund. (After all, the federal surplus is an overpayment of taxes.)

"The buzz in Washington is that Greenspan will endorse tax cuts," says Larry Kudlow, chief economist at ING Barings LLC. "He didn't oppose tax cuts a year ago. What he advocated was surplus accumulation during full employment. If Congress is going to spend it, he said he'd rather see lower taxes."

Spend Congress has. The budgetary spending caps, which provided some discipline for discretionary spending in the early and mid-1990s, are passé.

"The pressure is off on containing spending, and the opportunity is on to lift it," says Susan Hering, senior U.S. economist at UBS Warburg.

BIG, BIGGER, BIGGEST

Next week, the Congressional Budget Office will release new 10-year budget estimates. Senate Budget Committee Chairman Pete Domenici already let the cat out of the bag when he announced last week that the projected surplus will reach $5.7 trillion over the next 10 years, $1.1 trillion higher than CBO's previous forecast. Of that $5.7 trillion, $3.3 trillion is "on budget," or outside the surplus in the Social Security trust funds, where taxes exceed benefits through the middle of the next decade.

Normally, Greenspan would caution against relying on 10-year budget estimates. Since "most of the revision is based on raising potential GDP forecasts, and faster potential growth is something Greenspan has advocated for a long time, it's hard for him to argue against it," says Hering.

Budget Committee Democrats clearly hope the Fed chairman reiterates his priority of debt reduction *über alles*. Republicans want the Good Housekeeping seal of approval on their $1.6 trillion tax cut. Everyone wants to know what Greenspan thinks of the economy, although clearly fiscal policy will be in the spotlight.

"Greenspan has not spoken on the record about what changed his mind so quickly," Kudlow says.

WHEELIE

On Nov. 15, the Fed saw the balance of risks weighted toward higher inflation. On Dec. 5, Greenspan issued his first warning about the increased risks to an economy losing momentum. On Dec. 19, policy-makers officially determined that the risks were toward slower economic growth. And on Jan. 3, the Fed lowered the federal funds rate by 50 basis points between meetings.

Yet unlike other major government policy-makers, "Greenspan gets a free ride," Kudlow says. "He never has to face the press and answer questions."

The senators on the committee will ask Greenspan about the economy. Ever since the Jan. 3 rate cut, Fed policy-makers have been hawking a soft-landing scenario, implying no aggressive rate cuts, says Tom Gallagher, a political economist at International Strategy & Investment in Washington, D.C.

"The market has refused to be steered and still expects 50 basis points next week," Gallagher says. "It will be interesting to see how he reconciles the two views."

PUBLIC VS PRIVATE

The February fed funds futures contract, at an implied yield of 5.525 percent, puts the odds of a 50-basis-point move near 90 percent. The contract has a stellar track record of predicting the outcome of Fed meetings—35 out of 38 dating back to mid-1996—especially one week prior to a gathering, according to Jim Bianco, president of Bianco Research in Barrington, Illinois.

Greenspan will probably attempt to differentiate between his preferred method of macroeconomic management (interest rates) and countercyclical fiscal policy (cutting taxes when the economy is weak), which usually turns out to be a case of too little, too late because of the vagaries of the legislative process.

"He'll probably focus on the incentives created by tax cuts," Gallagher says. "Publicly he'll be neutral to positive on tax cuts, advocate a reduction in marginal tax rates, not targeted tax cuts, and try to protect his credibility" by not endorsing the Bush plan before it's been hammered out.

Behind the scenes, Greenspan will reach an accommodation with the White House, Gallagher says, even if publicly he sounds a lot like he did before.

Assuming the Fed chief does want to come out in favor of tax cuts, how will he negotiate the transition?

Easy. Given that all Greenspan's statements are highly nuanced and padded with conditionality, he can claim that Congress's appetite for spending and the size of the burgeoning budget surplus argue for a cut in marginal tax rates. One point six trillion may be too large for his palate, but he can advocate a combination of debt reduction and tax cuts without endorsing the Bush plan.

Pete Davis, president of Davis Capital Investment Ideas in Washington, D.C., thinks Greenspan will reiterate his preference for debt reduction.

"I suspect he will maintain his priority for debt reduction without closing the door on a tax cut," Davis says.

In other words, consummate Greenspan.

POSTSCRIPT: *On Jan. 25, 2001, Greenspan endorsed tax cuts, saying they were necessary to avoid a situation where, with no Treasuries left to buy, the government would be forced to accumulate private assets. He is still defending his endorsement to a partisan Congress.*

The Ghost of Arthur Burns Stalks Alan Greenspan
——————— July 16, 2001 ———————

THIS WEEK'S main event takes place on Wednesday, when Federal Reserve Chairman Alan Greenspan goes up to Capitol Hill to deliver the Fed's semiannual monetary report to Congress. His appearance will overshadow economic news on industrial production, consumer prices, housing, trade and regional manufacturing, all of which are expected to show a dead-in-the-water economy.

Here's where Arthur Burns comes in. Before his inauspicious tour of duty as Fed chairman from 1970 to 1978, where he was suspected of pumping up the money supply to ensure Richard Nixon's reelection in 1972, Burns had a distinguished economic career. A professor of economics at Columbia University, Burns and coauthor Wesley Mitchell published *Measuring Business Cycles* in 1946, which was as empirical as Keynes's *General Theory* was theoretical. Burns was one of the few anti-Keynesians in an era where, to quote Nixon, we're all Keynesians now.

Burns had a major influence on graduate student Greenspan, as documented in Justin Martin's biography, *Greenspan: The Man Behind the Money* (the "other" biography that came out at the same time as Bob Woodward's hero worship).

An anecdote from Martin's book is instructive. It answers a question that has long plagued me about Greenspan's thinking. In Martin's retelling, Burns used to ask his graduate students, "What causes inflation?" Burns would pause and pan the room, before answering his own question: "Excess government spending causes inflation."

REVELATIONS

That paragraph on page 29 was an epiphany for me. All these years of watching and listening to Alan Greenspan, I've never understood how the one-time member of Ayn Rand's collective could prefer debt reduction to tax cuts (at least until it was politically prudent for him to support them when George W. Bush became president).

While the idea that government spending was inflationary was popular at the time—the federal government borrows to finance its spending, and the central bank then monetizes it by buying the debt—the thinking is more sophisticated today. While spending by the government is less efficient than that of the private sector since it isn't sensitive to price signals, it doesn't matter who borrows and spends. The central bank always has the ability to offset it.

An increase in government spending, all things equal, would cause interest rates to rise. Nothing says the central bank has to accommodate the increased demand for credit, supplying sufficient reserves to prevent the short-term rate from rising.

INFLATION RATIONALIZATION

If Greenspan really believes that excess government spending causes inflation, not too much money chasing too few goods and services, everything falls into place. There is never any mention of inflation as a monetary phenomenon in Greenspan's speeches and testimonies. In fact, anyone whose sole source of insight into the Fed's thinking is the minutes of the policy deliberations would be convinced that higher energy prices cause inflation. Second in line would be a tight labor market and the higher wages it engenders.

"Widespread evidence of some lessening of pressures in most labor markets across the nation had not yet resulted in lower wage inflation, but the members expected that recent and anticipated ebbing of pressures on labor and other resources and associated slack in product markets in a period of continuing sub-par economic growth, along with projected declines in energy prices, would hold down inflation over the forecast horizon," the Fed said in the minutes from the May 15 meeting.

To be sure, Greenspan has gone out of his way in the past to explain that higher wages aren't inflationary per se, but only to the extent that they exceed productivity growth. But he never gets to what causes wages to rise—or a wage/price spiral to be maintained—in the first place. It's always something outside the Fed when in reality it's always and every-where inside the Fed, to paraphrase Milton Friedman.

FISCAL FORUM

Whatever Greenspan has to say on the outlook for the economy on Wednesday—he may be cautiously optimistic that the forces to produce a rebound are in place, or he may be guardedly pessimistic, saying risks remain but in a manner that will not upset the stock market—he surely will say that the outlook for inflation is benign, given the collapse in energy prices.

Congress, as always, will want to hear from the monetary authority on fiscal policy. Why is unclear, since Greenspan always warns against frittering away revenue on wasteful spending.

Congressional Democrats are whining about a return to budget defi-cits as a result of the $1.35 trillion Bush tax cut. The truth is the surplus for the year that ends Sept. 30 will be between $160 and $190 billion, according to budget director Mitch Daniels.

While that's shy of last year's $237 billion surplus, "it's still the second-largest surplus on record, allowing more than $125 billion of Treasury debt to be retired," economists at Salomon Smith Barney write in this week's *Comments on Credit*.

PRODUCTIVITY HOPES

Greenspan will probably hawk his optimistic view that the improve-ment in productivity growth since 1995 has been structural, not an offshoot of strong economic growth. And it's productivity growth—specifically the increase in the economy's potential noninflationary growth rate from a measly 1.4 percent in the two decades prior to 1995 to 2.5 percent from mid-1995 through mid-2000—that made federal deficits morph into federal surpluses.

The Fed chairman probably won't encounter tough questioning from the House Financial Services Committee Wednesday. The following week, when he repeats his testimony on the Senate side, Banking Committee Chairman Paul Sarbanes, an economist by training, should have a question or two on the subject.

Last February, Sarbanes drilled Greenspan on the reasons for his shift in stance on tax cuts. Greenspan said an increase in structural productivity growth meant reducing publicly held debt to zero by 2007 was a reality. In order to obviate the conflict of interest in the government's purchase of private securities, Greenspan decided a tax cut at this time was appropriate.

Senator Sarbanes: "You think the six-month period of a slowing economy is adequate to reach a conclusion that the productivity performance will track what it was in a growing and expanding economy?"

Sarbanes will return to the scene of the crime, now that the $1.35 trillion tax cut has been implemented and surplus forecasts are shrinking.

It used to seem strange that Congress was more interested in Greenspan's view on fiscal policy than on monetary policy, which is what he controls. In light of the insights shed by Justin Martin on Greenspan's mentor's view of what causes inflation, Greenspan seems perfectly suited to the task.

Alan Greenspan Is a Knight for All Ages

——————— Aug. 8, 2002 ———————

I've been brushing up on my medieval history, especially on the subjects of knighthood and chivalry, ever since it was announced that Federal Reserve Chairman Alan Greenspan would receive an honorary knighthood from Queen Elizabeth II for his "outstanding contribution to global economic stability."

Sir Alan won't actually be entitled to use his "Sir" name since he's not a British citizen. It will be Alan Greenspan, KBE, or Knight Commander of the British Empire.

That's a big step up from "Mr. Chairman."

In the olden days, a knight was a professional soldier. He needed to own and maintain at least three horses as well as a good suit of armor, so he had to be a man of some means.

Knighthood was an honor bestowed on men who proved worthy in battle. Knights were expected to live by a certain code of conduct and forced to do battle in the king's armies.

As a military institution, knighthood peaked in the 13th century. The rank of knight then acquired some of the status of nobility, except that it was bestowed for achievement rather than inherited.

Modern knighthood carries no military obligation. It's a form of recognition for significant contributions to national life bestowed by the British monarch on individuals from the arts and sciences, business and government.

MAN FOR ALL SEASONS

Alan Greenspan may be a knight in the modern-day sense, but Sir Alan (we'll call him that even though he can't use the title) could as easily have made the grade in the Middle Ages.

Over and over again, Sir Alan has proven himself to be the king's faithful servant. After King George II was crowned in January 2001, Sir Alan was called to testify before the king's Parliament on the proposed fiscal program, the key feature of which was a large tax cut.

Hitherto, Sir Alan had always advised the king's Treasury on the value of frugality, using the monies from the tithe imposed on the subjects of the realm to repay old debts.

Somewhere between the reign of King William and the reign of King George, Sir Alan had a change of heart. No longer should the king's stuffed coffers be used for debt retirement, Sir Alan told members of Parliament. Relying on 10-year budget forecasts that he had previously derided, Sir Alan said the fiscal situation was so good that unless King George cut taxes, there would be no sovereign debt for the kingdom to retire in the next five years.

KING'S RANSOM

At latest count, the government budget was projected to be in deficit by $165 billion for the fiscal year ending Sept. 30, compared with a $127 billion surplus in fiscal 2001.

Sir Alan wasn't always such a man of the people. In fact, under King William, Sir Alan gave his imprimatur to a package of spending cuts and tax increases, the basis of King William's program of fiscal responsibility.

"I even recall Sir Alan sitting in the Queen's box" when the king addressed Parliament for the first time, said Paul Kasriel, director of economic research at the Northern Trust Corp. in Chicago.

During King William's reign, Sir Alan breakfasted regularly with the king's Chancellor of the Exchequer, Robert, Earl of Citicorp. Sir Alan and Robert were never shy about offering up the public Treasury in service of the king, whether it was to help a far-off kingdom or to support the nobility at home.

SHINING ARMOR

Sir Alan has advised kings for decades. During the Dark Ages of the 1970s, Sir Alan served as chief economic adviser to King Gerald. His main contribution, according to historians, was his campaign to "whip inflation now," memorialized in "WIN" buttons.

"Of course, Greenspan was slaying the inflation dragon when it had already stopped breathing hot air," Kasriel said.

As a private citizen, Sir Alan was not above doing favors for those in the service of the crown. In 1985, he wrote letters to regulators and Congress in support of Charles Keating, president of Lincoln Savings and Loan, which collapsed under the weight of bad real estate loans at a cost of $3.4 billion to taxpayers. Keating was convicted of 17 counts of securities fraud in California in 1991 and 73 federal counts of fraud, racketeering and conspiracy two years later, and went to jail.

When the history of the era is finally written, Sir Alan may best be remembered for asking in December 1996 if the stock market was experiencing "irrational exuberance," and then answering his own question by justifying the inflated levels for the next four years.

If Sir Alan's knighthood is as distinguished as his life as a commoner, a peerage may be in his future.

9

What Would We Do
Without a Dollar Policy?

U NTIL A DECADE AGO, the U.S. had no dollar policy and no one cared.

All that changed when Robert Rubin became the Clinton administration's second Treasury secretary in 1995, single-handedly rescued the dollar from near-extinction and enunciated a dollar policy (a slogan, really) that we're stuck with for fear the buck will collapse.

"A strong dollar is in the best interest of the U.S." became the Rubin mantra, repeated so often that some folks started to believe the administration had something to do with the rise in the dollar's foreign-exchange value from 1995 to 2002.

There is an institution that can affect the dollar's value, but it's not the Treasury. It's the Federal Reserve. The central bank determines the supply of dollars in circulation, thanks to its magical powers to create reserves out of nowhere and destroy them with equal facility.

While the Treasury can instruct the Fed to buy or sell dollars in the foreign-exchange market, the Fed decides whether those dollar purchases or sales are sterilized, or neutralized by offsetting actions elsewhere in the banking system.

Running the mint (the Treasury's job) is symbolic compared with overseeing the money supply (the Fed's job).

For that reason, it took me a long time to figure out why the dollar would rally when Rubin repeated his mantra. There was never any suggestion the Fed would follow up the comments with tighter monetary policy. So why the reaction?

The Treasury secretary can affect the short-run *demand* for dollars, not the supply. Because there are always enough foreign-exchange traders leaning in the other direction, the reiteration of a silly slogan is enough to send them scurrying to cover short positions.

Once the markets were conditioned to respond to the Rubin mantra, the next logical step was to look for a Treasury secretary who could be a good salesman for all kinds of administration initiatives. So much for the once plum cabinet post.

Paul O'Neill Is No Bob Rubin. Get Used to It

———— July 31, 2001 ————

ROBERT RUBIN was everybody's favorite Treasury secretary. He was good-looking, wealthy, affable, savvy, a product of the Ivy League and Wall Street. They ate him up.

It didn't hurt that Rubin succeeded Lloyd Bentsen, the former senator from Texas and probably one of the worst Treasury secretaries in recent memory. Bentsen is credited with guiding the dollar to an all-time low of 79.75 yen, even though the dollar attained that nadir during Rubin's watch in April 1995.

Treasury Secretary Paul O'Neill was hardly a neophyte when he came to Washington in January, having done an eight-year stint at the Office of Management and Budget in the 1970s. Admired for a successful 13-year stewardship at the helm of Alcoa, Inc., O'Neill drew criticism—early and often—for the simple reason that he wasn't pre-programmed to recite the Rubin mantra: "A strong dollar is in the best interest of the U.S."

In February, O'Neill had to assuage fears that the Bush administration was reneging on the Clinton administration's strong-dollar policy. A German newspaper quoted him as saying the U.S. doesn't "follow, as is often said, a policy of a strong dollar."

Bravo. While O'Neill's statement was taken out of context—what he said was "a strong dollar is a reflection of a strong U.S. economy"—some might find his candor refreshing. Instead, he was chastised for his failure to understand his role as defender of the strong-dollar policy.

Shhhhhh!

The dirty little secret that no one in Washington or on Wall Street dares mention is that there is no—has never been any—U.S. foreign-exchange policy, says Lou Crandall, chief economist at Wrightson Associates.

"Unless you want to call Bretton Woods a foreign-exchange policy, the U.S. has never had an activist, interventionist foreign-exchange policy," Crandall says.

What became known as the Rubin mantra, repeated on prompting like some posthypnotic suggestion, was really a lot of hooey.

"What exactly is the U.S.'s strong-dollar policy other than a few words?" wonders Paul Kasriel, director of economic research at the Northern Trust Corp. in Chicago. "Rubin used to remind me of the bird in a cuckoo clock. Periodically, he would come out of his office, announce that he was maintaining the U.S.'s strong-dollar policy, then go back to work. No one ever asked him what policy levers he controlled to bring about a strong dollar, and he never volunteered the information."

Empty Words

Kasriel rightly points out that the Treasury secretary controls neither real interest rates (the Fed's job) nor tax and spending policy (Congress's bailiwick). The Treasury can order the Federal Reserve to buy or sell dollars in the foreign-exchange market, but it has no power to prevent the Fed from sterilizing the intervention, offsetting the dollar purchases/sales in the foreign-exchange market with sales/purchases of government securities in an open market operation.

"Other than expressing the preferences of the administration with regard to the dollar, the Treasury secretary has very little substantive power to implement policies that will bring the administration's preferences to fruition," Kasriel says.

Of course, government policies do come to bear on the value of a currency. An environment of low taxes and little regulation—an area where the U.S. still reigns supreme over its trading partners—provides an attractive environment for investment.

During his brief tenure, O'Neill has created a flap for, among other things, talking the economy down when the Bush administration took office, alienating our allies by countering European claims that the continent would be immune from the economic slowdown in the U.S. and remaining rosy on his outlook for U.S. economic growth.

Much Ado

The first case was, once again, a statement of the obvious, no doubt motivated by a desire to front-run Democratic accusations that the Bush administration's tax cut ruined an economy that slowed during Clinton's watch.

The second brouhaha was another reality check that proved prescient. The optimistic outlook on the U.S. economy remains a forecast.

Two weeks ago, there was yet another flutter when President Bush failed to do the Rubin cuckoo routine. En route to a meeting of the Group of Eight industrialized nations, Bush told reporters that the market should determine the foreign-exchange value of the dollar.

Given the pressure from manufacturing trade groups in the U.S., for whom the strong dollar is an impediment to exports, Bush's plain-spoken comments created speculation the administration might be going soft on the strong dollar.

Enter Secretary O'Neill to claim he was the sole spokesman for the dollar, and that a strong dollar was still the name of the game (that's what it is: a game).

So great was the confusion as to who was in charge (at the gaming tables) that a White House spokesman had to clarify that there was no split in the administration on dollar policy, that O'Neill was the point man on the dollar.

Fool's Gold

What's surprising is that so many analysts and traders seem to prefer meaningless words that aren't backed up by actions to straight, unscripted talk. Anyone who thinks the U.S. is crazy enough to start talking the dollar down when it needs to import more than $1 billion a day to finance its gaping current account deficit, which totaled $445 billion last year, is, well, crazy.

What people need to understand is that Paul O'Neill is no Bob Rubin. And that's not meant in a pejorative sense.

"O'Neill can't pull off the Rubin mantra," Crandall says. "Rubin is a lawyer. He's well-practiced in saying something meaningless with a straight face."

Not everyone is so adept.

❈ ❈ ❈

The Foreign-Exchange Market
Can't Handle the Truth

————— May 6, 2002 —————

IN SEARCH of a scapegoat for the dollar's latest bout of dyspepsia, the foreign-exchange market settled on U.S. Treasury Secretary Paul O'Neill.

O'Neill is something of an original in a town where ideas are cut to fit this year's fashions. He speaks the truth. His audience might prefer that he recite on command his predecessor Bob Rubin's mantra—"a strong dollar is in the best interest of the U.S."—but O'Neill refuses to play the game.

You've got to admire a guy who is honest enough to admit that the foreign-exchange value of the dollar is a reflection of policy, not a policy in and of itself. Run a good country, create an environment for the private sector to thrive and prosper, and a strong dollar will be the result, not the other way around.

"It's a candid admission of the view that a strong dollar is a good thing, but that we don't set it," said Neal Soss, chief economist at Credit Suisse First Boston.

O'Neill went up to Capitol Hill last week to testify on international economic policy. His prepared text had nary a mention of the dollar. He went out of his way to disabuse his audience—the Senate Banking Committee, the American people and currency traders—of the notion that U.S. manufacturers had prevailed on the administration to weaken the dollar.

"There's apparently some breathless anticipation that I'm going to say something to intentionally indicate a change in policy, position or direction," O'Neill said last Wednesday. "That is not the intent."

UNDESIRED OUTCOME

It was, however, the outcome. Wednesday's fall in the dollar versus major world currencies was just the continuation of a slide that began in earnest in April.

Senate Banking Committee Chairman Paul Sarbanes, a Maryland Democrat, hammered away at what he saw as O'Neill's cavalier attitude toward the large and growing current account deficit, which is close to 4 percent of gross domestic product. Given the strong growth in the U.S.

relative to our trading partners, and given the U.S.'s strong propensity to consume, the current account deficit is projected to balloon to some 6 percent of GDP by the end of next year, according to some analysts. That would be, in economists' parlance, "unsustainable."

Clearly Sarbanes doesn't want to wait to see if it can be sustained. After many attempts to rattle the Treasury secretary, the senator resorted to that favorite argument children use with their parents: Everybody else does it.

GROUCHO'S CLUB

"I am really taken aback that we have a secretary of the Treasury who doesn't perceive any problems associated with this large current account deficit," Sarbanes said. "Now, that flies directly contrary to what virtually every other economic observer is telling us."

Those observers include the International Monetary Fund, the *Economist* and *Business Week* magazines, previous Treasury secretaries, Secretary O'Neill in his former life as a corporate chieftain, U.S. manufacturers and a host of others.

It was a delicious moment when O'Neill took Sarbanes's opening to point out that the IMF's forecasts have been somewhat wide of the mark.

He went on to ask Sarbanes about his solution to the problem.

"If you don't like the current account deficit, we could say bugger them, the U.S. citizens, we here in Washington know better," O'Neill said. "They shouldn't be buying so much stuff from outside the country. That would fix the current account deficit. It doesn't seem like a brilliant thing to me to do."

REVERSAL OF FORTUNE

During the latter part of the 1990s, the flow of capital into the United States "was greater than the appetite for foreign goods that underwrite it," said Bob DiClemente, an economist at Salomon Smith Barney. "The value of the dollar was pushed higher to regulate the flow of traffic."

The fact that the dollar was appreciating as the current account deficit was widening was proof positive that capital flows were dominant, DiClemente said.

Capital flowed into the U.S. because the U.S. delivered the best return to capital. Economic growth was strong, productivity growth was the envy of the world, real short-term rates were high and the government's fiscal house was in order, said Bob Barbera, chief economist at Hoenig & Co. in Rye Brook, New York.

"The productivity piece, so far, remains in place," Barbera said. "But much of the rest of the story is gone."

Many overseas stock markets have outperformed those in the U.S. this year. Budget surpluses are gone for now and doubtful for the future. Money market funds pay a pittance, and "the case for an extended period of easy money suggests they will continue to yield little for some time to come," Barbera said.

SUPPLY AND DEMAND

Add to that some bad policy decisions, such as trade protectionism (steel and lumber) and farm subsidies, and a surfeit of dollars sloshing around, courtesy of the Fed's extended period of easy monetary policy, and the elements are in place for the dollar to come down from its lofty heights.

Academics would have you believe that the U.S.'s huge unsustainable current account deficit leaves the dollar vulnerable to a destabilizing plunge. (They've had this view for about three years.)

"'Unsustainable' is not a sufficient condition for anything," DiClemente said. "In academia, they don't have to mark-to-market their views."

The fact of the dollar's vulnerability "is not a condition that creates a crisis or an abrupt downturn," DiClemente said. "The same market forces that brought about the dollar's rise will bring about the dollar's fall over time. It may happen while we sleep."

Arguing against a precipitous decline in the dollar is "the amazing mediocrity of Europe and fumbling in Japan," DiClemente said.

If Senator Sarbanes is really interested in helping U.S. manufacturers compete, he would be well advised to let market forces do the job for him.

And as for Paul O'Neill, here's an audience of one for the truth any day, any time, even if the foreign-exchange market can't handle it.

✿   ✿   ✿

Wanted: One Willy Loman with Wall St. Savvy
———— Dec. 11, 2002 ————

I HAD barely finished reading about Paul O'Neill's shortcomings as Treasury secretary when there was a new résumé to digest.

John Snow, lawyer, Ph.D. economist, chief executive officer of CSX Corp., business leader and public servant in the Ford administration, was President Bush's choice to replace O'Neill.

So many people had so many flattering things to say about Snow instantaneously I had to wonder why he wasn't on anybody's short list of candidates. Most folks in the financial markets had never heard of him.

On paper, the former Treasury secretary and secretary-designate look surprisingly similar. They both ran Old Economy companies: O'Neill, Alcoa, Inc.; Snow, CSX Corp. They both had a previous tour of duty with the federal government: O'Neill at the Office of Management and Budget; Snow at the Department of Transportation.

What seems to differentiate the two gentlemen is their salesmanship ability, which most of the encomiums on Snow were quick to mention.

"In terms of selling the program and spinning the story, he'll be very good," Greg Valliere, chief strategist at Schwab Capital Markets LP, told Bloomberg News on Monday. "They need a salesman."

"He's very plain-spoken, very plain-talking; he's a bit like the president in the way he talks," said Pete Peterson, chairman of the Blackstone Group LP. "I think he will be a good salesman."

HELP WANTED

Is this what the country really needs? If someone is that slick a salesman, potential buyers generally want to know what's wrong with the goods.

To the extent that the Republicans have never been good at selling ideas—compelling ideas like low taxes, limited government and individual responsibility—they could use a good public relations firm. It's not clear the job description for Treasury secretary includes peddler and spin artist.

I'd like to think of the Treasury secretary, one of the choicest cabinet positions, as a person of stature who understands the issues facing the U.S. and world economy and who has the ability to formulate and communicate policy, the gravitas to command attention on the world stage, the skill to work with the president and Congress, and, most important, the sense to know when doing nothing is better than the appearance of doing something.

SENIOR STATESMAN

The Treasury secretary is the president's point man on economic policy, along with the chairman of the Council of Economic Advisers and the arguably useless chairman of the National Economic Council, a Clinton creation intended as a companion piece to the National Security Council. No one has ever explained why we needed another individual to coordinate economic policy instead of letting the Treasury and CEA talk directly to each other.

I doubt the American people think, or want to think, of the Treasury secretary as a detail salesman. It's not how finance ministers, as Treasury secretaries are known overseas, see themselves.

So it seems unfair, if not demeaning, to position John Snow as some sort of snow job for Bush's economic policies. It may lead some folks to wonder about the soundness of the policies themselves.

ELECTION 2004

"It gives you a window into what's going on in the Bush administration," said Tom Gallagher, a political economist with the ISI Group in Washington. "The message is that Bush is in full election mode. What one looks for in a Treasury secretary in the first two years of an administration—someone to formulate and communicate economic policy— is different than what one looks for in the two years leading up to the election—someone who can present it better."

Selling tax cuts has never been easy for the GOP. The Democrats say "tax cuts" followed by "for the rich," and the debate ends there.

It isn't rocket science. In fact, the story could be sold in a three-column, six-line table.

PERCENTILE	AGI THRESHOLD	FEDERAL PERSONAL INCOME TAX PAID
Top 1%	$313,469	37.42%
Top 5	128,336	56.47
Top 10	92,144	67.33
Top 25	55,225	84.01
Top 50	27,682	96.09
Bottom 50	<27,682	3.91

The top 5 percent of income earners pay 56.5 percent of all federal personal income taxes, according to Internal Revenue Service data from 2000. The top 25 percent—those with an adjusted gross income of $55,225 or more—pay 84 percent. The top 50 percent shoulder 96 percent of the personal income tax burden.

"If you want to cut taxes, you have to cut taxes on the people who pay them," said Neal Soss, chief economist at Credit Suisse First Boston.

Paul O'Neill was sacked because he spoke his mind and wasn't interested in currying favor with Wall Street. His outspoken honesty on issues, even if he disagreed with the president, was considered his most valuable asset, according to O'Neill. At least it was until the president decided it was a liability.

John Snow sounds like a smart man, an accomplished business executive and an able public servant. It does a disservice, to him and to the administration's agenda, to package and sell him as a salesman—even if that's Snow's intended role as Treasury secretary.

POSTSCRIPT: *Following the Bush tax cuts, upper-income earners saw their share of the tax burden reduced. For the tax year 2002, the top 5 percent of income earners paid 53.8 percent of all federal personal income taxes compared with 56.47 percent in 2000, according to the IRS. The top 25 percent—those with an adjusted gross income of $56,401 or more—paid 83.9 percent, about the same as in 2000. The bottom 50 percent paid 3.5 percent in 2002 compared with 3.9 percent in 2000.*

Treasury Trapped in Faustian Bargain with Dollar

———— Dec. 20, 2002 ————

SHHHHH. Don't tell anyone. The dollar has no spokesperson. How will it know what to do?

The insight that the dollar is without official representation comes from the G7 Group, a consultancy that bills itself as plugged into the movers and shakers in Washington. As a statement of fact, one can't take issue with it: Treasury Secretary-designate John Snow has to be confirmed by the Senate, and White House economic adviser Stephen Friedman comes on board in the new year.

Deputy Treasury Secretary Kenneth Dam's lame-duck status apparently disqualifies him from speaking on behalf of the mute currency. Which is why White House spokesman Ari Fleischer, an ad hoc dollar spinmeister (the line of succession probably stops with Dam), had to confirm Tuesday that the "strong dollar policy" was intact.

As a statement of policy, to say the dollar is without a spokesperson is silly and perpetuates the myth that the Treasury is instrumental in setting the foreign-exchange value of the dollar.

It's scary that so many smart people believe the pulp fiction about U.S. dollar policy.

"If the U.S. had a dollar policy, the apparatus at the Treasury Department could implement it," says Lou Crandall, chief economist at Wrightson Associates. "All they have is a slogan."

And every good slogan needs a good sloganeer, Crandall says.

SAY WHAT?

The G7 Group's daily briefing for Thursday goes on to say that the strong-dollar policy "does not serve the currency well" (it doesn't serve the country well either). While a gradually weakening dollar might be desirable in the current circumstances, officials "can't say that beyond the walls of the Treasury without prompting a nosedive in the currency," the G7 Group says.

Instead, Treasury officials are subtly moving toward a "market-based dollar" (from a nonconvertible currency?).

I was curious why the G7 Group would knowingly reinforce the notion that the Treasury sets the foreign-exchange value of the dollar by implying officials will let the market be the determinant in the future. Nancy Roman, the author of the report, was traveling and couldn't be reached for comment, according to her office. No one else at the G7 Group was willing to speak on her behalf.

TRUTH HURTS

The idea that the Bush administration would be happy with, or not upset by, a weaker dollar is not new. The problem is, the market got hooked on the empty words uttered by former Treasury secretary Robert Rubin: "A strong dollar is in the best interest of the U.S." The market's addiction to the Rubin mantra and the administration's willingness to comply have locked all parties into a dangerous game.

Treasury Secretary Paul O'Neill lost his job because he dared to speak the truth about dollar policy (among other things). Even someone as idiosyncratic as O'Neill had to be brought into line: Destabilizing the currency market was unacceptable at any price.

The first peep that the U.S. may be softening or abandoning its "strong-dollar policy," and the dollar might plummet. That would satisfy the economists and strategists, not to mention hedge funds, who have been predicting the dollar's demise for a few years. And it would be a gift to manufacturers, given the factory sector's depressed state. But the collateral damage on the stock market might be more than policy-makers can stomach as the U.S. prepares for war with Iraq.

Risk Factors

The dollar is down 8 percent year-to-date against a basket of weighted currencies of the U.S.'s largest trading partners. That's an impressive performance given that the U.S. current account deficit, near a record high of almost 5 percent of gross domestic product, was supposed to mean death to the dollar—one of these years.

The U.S. overnight interest rate adjusted for inflation is negative, which is a disincentive for overseas investors to park money here. The U.S. stock market is finishing its third consecutive year with losses, the first such occurrence in 60 years. Commodity prices are behaving as if stimulative monetary policy is starting to find its way into hard assets. So there are a lot of reasons the dollar might be feeling queasy on its own, without any official guidance.

The Treasury may very well be looking for a new dollar slogan, as opposed to a new dollar policy, since "the old one doesn't make sense," Crandall says. "But they need a slogan that is not destabilizing. And they need a slogan they can say with a straight face."

The trouble is, they made a Faustian bargain, and those sorts of wagers aren't easily reversed—at least not without dire consequences.

Postscript: *By the end of 2004, the dollar had fallen 30 percent from its January 2002 high against a basket of weighted currencies.*

✿   ✿   ✿

You Get What You Pay for in Treasury Secretaries
—————— Oct. 22, 2003 ——————

THEY RAN Paul O'Neill out of town because he spoke the truth. They installed a new Treasury secretary, John Snow, about whom the nicest thing anyone could say was, "He's a good salesman." And now they're upset because the salesman got a little carried away with his wares?

Snow created a kerfuffle Monday when he told the *Times* of London he would welcome higher interest rates.

He was stating the obvious, of course, but bond and currency traders prefer their Treasury secretaries to spoon-feed them carefully crafted pablum on a daily basis. Snow is in the unenviable position of having to pay lip service to a strong-dollar policy as he pushes for a weaker dollar, pressuring Japan and China to let their manipulated currencies rise.

The market's interpretation of this two-step is that the Bush administration wants a weaker dollar to help U.S. exporters; it just wants to make sure the decline is orderly.

Foreign-exchange markets play along with this patent nonsense, at least until someone digresses from the script.

Monday's heresy was Snow's comment on interest rates. It's a basic tenet of economics—the law of supply and demand—that an increase in demand pushes the equilibrium price up, assuming no change in supply. A strengthening economy requires more credit. The price of credit—the interest rate—has to rise.

LIFE EXPERIENCE

When Snow said he'd be "frustrated and concerned" if there were no rise in rates, he was merely relating a former railroad executive's real-world experience of the business cycle.

In welcoming higher interest rates—a statement qualified later to mean market rates, not the funds rate under the aegis of the Fed—Snow was saying rising rates are confirmation of a strengthening economy, as are rising commodity prices.

Snow also predicted economic growth close to 4 percent next year and new job creation of 200,000 a month starting in the fourth quarter, which is "typical rah-rah cheerleader stuff," said Don Luskin, chief investment officer at Trend Macrolytics LLC, an independent economics and investment-research firm in Menlo Park, California. "I don't fault Snow one bit for what he said. Nobody would have even reported it if it weren't for all this currency bashing."

JOHN LOMAN

Anyone listening to Salesman Snow in recent weeks knows he's been handed an impossible task. With a straight face, he's had to mouth the Rubin mantra of a strong-dollar policy—the legacy of everyone's favorite Treasury secretary, Bob Rubin. At the same time, he's advocated more "flexibility" in exchange rates for China and Japan, which is a euphemism for a weaker dollar. Not even the magician David Blaine could pull that off.

Japan intervenes regularly in the currency market to prevent the yen from strengthening. China pegs its currency, the yuan, at 8.3 to the dollar, exchanging all the dollars that find their way to the People's Bank of China at that rate. Most economists agree that it would be suicidal to lift China's currency peg with its banking system insolvent. And it's far from clear the yuan would rise if allowed to float. Maybe the folks in China would want to convert their yuan deposits into dollars.

In the eight years since the yuan has been pegged to the dollar, "the dollar has retained its purchasing power versus gold, with some zigs and zags," Luskin said. "So you could say that the yuan is perfectly pegged."

A BILLION CONSUMERS

All the China-bashing for its stealing of manufacturing jobs overlooks China's role as a huge consumer of goods from the rest of the world. China's imports rose to a record $41.7 billion in September, a 40 percent increase from a year earlier. Exports were up 31 percent.

China's trade surplus narrowed to $290 million last month, the smallest since it ran a deficit in March. The third-quarter trade surplus totaled $4.68 billion compared with $6.57 billion in 2002, a decline of 29 percent.

China does run a big trade surplus with the U.S. In the first eight months of the year, the U.S. trade deficit with China swelled to $77 billion, a 22 percent increase from the same period a year earlier. China's deficit with the rest of the world is no consolation for U.S. politicians wanting to appear proactive on disappearing manufacturing jobs in an election year.

Neither China nor Japan has shown any interest in obliging Snow's request for more flexible currencies right now.

JOB DESCRIPTION

Snow was roundly spanked for his comments Monday.

"He should act with more caution in future," the *Financial Times* wrote in its lead editorial Tuesday. "The world economy is in a volatile enough state without a loose cannon at the U.S. Treasury."

That's certainly the prevailing view among traders, investors and analysts.

"You want someone [as Treasury secretary] who understands financial markets and the psychology of traders," said David Gilmore, a partner at Foreign Exchange Analytics in Essex, Connecticut.

I'm not sure that was the job description handed to Alexander Hamilton.

The administration wanted a salesman. It got a salesman. The salesman happened to get a little enthusiastic about the product he's selling, veering from the marketing manual.

"If things go awry, the White House has set up Snow to take the fall," Luskin said.

In other words, we could be witnessing the death of a salesman.

POSTSCRIPT: Snow wasn't far off the mark in his growth estimate. The U.S. economy grew 3.9 percent in 2004 on a fourth-quarter-over-fourth-quarter basis. Job growth fell short of his prediction, with an average of 166,000 jobs created a month from the fourth quarter of 2003 through the end of 2004. All data are subject to revisions.

10

Off the Charts

TRADERS SUBDIVIDE into one of two categories: those who follow the fundamentals and those who track the technicals.

Fundamentals include things like economic growth and inflation, monetary and fiscal policy, corporate profits and crude oil inventories, all of which determine the supply and demand for a particular commodity, asset or asset class.

Technicians study price patterns. They don't care how many jobs were created last month, who wins the presidential election or what OPEC will do with production quotas. Technical analysis is based on the premise that all known information, be it economic, political or psychological, is immediately incorporated into the price of a particular commodity. The price action provides everything a technical trader needs.

Instead of looking at things like economic data or quarterly earnings reports, technicians study an array of price charts, as well as data on volume and open interest (in futures contracts), to divine a market's momentum and relative strength and to determine whether a trend has legs.

A technician doesn't need to know anything about the soybean harvest to trade beans. Crop expectations are already discounted in the price. Beans, bonds, bellies—they're all the same to a technician. Just give him a price chart, and he can figure out whether to buy or to sell.

Even fundamentally oriented traders have to be cognizant of the technicals. Fundamental analysis may tell a trader to sell, but if the market is going up in his face day after day, the market is telling him he's wrong.

I write mostly about the fundamentals for a couple of reasons. One, it's how I think: The challenge is to figure out the "why" from the "what." And two, technical analysis makes for dull copy.

Early in my career, I was intrigued by the work of some self-described technicians whose technical indicators went well beyond lines on graph paper. For example, Paul McCrae Montgomery, president of Montgomery Capital in Newport News, Virginia, studied magazine covers going back to the 1920s and found that when a financial phenomenon graces the cover of the news weeklies, it's a clear contrarian signal.

Caveat emptor: The columns in this chapter are not for the average point-and-figure chart trader.

Can Jeff Bezos Defy the Time *Magazine Cover Curse?*

—————— Dec. 20, 1999 ——————

NORMALLY IT'S CONSIDERED an honor to be selected to grace the cover of a weekly news magazine. If, however, your métier happens to be business or finance or economics, the last place you want to be is on the cover of *Time* magazine.

Call it the curse of the magazine covers. There is an entire body of work devoted to analyzing the information on magazine covers. The bottom line? By the time a person or a phenomenon acquires magazine-cover status, the news is, as they say, already "in the market."

What, then, are we to make of Jeff Bezos's designation as *Time* magazine's Man (oops! Person) of the Year? The 35-year-old chief executive officer of Amazon.com Inc., an online bookseller that has transformed itself to an anythingyouwant.com online retailer, is the fourth-youngest individual ever to be given that distinction by the editors at *Time*.

Surely no one will quibble with *Time*'s choice in honoring someone who has been at the forefront of the Internet revolution. That the five-year-old Amazon.com hasn't earned a penny yet, nor is it projected to until 2001 or 2002, hasn't stopped Amazon stock from returning 83 percent this year, outpacing the high-flying Nasdaq by more than 10 percentage points.

If history is any guide, bad times may be in store for Amazon's stock, even though by all counts Christmas sales are booming.

Magazine covers "reflect the extent to which the bullish, or bearish, news is in the public domain and has been acted upon," says Paul McCrae Montgomery, a money manager and market analyst at Legg Mason Wood Walker, Inc. in Newport News, Virginia, who has studied magazine covers going back to 1923. "By the time something's on the cover of *Time,* the story is widely shared."

Fade the Cover

Unlike *Business Week* and *Barron's,* which "give some good contrarian signals but also emit a lot of noise because they cover business every week," *Time* doesn't venture into the world of finance for its cover story that often, Montgomery explains.

When it does, investors should take note. Montgomery's comprehensive study has found that the market goes in the direction of the cover for anywhere from one week to two months and is 60–65 percent reliable.

One year later, the market has gone in the exact opposite direction of that suggested by the cover more than 85 percent of the time, Montgomery says.

Other notable examples of contrarian *Time* covers include "Interest Rate Anguish" in 1982, with then Fed chairman Paul Volcker on the cover, along with his ubiquitous cigar. That was right before the secular bull market in bonds took 30-year yields from 14 percent to 4.69 percent in October 1998.

Once Bitten, Twice Wrong

"Can GM Survive?" on Nov. 9, 1992, arrived when the stock of the No. 1 U.S. auto manufacturer was hovering near 25. One year later, General Motors' stock was up 52 percent.

Attempting to redeem itself, *Time* went back to the drawing board and produced "Detroit Shifting Into High Gear" in December 1993.

Just about that time, GM stock shifted into reverse. One year after the bullish magazine cover, GM was trading below 30 again.

Montgomery noted two other *Time* classics that ran within a week either side of the 1929 crash. One featured Samuel Insull, the British-born American public utilities magnate; the other profiled Ivar Kreuger, the match king. Insull was tried three times (and acquitted) for fraud, violation of federal bankruptcy laws and embezzlement before fleeing the country. Kreuger shot himself.

Time magazine is not alone in penning big bloopers. The editors of the *Economist* went out of their way in this week's edition to apologize for some of their blunders this year in a piece titled "We woz wrong."

CRUDE CALL

First among the cover stories that didn't turn out the way they predicted was the March 6 cover, "Drowning in Oil," predicting $5 crude. That was right before crude oil prices took off in earnest. The price of West Texas intermediate, the benchmark U.S. crude, averaged $12.25 in the first two months of 1999 compared with an average price of $25.30 in November and the first 20 days of December.

The *Economist* is no different than other forecasters when it comes to being victimized by one-way-itis: It went down, so it will continue to go down. Who can forget the *Wall Street Journal*'s currency outlook on the Monday after the dollar slumped to an all-time low of 79.75 yen in April 1995? Every analyst predicted that the dollar could only go lower.

Oil has almost doubled in price since the *Economist* predicted its demise. The editors do their obligatory mea culpas, though not before offering an excuse—Who knew that OPEC would stick to its production cuts?—and a bit of self-praise. After all, the shock of $5 oil may have persuaded ministers from the Organization of Petroleum Exporting Countries to take action.

The *Economist* editors were hardly contrite about their view of the U.S. as a "bubble economy" with a bubble stock market, another eye-catching cover. They hold out hope that they may yet be proved right in their forecast.

The good news for the *Economist* this time around is that *Time* is on their side.

POSTSCRIPT: *Amazon.com hit a record of $113, adjusted for stock splits, on Dec. 9, 1999. The stock bottomed at $5.51 on Oct. 1, 2001, a loss of 95 percent. Amazon stock finished 2004 at $44.29. My advice to the perennially perky Bezos: Beware of representatives from magazines bearing anything other than free subscriptions.*

✿　✿　✿

Baby Abandoned in a Canoe with a Hockey Stick
———————   Dec. 19, 2001   ———————

NEWS FLASH: Abandoned Baby!

No, this column hasn't gone tabloid. The reference to an abandoned baby was contained in a communication I received from a Tokyo trader overnight.

"A quick spurt higher on the back of some Japanese buying in the belly of the [Treasury] curve," my friend writes. "I'm hearing the reason for the Japanese buying is that the price action of the past two days has generated an 'abandoned baby' formation, a rare but extremely bullish candlestick formation currently targeting the mid-104s on the bond contract."

Immediately I went to my copy of *Japanese Candlestick Charting Techniques*, by Steve Nison. There it was on page 64, plain as day: the abandoned-baby top and bottom formations, both "extremely rare," considered a signal of a major top or bottom in a market.

The abandoned baby consists of a "doji star that has a gap before and after it where the shadows do not touch," Nison says.

Glad he clarified that.

Next, I went to the smartest person I know for some insight. Paul DeRosa, a partner at Mt. Lucas Management Co. and an unregistered technician, was intrigued.

"I can't say I'm familiar with the abandoned baby, but I've been thinking that the yen looks a lot like the canoe over the waterfall," DeRosa says.

THAR SHE GOES!

Traders versed in technical formations such as head and shoulders or pennants ascending or descending might be unfamiliar with the canoe (it's something of a proprietary indicator that DeRosa was willing to share with me).

The canoe-over-the-waterfall pattern is very simple. It requires no wave counts, complicated chart construction or arduous calculations. What you see is what you get—if it doesn't get you first.

"It's something that happens frequently with common stocks," DeRosa says. "First they get cheap. Then they really go down."

DeRosa says the canoe over the waterfall is "one of the most treacherous patterns for value traders," not to mention a "speculator's nightmare."

Speculators buy when everyone else is selling, and vice versa. The canoe has been known to tempt speculators to dip an oar into the water (sorry) when they should really be going downstream with the other boats.

The yen has been gradually losing ground against the dollar for two months now. A speculator would want to fade the move (buy yen), but DeRosa sees the yen as a potential canoe candidate.

SPORTING TYPES

He recalled the dollar's movement in the first half of 1995 as the "connoisseur's canoe over the waterfall." The dollar spent the first three months of the year edging lower from 112 yen to 100 yen, he says. "Then it went from 98 yen to 88 yen in a few days" before finally hitting the riverbed at 79.75 yen in mid-April.

Only expert canoers will be familiar with the mirror image of that pattern: the hockey stick. As in nature, where gravity dictates that objects fall faster than they rise, "you rarely get a 'V' on the upside—the hockey stick—as steep as the canoe going over the waterfall," DeRosa says.

So how did he come to identify such simple yet scarcely recognized patterns?

"I have no claim to an exhaustive catalog," says this veteran. "We used to classify patterns as to which ones we were good at figuring out. The mountain peak and sharp valley—we got those. The canoe over the waterfall always got us."

Gunman, Arsonist Bracket Bull Market in Bonds

———— July 25, 2003 ————

AT 10:30 A.M. on Dec. 7, 1981, a 61-year-old man carrying a .38 caliber pistol, two sawed-off shotguns and a hunting knife walked into a building at Constitution Avenue NW and 21st Street in Washington.

The New Hampshire resident proceeded to the second floor of the Marriner Eccles Building, where he intended to take the cloistered members of the Federal Reserve Board hostage to focus media attention on the damage near-record interest rates were having on the U.S. economy.

Little did he know that "interest rates had peaked some nine weeks previous and had embarked on their greatest down move in history," says

Paul McCrae Montgomery, a market analyst in Newport News, Virginia, who publishes *Universal Economics.*

Two weeks ago, a 63-year-old Hong Kong man burned 22,000 Hong Kong dollars (US$2,821) to protest near-record low interest rates. His nest egg of HK$346,580.05 had generated a paltry HK$17.50 in interest at HSBC Bank during the past six months. Interest rates have plummeted in Hong Kong, which links its currency to the U.S. dollar.

The two sexagenarian interest-rate protesters may be bookends to the biggest bond bull market in history, which started in September 1981 with the 10-year note yield at 15.84 percent and the 30-year bond yield at 15.31 percent.

'TIDAL AFFAIRS'

The bull market may have ended on June 16, 2003, when the yield on the 10-year note and 30-year bond touched a 45-year low of 3.07 percent and 4.14 percent, respectively.

"The price structure is compatible with the end of the bull market," Montgomery says. "You get confirmation when all markets are moving together."

What greater confirmation can there be than all the world bond markets turning in sync? Since last month's low in yield/high in price, bond markets in the U.K., Germany, France, Spain, Canada, Japan and Australia, to name a few, have all declined.

"We worry too much about what [Fed chairman Alan] Greenspan says and what our economy is doing, because the world's credit markets are not nearly that parochial," Montgomery says. "Major movements in interest rates are tidal affairs."

In retrospect, the final leg of the rally that kicked off with the Fed's statement on May 6 about "an unwelcome substantial fall in inflation" had such force it couldn't have been sparked by fears of deflation.

CONCEPT RALLY?

"You don't get a rally like that on a concept," says Jim Glassman, senior U.S. economist at J.P. Morgan Chase & Co. "Inflation expectations don't change that rapidly," which is something Fed governor Ben Bernanke pointed out in a speech on Wednesday.

Rather, the rally was driven by an expectation the Fed would resort to "unconventional measures" to stimulate the economy (buy long-term bonds) and by what Montgomery described at the time as the law of increasing returns.

Normal market dynamics can be defined by the law of diminishing returns, "wherein a rally in prices and a drop in yields decreases demand," he says. "The type of buying that drove bonds to their June 16 top was of a dangerous sort and subject to reverse itself in an equally dynamic move to the downside."

Higher prices begat more buying as mortgage portfolios were forced to beef up their duration, a measure of risk, by buying non-callable Treasuries to offset the mortgage-backed securities being called away when homeowners prepaid their mortgages and refinanced at a lower rate.

ROUND TRIP

The second kicker came from the pools of commodity trading advisers, whose black-box models are driven by market momentum and other technical indicators.

A third supercharger came from the "carry trade," with traders borrowing money at low short-term rates and buying long-term notes and bonds to benefit from the steep yield curve.

"The problem comes when one isn't satisfied to earn 100 to 200 basis points of spread and decides to leverage up 10 or 20 to one," Montgomery says.

The force of the rally drove Treasury yields below those on tax-free municipal bonds, a rare occurrence.

"Once the market gets leveraged up in this fashion, it doesn't take much price weakness to generate a cascade of selling," Montgomery says.

WELCOME BACK

And it didn't. Yields rose further, faster than anyone expected. Now there's seven times as much money invested in Treasury bond puts as in calls, Montgomery says. That compares with a 13-to-1 weighting in favor of calls, a bet on higher prices, at the June top.

The rise in yields is already sparking the usual warnings that higher rates are going to nip the nascent economic recovery in the bud. To put the 100-basis-point rise in long yields in perspective, for anyone who left the country on May 6 to go trekking in Nepal and came back this week, interest rates are still historically low.

That's what the Hong Kong protester was saying when he put match to money.

11

Odd Ducks

S OMETIMES THE conventional prose format doesn't lend itself to what I have to say. It's as if the content cries out for a new and different form, and I'm right there to answer the call.

This chapter is home to some of those quirkier columns. It includes a couple of year-in-review columns, which are always a challenge once you accept that you will not be setting the year's events to the rhyme scheme of Clement Clarke Moore's "A Visit from St. Nicholas," an age-old formula for financial writers.

It includes a sample of the letter-as-column format, which is a back-door way of sharing your thoughts with a public figure who might otherwise not give you the time of day.

You'll find columns I've written to exorcise a particular bugaboo, such as the lack of customer service in the high-tech age. This is a productive way to vent frustration, especially for someone like me who's never shy about telling a CEO when his product or service doesn't live up to my standards.

You'll meet Dr. I.C. Clearlie, an economist with some unconventional views who sat down with me for an exclusive interview. (Before you start reading, say his name slowly out loud.)

Finally, this chapter features a column written in response to Petsmart's rationalization for lousy earnings. It wasn't my superior ability to decipher the footnotes in the company's financial statements that gave it away. As a pet owner, I can smell a lame excuse as well as the next dog.

BOJ Officials Should Buy Luxury Cars, Not Bonds
—————— Oct. 4, 1999 ——————

MR. MASARU HAYAMI
Bank of Japan 2-1-1
Hongoku-Cho Nihonbashi,
Chuo-Ku Tokyo, Japan

Dear Mr. Hayami:

I am taking the liberty of writing to you because I think I have come up with a way to get you out of your pickle.

Let me start by first saying that I feel terrible about the way you were treated at the Group of Seven meeting in Washington last week. I mean, I wouldn't want to be on the receiving end of Larry Summers's wrath! To be humiliated in front of your fellow central bankers and finance ministers, and to be forced to give a press conference and repeat words that someone else crafted—no wonder you were upset.

Your refusal to cave in to pressure from Japan's ruling Liberal Democratic Party and the powerful Ministry of Finance, from whom you recently won your independence, for a "quantitative easing" of monetary policy is admirable.

But it's not good politics to defend bad policies. Japan needs to increase bank reserves and the broad money supply to ensure that the nascent recovery isn't derailed again. The offshoot of creating more yen to satisfy the increasing demand would be to halt the yen's appreciation against every other world currency.

THE OLD-FASHIONED WAY

What you need to do, Governor Hayami, is to find a new way to increase the money supply. Monetization, or the process whereby the central bank buys its country's debt and creates money out of nowhere, has acquired a bad name. It brings to mind some banana republic that creates money the old-fashioned way: It prints it.

On that score, you gotta hand it to those Russkies. Western governments have been shuttling advisers into and out of Moscow for years to try and help with the transition to a market-based economy.

But in this area, Mr. Hayami, they could teach you a thing or two! When the Russian central bank wants to expand its domestic money supply, it isn't constrained by fledgling capital markets or a lack of money demand (surely there can't be much money demand during hyperinflation, and it doesn't prevent the central bank from increasing the money supply). What they do is crank up the printing press.

Here's where my idea comes in. You can increase the money supply without being viewed as a wimp for capitulating to the MOF. You can do it without resorting to monetization, even though the Bank of Japan could buy securities in the secondary market, in full view, rather than transact business with the MOF directly.

STRANGERS BEARING GIFTS

First you write a check, drawn off the Bank of Japan, to every Japanese citizen for, say, 100,000 yen, or any amount you calculate will increase bank reserves significantly.

Don't laugh: The state of Alaska distributes a check from oil revenues to its residents every year.

Ignore the chorus of objections that 1) the Japanese won't spend the money but will save it; and 2) the Japanese government already tried that last year, issuing vouchers to stimulate spending.

They did try it, but those vouchers were drawn from general revenues. Issuing the vouchers didn't increase the money supply; only the ownership of the deposits changed hands, from the government via the individual to the merchant.

Second, even if the Japanese are savers by nature, the very act of depositing the checks in the bank will increase the money supply. Besides, at the margin some folks will spend.

WHO NEEDS DEMAND?

Simply put, the BOJ creates money by bearing gifts. It's the old Milton Friedman helicopter story. The Nobel laureate used to illustrate the money creation process to his classes at the University of Chicago by asking them what would happen if a helicopter flew over the city and dropped $100 bills. Assuming that folks are already holding the money balances they want to hold (that's money demand), they would pick up the $100 bills and spend them.

The central bank increases the money supply in the same way, even if there is no demand for money, credit or Toyotas. In fact, if there is no demand for money (a desire to hold money balances), then people are more likely to spend the windfall.

While we're on the subject of Toyotas, to ensure a successful launch of the new program, may I suggest that you and your fellow board members at the BOJ set an example by doing some conspicuous consumption? You'd look marvelous behind the wheel of a Lexus LS 400 equivalent. Smile. Make it look as if you are enjoying yourself. None of this bowing stuff. As you slither behind the wheel and feel the plush leather seat, think of all the horsepower.

You might even want to pick up a second car—a Nissan Infiniti, perhaps—for the missus.

I understand that this is a little different from the standard approach for increasing bank reserves. But what have you got to lose?

Look at it this way: This is one tactic Larry Summers hasn't thought of just yet.

Very truly yours,

Caroline Baum

Economist I.C. Clearlie Looks Forward to 2000

—————— Dec. 17, 1999 ——————

WITH THE MILLENNIUM fast approaching and everyone from chief economists to chief executives to the commander in chief weighing in with a view, it seemed like a good time to corral an old acquaintance, the noted economist I.C. Clearlie, for an interview.

Dr. Clearlie was born "sometime in the early part of this century," has a sharp mind and an astute memory, and has seen his share of financial bubbles and crises. His unconventional views are guaranteed to pique your interest.

CB: Dr. Clearlie, thank you for taking time out of your busy schedule to stop by for a chat.

IC: Call me I.C. I'm happy to oblige. Not much demand for nonagenarians these days. Haven't you heard that the average age at Microsoft is 30?

CB: Certainly, I.C. I want to start by asking you about your economic outlook going forward. Do you think that …

IC: You and your ilk have this passion for asking armchair economists about the future. They can't even agree about the present. If you don't know where you are, how the hell are you gonna figure out where you're going?

CB: You have a point. Let me be more specific. After almost four years of 4 percent economic growth and with unemployment at a generation low, do you expect that inflation will finally accelerate next year?

IC: Watch the price of pizza.

CB: Pizza?

IC: Yup. A slice still costs $1.40 at my local pizza parlor. The demand curve for pizza is totally inelastic—completely vertical. No matter what the price—within reason, of course—people will still pony up for a slice. So if the price of pizza isn't going up, I doubt there's any pepperoni cost-push.

CB: Pepperoni cost-push?

IC: Do you have some kind of hearing problem? You're awfully young to be hearing-impaired.

CB: No, sir. I just don't get your drift.

IC: Look, some guy slaving over a 500-degree brick oven all day isn't going to charge less for a slice or a pie than his ingredients cost. You don't need an econometric model to figure that one out.

CB: So, pizza price unchanged. No inflation ahead.

IC: You are dense, aren't you? No inflation now. To see what's ahead, you have to know what leads pizza.

CB: Something tells me pepperoni is not the correct answer.

IC: Bravo! You got one right. Something leads pepperoni.

CB: Okay. Moving right along, there's been a lot of talk about the soaring Nasdaq—about a select group of high-flying tech stocks—and whether it constitutes a bubble. What do you think? I can't imagine you use a simple price/earnings model.

IC: You'd be right again. Look, value investing this isn't. But you have to be careful when folks start tossing out the rules and declaring that this time is different. It's always different this time, until one day it's the same. Pay close attention to the babble.

CB: The bubble?

IC: No, the babble about the bubble. Just this morning, I heard someone on TV say that technology spending is impermeable to higher interest rates. An alarm went off in my head. By all rights these new tech companies, which will deliver earnings some five, six years in the future, should be more sensitive to higher interest rates than companies with actual earnings. The higher long-term rates, the less earnings are worth in the future. If you don't have any earnings, and the discount factor goes up, well, you do the math.

CB: This period of technological innovation is being compared to the Industrial Revolution, which changed the world.

IC: Electricity was a big deal once, too; it changed the world. Same with the rails. Did that prevent the stocks from taking a tumble when valuations got out of whack?

CB: I guess not. So what's your outlook for the stock market?

IC: The mania will end. It always does. And not with a whimper, with a bang.

CB: But if things get too dicey—if stocks go down too far too fast, decimating consumers' wealth and putting the financial system at risk—then the Federal Reserve will lower interest rates and provide adequate liquidity.

IC: Right. Give the alcoholic a drink.

CB: So in a perverse way, a crash is better than an orderly decline?

IC: To the extent that a crash means help is on the way, then yes, I guess it is better for shareholders. But not for the economy.

The lesson learned over the past few years is, if you're going to make risky loans, make sure you're in good company. Because if everyone makes risky loans that go bad, it introduces the specter of systemic risk. And there's nothing that sends central bankers into a state of apoplexy more than the mention of systemic risk.

CB: So I've heard. Which brings me to one last question. When it comes to your own money, what rules of investing do you follow?

IC: My dear, at my age, I have one simple rule: Don't buy green bananas.

✻   ✻   ✻

Remembering a Year That's Better Left Forgotten
Dec. 26, 2001

WHAT A YEAR IT WAS.

Enron collapsed, the Twin Towers collapsed, Argentina collapsed, the Middle East peace process collapsed, the U.S. budget surplus collapsed, the tech bubble collapsed some more.

The U.S. entered recession. Europe felt like it was in recession. Japan re-entered recession, the fourth time since 1990.

The Treasury stopped issuing 30-year bonds. The SEC started issuing subpoenas—in its investigation of how initial public offerings were allocated.

President Bush cut taxes. The Federal Reserve cut interest rates. Corporate America cut payrolls.

The euro failed to reach parity with the dollar for the second year in its three-year life. The fiscal stimulus package failed to get off the ground. Alan Greenspan failed to get the economy moving.

Japan experienced deflation. The U.S. experienced disinflation. Harvard experienced grade inflation.

The lights stayed on in California. The lights went off at Pets.com and a host of other bad Internet retailing ideas.

Oil prices headed south. Long rates headed north. East-West relations headed nowhere, strained by the Sept. 11 terrorist attacks.

Auto sales were hot. Christmas sales were not.

Kraft went public. Tech gurus avoided the public.

The dollar bears got hosed. Accounting frauds were exposed.

Al Gore grew a beard.

The U.S. went to war. Geraldo went to cover the war. Wall Street went to pot. Hillary Clinton went to the Senate. And I'm still here, wishing you a better 2002.

✿   ✿   ✿

Grasso Heads the Parade in 2003's Animal Kingdom
―――――― Dec. 30, 2003 ――――――

ACCORDING TO the Chinese lunar calendar, 2003 was the year of the ram.

Former New York Stock Exchange chairman Dick Grasso will attest to that. Grasso went unwillingly to the slaughter when revelations about his $140 million pay package created an uproar.

The NYSE's asleep-at-the-wheel board of directors met a similar fate. The specialist system, a relic of the pre-electronic age, may be another casualty of the shake-up.

Not everyone was bleating in 2003. All 12 animals of the Chinese calendar, which are assigned in rotating order to sequential years, found representation in the year gone by.

For U.S. Treasury Secretary John Snow, it was the year of the rooster. Snow was put in the uncomfortable and unenviable position of having to crow about the strong-dollar policy, even as the Bush administration's body language suggested a weaker dollar was in order.

The dollar fell more than 14 percent against a basket of currencies and 16 percent against the euro, but the strong-dollar policy lives on.

For Saddam Hussein, 2003 was the year of the rat. The former Iraqi dictator was discovered in a hole in the ground in a farmhouse near his hometown of Tikrit seven months after the official hostilities ended. The armed and unshaven dictator surrendered to U.S. authorities without a fight. The videotape beamed around the world of a U.S. Army doctor examining Saddam's scalp for lice was an image befitting the butcher of Baghdad.

BREATHING FIRE

For New York Attorney General Eliot Spitzer, it was the year of the dragon. After extracting his pound of flesh from Wall Street in a $1.4 billion settlement last April, Spitzer breathed fire at the mutual funds.

Not content to limit himself to the fund abuses of late trading and market timing, Spitzer set his sights on mutual fund fees. He got Alliance Capital Management to cut them by about $50 million and pay a $250 million penalty.

Few criticize Spitzer publicly for overreach, fearing the fiery dragon will turn on them.

For Alan Greenspan, 2003 was the year of the ox. The Federal Reserve chairman carried the weight of the economy on his shoulders, keeping interest rates low and promising to hold them there for an extended period, dissuading traders from pushing up long-term rates.

Ox BEFORE THE CART

Greenspan's easy monetary policy was only one half of a team of oxen drawing the U.S. and global economy. The Bush administration cut taxes for a third time, which turned out to be the magic number. The economy came roaring back in the third quarter, expanding at an 8.2 percent annualized rate, the fastest in 20 years.

There are tentative signs easy money has overstayed its welcome. The dollar has been falling, and industrial commodity prices have been soaring. The overnight federal funds rate, adjusted for inflation, is negative, a state of affairs that historically has produced inflationary outcomes.

Time will tell if the ox gets gored.

For Frank Quattrone, the banker who headed up Credit Suisse First Boston's technology group, it was the year of the serpent. Quattrone slithered through his first trial for allegedly obstructing an investigation into the allocation of initial public offerings.

The prosecution coiled around the defendant, presenting evidence of Quattrone's involvement in IPO allocations that contradicted his earlier testimony.

NO SLEEPING TIGER

In the end, there was enough uncertainty about Quattrone's intent in his instruction to associates to clean up their e-mails to prevent the jury from reaching a unanimous verdict.

Quattrone's retrial is scheduled for March.

For China, it was the year of the tiger. China's roar resonated around the world—driving up the prices of raw materials, driving down the prices of consumer goods.

China's commanding presence comes with a cost. Manufacturing job losses? It's China's fault. A record U.S. trade and current account deficit? Blame China's currency, which is pegged to the dollar at too low an exchange rate.

The pressure for a response to market forces—productivity, not China, is "stealing" manufacturing jobs globally—got so intense, the Bush administration slapped quotas on bras, robes and knit fabric last month.

China's loss will benefit another low-cost producer, not the U.S.

FLEET OF FOOT

For the U.S. stock market, it was the year of the hare. The U.S. stock market bottomed in March and never looked back, breaking a three-year losing streak. The Wilshire 5000, the broadest index of U.S. publicly traded companies, rose 29.4 percent this year.

Small companies outperformed large ones, with the Russell 2000 Index up 47.2 percent. Technology stocks were even hotter. The Nasdaq Composite Index rose 50 percent in 2003. At 2006, the index is a shadow of its former self: Its peak was 5133 in March 2000.

Overseas stock markets—from Latin America to India to Russia to Australia—did even better. Crossing the finish line first isn't the only way to win the race.

For Parmalat Finanziaria SpA, Italy's biggest food company, it was the year of the monkey—monkey business. If Enron was devious and WorldCom was dishonest, Parmalat was a magician. Following an audit in November, the company was forced to admit that a $4.9 billion bank account, 38 percent of its assets, didn't exist.

In filing for bankruptcy protection last week, Parmalat couldn't account for $11 billion. Not even a good magician can pull that much money out of a hat.

DOGGEDLY BORING

For U.S. Senator Joe Lieberman, it was the year of the dog. Faithful to his 2000 running mate, Al Gore, the Connecticut Democrat deferred his ambitions of a presidential run until he knew his former No. 1 wasn't a candidate.

Gore's response to Lieberman was a gentle knife in the back. Gore endorsed front-runner Howard Dean, former Vermont governor, without even a heads-up to his former running mate.

Come to think of it, Lieberman's candidacy is something of a dog.

For Arnold Schwarzenegger, 2003 was the year of the horse. The former bodybuilder-turned-actor rode in to save California from fiscal disaster, defeating the unpopular Democratic governor Gray Davis in an October recall election.

Schwarzenegger hopes to enlist the support of the state's voters to help him. Californians will get a chance to vote on the governor's balanced-budget proposal in a March referendum.

DENNIS THE BOAR

For Dennis Kozlowski, it was the year of the boar. The former chairman and CEO of Tyco International Ltd. is on trial for allegedly looting the company of $600 million.

Kozlowski's purchases of a $6,000 shower curtain and a $15,000 umbrella stand were legendary before the trial began. The trial produced the picture that was worth a thousand words.

The jury was treated to a video of a $2 million birthday party Kozlowski threw for his wife on the island of Sardinia—with Tyco allegedly picking up half the tab—complete with scantily clad male dancers. The tape gave new meaning to the phrase "corporate pig."

For what it's worth, the Chinese calendar designates 2004 as the year of the monkey. Don't be surprised if all the animals are out again.

If Only Computers Functioned More Like Cars

——————— Nov. 20, 2002 ———————

IMAGINE THIS SITUATION: You are cruising along Interstate 95 at 65 miles an hour when your brakes freeze and your engine stalls. You reach for your cell phone and, assuming you have a signal, dial General Motors technical support, only to be told to reboot your car.

Fortunately, cars work well. If you ever need service—that's customer service—from one of the newer high-tech industries, you might as well just throw the damned product out.

Every month when the consumer price index comes out, I'm struck by the disconnect between reported inflation (low) and my real-world experience of inflation (not so low), manifested by the degradation of services.

The trend in goods prices, which have been falling for a year, may be changing. Excluding volatile food and energy prices, core commodities prices rose 0.3 percent on a three-month annualized basis in September and October. With services prices, which make up 59 percent of the CPI, accelerating at a 3.5 percent pace (with and without food and energy) and commodity price changes flattening out, the deflation case may be losing its one standing leg.

"There is evidence that the softer dollar has eased the downward pressure on some goods prices, especially apparel prices, which haven't

fallen since July," says Ian Shepherdson, chief U.S. economist at High
Frequency Economics in Valhalla, New York.

In the last three months, apparel prices rose an outsized 4.7 percent
annualized, matching the increase in medical care, one of the usual CPI
offenders.

ONE-WAY ADJUSTMENT

The discrepancy between goods and services prices is even more
glaring when one considers the quality adjustment made for the former. The Bureau of Labor Statistics determines how much of the
price change in a good is improved quality: You pay more for a car
but get more car for the money. It makes no equivalent adjustment
for services. (We don't know the amount, but I think we know the
direction.)

The BLS said last week that the retail value of quality changes for
a sample of 2003 domestic light trucks was 39.9 percent of the average
$583 increase in the manufacturers' suggested list price. In other words,
an average $233 price increase on 2003 light trucks would show up as no
change in that component of the CPI.

Airfares are 5.1 percent lower than a year ago, according to the BLS.
Since the service provided is, say, 10 to 15 percent worse—long check-
in lines, delayed flights, skimpy (if any) meals—adjusted airfare prices
should be up, not down.

REACH OUT, TOUCH WHOM?

On that score, I marveled at the report this week that consumer satisfaction rose in the third quarter and has been rising ever so slightly all
year. I don't know any consumer who is more satisfied about anything
except a complete refund. I have three Kyocera phones from Sprint PCS
at home (two are awaiting a bubble-wrap kit for return) and a new Dell
laptop that, after two hours of dithering on my own and three with various Dell technicians, I'm sending back.

How can consumers be satisfied with these presumably productivity-
enhancing devices when they don't work well enough to enhance productivity? Take my cell phone (please!). The Kyocera model 2255 comes with
a unique feature (you don't pay extra for it): The video display panel dies
after several months. You have sound but no picture, which makes access-
ing your contact list or settings something of a challenge.

Satisfaction

The good news is the first two phones went bad while under warranty. Sprint PCS is "well aware of the problem," which affects only some Kyocera model 2255 phones, according to everyone I spoke with at the Sprint PCS store and at customer support on the phone. (Claire, my Sprint PCS virtual service representative, is the only one who's unaware of the problem.)

The fact that I've had two lemons in less than a year tells me either I'm extremely unlucky or there's a lot more lemonade than Sprint lets on. (Whatever happened to quality assurance?)

Everyone has similar stories, so what could the consumer possibly be satisfied about?

Lower prices, according to Claes Fornell, director of the National Quality Research Center at the University of Michigan's business school, which helps produce the quarterly American Customer Satisfaction Index.

"The increase since last year is not from better service but from lower prices or a lack of price increases," Fornell says.

Am I weird? If I get $200 off the price of a computer and spend five hours in a high-anxiety state either on hold or in conversation with a representative, waste a couple of evenings and weekend time, and am so stressed that I perform poorly at work, the attraction of the discount fades.

I'm happy to pay full retail for service. That's not an option nowadays.

POSTSCRIPT: *The Kyocera 2255 saga didn't end there. After the fourth phone manifested the same defect as the previous three, I sent a letter to the president of Sprint PCS, along with this column, and promptly received a $100 credit, which I applied to the purchase of a new phone by a different manufacturer.*

✿   ✿   ✿

Here's an Area Where Technology Could Clean Up

———————   May 23, 2002   ———————

I SPEND a good deal of time off the job thinking about the same kinds of issues I write about on a daily basis. To get a read on the economy, I ask retailers about sales (the answer I get depends on whether I'm perceived as an interested shopper or reveal myself to be a journalist); I note if the places I frequent—theaters, restaurants—are crowded or empty; I question service providers on how their business is doing.

So it should come as no surprise that I've taken up the cause of technology—with somewhat of a different slant than Federal Reserve Chairman Alan Greenspan, who wants to know when it's coming back.

For me, the burning technology question of the day is: Can't anyone design a better mop?

I'd been through what I thought were all the brands on the market, from sponge-type to string-type. They all start strong and end weak. The dirt absorbed from the first area of mopped floor is redeposited at the opposite end of the room. Unless you change the water in your bucket constantly, sponge- or string-mopping is an effort in futility.

Last year, I took up my dilemma with one of my colleagues, Steve Matthews, a Bloomberg consumer products reporter based in Atlanta. One of the advantages of working for a news organization is that someone always has the answer you're looking for or can tell you where to find it.

STUCK ON SWIFFER

Matthews suggested I try Swiffer. (OK, so I'm a little out of the mop loop not to have heard of Swiffer before then.)

"A Swiffer home is a cleaner home," Procter & Gamble promises on the Swiffer Web site. "Transform your home. Transform your life."

I was looking for a better mop; Swiffer promised to change my life.

I immediately went out and bought a Swiffer (the hardware—aluminum shaft with swivel head—comes packaged with the dry mop) and a Swiffer Wet, which is what I needed for hardwood floors. I decided against the Swiffer WetJet, a powered version, for reasons I can no longer remember. (Matthews reports that the big battle right now is between the powered Clorox ReadyMop and Swiffer WetJet.)

The Swiffer wet-mop system consists of the hardware purchased with the dry mop plus a package of wet, disposable cloths (soaked in cleaning solution) that wrap around and attach to the head.

'SOFTWARE' WORKS

That part of the concept and design is excellent. We live in a disposable culture. The philosophy of planned obsolescence predated high-tech equipment: When was the last time you chose to have a toaster oven repaired?

The Swiffer is great for quick mop-ups on bathroom floors. Dust and hair (human and dog) adhere to the wet cloth, although the wet goes out of the mop quickly, leaving the detritus on the floor in a nice little line along the mop edge.

Where the Swiffer doesn't pass muster with this consumer is on those tough spills on hardwood floors. I need a man's mop, something that can take the pressure when applied. The Swiffer is just too flimsy for the tough jobs.

Some of the product endorsements on the Web site—"best thing ever," "awesome," "a godsend"—suggest Swiffer won't be contacting me as a spokeswoman anytime soon. Surely I can't be the only person who finds mop technology unequal to the task.

MOPPING UP

We are producing faster chips, more-powerful computers, higher-speed phone lines and cars with global positioning systems to tell us where we are at any given moment (in case we forget). Yet basic home products remain in a technological backwater state.

Mopping may not be new or sexy, but it has huge potential for technological innovation, not to mention a ready-made audience. I'd venture that more households own a mop—and would spring for a new and improved one—than a computer.

Mops and brooms are a $450 million market, according to Information Resources Inc. The profit margins on the Swiffer Wet replacement cloths and Swiffer WetJet are high, Matthews tells me. P&G derived 30 percent of its sales and 37 percent of its profit from household cleaning products in the fiscal year ended June 2001.

Moore's Law—the idea that the capacity of semiconductor chips doubles every 18 months—may be the operative philosophy in the high-tech arena. Wouldn't it be nice if there were a Swiffer protocol?

POSTSCRIPT: *I eventually sprang for the Swiffer WetJet, a big improvement over the Swiffer Wet (especially after the connection holding the two parts of the steel shaft together broke). The WetJet is great for bathroom floors but isn't up to the tough jobs. And I'm still waiting for Swiffer to transform my life.*

No Bones for Fido While Iraq War Fears Loom

————— March 5, 2003 —————

PITY POOR FIDO.

You'd think the family pooch would be immune from the geopolitical risks buffeting the stock market, the U.S. dollar, business investment, consumer confidence and retail sales.

Think again. Spot, Sparky and Samantha are feeling the pinch. They get only an occasional pig's ear for good behavior and a new chew toy on their birthdays. And forget those perky, preppy navy-and-green cotton leashes.

Petsmart Inc., the biggest U.S. pet-supplies retailer, said fourth-quarter profit fell 17 percent from the same quarter a year earlier. "A combination of political uncertainty in the Middle East and some very tough winter weather" depressed sales, Chief Executive Officer Philip Francis told Bloomberg Radio.

Come again? We are cutting back on our pet pampering because the looming war with Iraq will, what? Trigger anti-war pet protests that destabilize the local dog population and cause mass riots and destruction of pet infrastructure? Make Fido turn up his nose at kibble and refuse to play tug?

This is getting tiresome. What will CEOs say once the Iraq threat is defused, either through peaceful disarmament and regime change or a war?

I may not be a typical consumer (I pay for service), but when it comes to my status as a pet owner, I'm as close to typical as it gets. My dachshund Lillie hasn't missed one treat, one toy or one trip to the groomer. (As it happens, she doesn't go to be groomed. If she did, I wouldn't deny her now.)

SPOIL THE DOG

Pets provide company and comfort. They lower our blood pressure. They love us unconditionally, or so we're told. (Just in case it isn't true, we buy them lots of stuff to make sure.)

I bet if I asked fellow dog owners about a decline in canine purchases because of geopolitical risks, I'd get some weird stares in the neighborhood.

In recent days, news outlets have started to hedge their bets on whether geopolitical risks are the economy's sole source of angst, hinting that a resolution to the Iraq situation may not usher in the Era of Good Feeling. Stocks may still be expensive. (Warren Buffett thinks they are.) Businesses may be keeping a lid on investment because they've got excess capacity.

Until six months ago, there were plenty of legitimate reasons for the stock market to be weak and business investment to be soft. They've given way to the catchier "geopolitical risks."

Whatever happened to the over-investment of the late 1990s, the over-valuation of the stock market and the over-leveraging of the corporate and household balance sheet? These used to be necessary and sufficient explanations for the bear market in stocks, the extended contraction in business investment and more restrained spending on the part of consumers.

Why do we need a new excuse?

Petsmart was barking up the wrong tree when it blamed Iraq for soft sales. It's enough to give investors paws.

12

Oil Things to Oil People

I T'S TOO BAD oil is such a vital commodity because gross misunder-
standings of its economic impact are compounded by the attention
attached to its every ebb and flow.

As you'll see from the third column in this chapter, the Federal
Reserve can't even decide if a rise in the price of oil is inflationary
or deflationary! Is there any other commodity that is all things to all
people?

The analysis of the impact of a change in oil prices is invariably one-
sided (and the one side is always bad).

When oil prices rise, there's no question it's a transfer of wealth
from consumers to producers. What do the producers do with the additional revenue? The profits don't disappear. They're recycled into the
economy.

Domestic energy companies invest in new plants and equipment
(the U.S. could use some new refineries). They use the revenue for oil
and gas exploration, with the goal of lessening the U.S.'s dependence on
foreign oil. They hire new workers. Or they pay the profits out to shareholders, who happen to be consumers.

In other words, the money is invested or spent.

But the U.S. is a net importer of oil. Higher oil prices don't do us
any good, right?

Once again, the money doesn't go into a hole in the ground in the
Middle East. The Organization of Petroleum Exporting Countries uses
those dollars to buy U.S. goods or to invest in the U.S.—in real estate,

stocks or bonds. In so doing, it lowers U.S. interest rates and boosts our wealth.

Granted, these oil-producing nations may not invest their windfall profits efficiently. And the second-order effects may be slow in coming. But the oil revenues that accrue to domestic and foreign producers aren't the dead-weight loss they're made out to be.

The rise in U.S. light, sweet crude oil prices to $55 a barrel in the fall of 2004 produced warnings of an imminent global recession. Maybe I'm missing something, but for every oil-importing country hurt by higher prices, isn't there an exporter laughing all the way to the bank?

How Oil Becomes More Than Price of Gasoline

———— June 30, 2000 ————

OIL IS a commodity, a necessity, an occasional calamity to the polity—and it has a propensity to morph into a tax when it can be used to advance a particular argument.

One of the popular theories making the rounds right now is that the spurt in oil and gas prices is acting like a tax on the consumer and will slow spending and economic growth.

"The important point about oil and gasoline pump price increases is the tax hike effect that will temporarily depress economic growth," writes ING Barings chief economist Larry Kudlow in a recent commentary.

Kudlow's hardly alone in his view. A gaggle of equity fund managers, ever quick to find a new reason to see the Promised Land of slower growth and an idle Fed, have been spouting the same pap on TV for weeks.

Let's see how the tax works. Gas prices have soared in recent weeks because (take your pick): OPEC isn't producing enough crude oil; oil refiners are colluding to pump up prices; pipeline problems are disrupting distribution; reformulated gas, as mandated by the Environmental Protection Agency, is more expensive to produce, especially if ethanol is used as the oxygenate; demand is rising (American preference for big, gas-guzzling cars); or all of the above.

The bottom line is that you and I have to pay more to fill the tank because the price of fuel has risen relative to the price of other goods. In order to keep our household spending constant, we have to cut back on the purchase of other discretionary goods and services. Our spending, however, will remain the same. So will total spending in the economy.

RUNNING INTERFERENCE

Where is the tax effect?

The tax effect is a case of "loose use of words," an economist says. A tax stands between a buyer and seller. A buyer may be willing to pay $1.50 a gallon for gasoline, and the seller may be willing to sell at that price, but the government imposes, say, a 25-cents-a-gallon tax. At a price of $1.75 a gallon, the market doesn't "clear," which means that neither buyers nor sellers are satisfied.

The gasoline story is so convoluted that it's impossible to determine whether the 30 percent rise since the beginning of the year to a record $1.681 a gallon in the week ended June 19 is the result of increased demand or reduced supply. What is clear is that no new tax was imposed on a commodity that is already highly taxed by both the federal and state government.

The idea of higher oil prices being a tax is "an old-fashioned idea, a holdover from the 1970s, when the OPEC nations recycled their petro-dollars into financial securities," says Jim Glassman, senior economist at Chase Securities. "It was considered to be a leakage out of the spending stream in the Keynesian framework."

KUDLOW AND KEYNES?

With the development of the oil-producing nations as consuming nations, the dollars sent overseas to pay for oil nowadays probably get recycled as purchases of consumer goods, Glassman says. "So it shouldn't do anything to the economy domestically."

Kudlow isn't using Lord Keynes as his framework for this or any other analysis, except to poke holes in the general theory. In a phone interview today, Kudlow conceded that total spending growth in the economy would remain constant, even in the face of higher oil prices, and made an efficiency argument instead.

"Energy is not a high-multiplier industry, so in terms of the money that circulates through the economy, more money spent on oil is less efficient," he says.

As for the higher prices OPEC gets for its major export, it's "an income transfer to some of the least economically efficient economies in the world," Kudlow says.

Usual Suspect

This isn't the first time that a change in oil prices has been regarded as a tax increase or tax cut and anointed with the ability to help or hinder economic growth. Time-trip back to early 1986, when oil prices plunged to $10 a barrel in April from $30 at the end of 1985. This was hailed as good news—a tax cut!—for consumers, which was guaranteed to boost U.S. economic growth.

It didn't turn out that way. Following the plunge in oil prices, gross domestic product growth slipped to an anemic 1.7 percent in the second quarter of 1986, the weakest quarter from the time the economy emerged from recession in 1982 until it started to falter again in 1989.

Considering that the Federal Reserve was aggressively lowering interest rates—it dropped the discount rate by 100 basis points in a span of less than two months in March and April 1986—the "tax cut" from cheap oil is certainly suspect.

Nothing like hindsight to provide the perfect ex-post explanation. In 1986, it was the oil patch, of course. The plunge in oil prices hurt the regions of the country that were dependent on oil for their revenue.

Maybe it's time to look at something for what it is. At present, the rise in oil prices is a relative price increase. Only when the central bank does what is politically expedient and accommodates the rise by increasing the money supply, as it did in the 1970s, do higher oil prices become higher inflation.

That's when consumers and the country as a whole pay a price (or is it a tax?).

Postscript: The average retail price for unleaded gasoline set a record of $2.28 a gallon in the week of April 11, 2005, according to the U.S. Department of Energy.

❀ ❀ ❀

Fed Chairman Ali al-Naimi Has a Nice Ring to It

————— July 5, 2000 —————

ONCE AGAIN, those pesky Arab oil producers are having their way with the U.S. economy, just as they purportedly did in 1990 when Iraq's invasion of Kuwait sent crude oil prices soaring to $40 a barrel.

Sky-high gas prices are being viewed as Public Enemy No. 1, allegedly causing consumers enough economic hardship to induce them to cut back spending in the second quarter to a pace estimated at less than half the 7.7 percent in the first quarter. (Never mind that auto manufacturers reported sales of gas-guzzling sport utility vehicles are holding up well.)

Clinton administration officials have warned that the surge in gas prices poses a risk to the U.S. economy, not to mention Al Gore's election prospects in November.

If the Organization of Petroleum Exporting Countries is so adept at managing our economy, why not get rid of the central bank and leave the driving to them? Instead of using interest rates to affect aggregate demand, encourage OPEC to manipulate aggregate supply and, hence, the price of gas. After all, most people need to drive regardless of their immediate financial straits.

Reduce the supply of something and, all else equal, the result is a higher price and lower quantity (output)—hardly the Fed's desired growth-and-inflation mix.

For some inexplicable reason, the Fed gets almost no credit for engineering a slowdown in U.S. economic growth (rest assured policymakers will get all the blame if the economy slumps). The central bank controls one measly short-term rate—the federal funds rate, at which banks make overnight uncollateralized loans to one another—that is considered insignificant, while gasoline prices are posted in big numbers on practically every street corner in America.

INVISIBLE HAND

"It's hard for people to add up the nickels and dimes, to see the many different ways the domestic and world economy responds to the Fed," says Jim Glassman, senior economist at Chase Securities. "It's not really visible, and it takes a long time."

The Federal Reserve has been raising the overnight interbank lending rate for a full year. Yet the cumulative 175-basis-point effort since

June 1999 was considered to be in vain—at least until the May economic reports landed with a thud. Now everything from retail sales to manufacturing and housing is losing altitude with alarming alacrity and stunning synchronicity.

To be sure, manufacturing and housing, the economy's traditional leaders because of their sensitivity to—no, not gas prices—interest rates, have been emitting early warning signs for some time now. New home sales peaked in November 1998, home resales in June 1999, and the National Association of Purchasing Management's monthly business barometer has been trending lower after hitting a two-year high last September.

New Gushers

Still, it's much easier to blame the price of gas than the efforts of an institution that determines banks' marginal cost of funds.

I'm just waiting for someone to say that Saudi Arabia's initiative, announced by Oil Minister Ali al-Naimi Monday, to pump an additional 500,000 barrels of crude oil daily will make the Fed's job harder. If the price of gas is what has consumer spirits and buying power on the wane, then by all rights motorists should be rushing to top off the tank, what with oil and gas prices down 6 percent and 7.5 percent, respectively, since Monday's announcement.

More likely, Saudi Arabia is acting in its own self-interest, Glassman suggests.

"They're concerned about their market share," he says. "High oil prices induce marginal projects to come on line. Industrial production of exploration equipment has exploded."

In the past year, the output of equipment for oil- and gas-well drilling is up 40 percent, according to the Fed's industrial production report for May. Because it's so much more expensive to pull oil out of the ground in the U.S. than in the Middle East, a sustained high oil price actually hurts the Saudis because it encourages more oil and gas exploration in the U.S.

Revisionist History

Sometimes the easy answer isn't the correct answer. Nor does it always square with the facts. For example, when Iraq invaded Kuwait on Aug. 1, 1990, crude oil prices were at $22 a barrel. As it turned out, the U.S. economy was already in recession, which is something the dating committee of the National Bureau of Economic Research, the arbiter of all things cyclical, determines well after the fact.

The Fed had been lowering interest rates for a year, paring them from 9.875 percent in June 1989 to 8 percent in July 1990, by the time Saddam Hussein acted on what he believed to be his territorial imperative.

The Treasury yield curve was no longer inverted; it already had some positive slope between short- and long-term rates.

Yet to this day, higher oil prices are assigned the role of 1980s expansion killer. The real "cause," if you can call it that, was the banking system, which was buckling under the weight of bad real estate loans and forced to contract its balance sheet to meet the required capital-to-asset ratios. With banks unable to perform the function for which they were created, the economy fell into recession and bounced along the bottom until financial institutions were restored to good health. Fed chairman Alan Greenspan presented the banks with a steep U.S. yield curve and said, go to it.

The U.S.'s willingness to close insolvent institutions and sell their assets stands in stark contrast to the Japanese government's foot-dragging in the 1990s. But that's a story for another day.

The Fed's Love/Hate Relationship with Energy Prices

Jan. 12, 2001

IN THE 12 MONTHS ended December, the producer price index for crude energy goods, which includes petroleum, natural gas and coal, rose 76 percent, the biggest increase in at least 25 years.

Until recently, the Federal Reserve was concerned that the surge in energy prices would lift the overall price level, better known as inflation. In addition, policy-makers were afraid that inflation expectations would work their way through the economy, causing businesses and consumers to behave like drunken sailors, which is what they were doing anyway.

On Nov. 15, the Fed still saw the risks to the economy as weighted toward higher inflation. Energy prices were a key consideration.

"The longer relatively high energy prices persisted, of course, the greater might be their imprint on both inflation expectations and core prices," the Fed said in the minutes from that meeting. "... [M]embers continued to view the prospects as weighted on balance in the direction of a gradual uptrend in core inflation."

By Jan. 3, higher oil prices had morphed into a deflationary concern. The Fed lowered the federal funds rate by 50 basis points in a surprise inter-meeting move, citing as the reason for its action a "further weakening of sales and production, and in the context of lower consumer confidence, tight conditions in some segments of financial markets, and high energy prices sapping household and business purchasing power."

EITHER/OR

Which is it? The same phenomenon—higher energy prices—generated a different analysis and produced a different answer. In a little over a month's time the relationship between energy prices and the economy did an about-face, the Fed went from inflation fighting to easing, yet higher energy prices were very much in place. There must be something unique about energy prices that gives them such a schizophrenic characteristic.

"Final demand has weakened; that's what's changed," says Susan Hering, senior U.S. economist at UBS Warburg. "Prices don't continue to rise when demand is weak."

That may be true, but the Fed didn't say that. Perhaps the Fed needs to do a better job of explaining just how its econometric model works. Or is this another case where the Fed justifies its actions with anything that fits the bill?

UNIQUELY INELASTIC

Actually, higher oil prices aren't inflationary per se. They reflect a change in relative prices, not a change in the price level. For a given stock of money, higher oil prices mean less money allocated toward something else, the price of which will fall. By all rights, higher energy prices are no more inflationary than higher wages, another concern for the Fed until recently.

What makes energy prices unique is that in the short run both demand and supply are inelastic. Higher prices normally encourage producers to supply more of a commodity to the market, but energy exploration and production are a long-term proposition.

Similarly, while higher prices normally send a message to consumers to demand less, people need to heat their homes and fill their gas tanks regardless of the price. That's one reason why the supply and demand for energy is different from that for commodities like automobiles, computers and apparel.

RAPID RESPONSE

Looking at some of those other items in today's producer price index report, passenger car prices rose 0.5 percent, which will be tough to sustain with demand collapsing. The rise in price was even more curious than the 0.3 percent increase in auto sales in December, as reported in today's retail sales report. Last week, auto manufacturers reported that sales fell to 15.5 million annual units in December from 16.6 million the month before—the third consecutive monthly drop.

The PPI for computer prices fell 2 percent last month, which seems to bear a real-life resemblance to the warnings from the computer industry about softening demand. December saw the rate of decline in computer prices accelerate after several months of smaller drops.

"We're seeing an aggressive price response from business, which is the old classical model," says Jim Glassman, senior U.S. economist at J.P. Morgan. "The quicker firms respond [by slashing prices], the less disruptive it is to the economy."

While price-cutting is not good news for corporate profits, the slash-and-burn response is, as Glassman says, better than the alternative.

"It's a profit story, not a spending story," he says.

Salvation Through Lower Oil Prices? Think Again.

—————— Nov. 19, 2001 ——————

EVERYWHERE YOU TURN, there's another article touting the boost lower oil prices are giving to the U.S. economy.

What about Japan? Doesn't that country get the benefit of what is widely viewed as a "tax cut" for consumers? Here's a country that imports all of its energy, not to mention most of its raw materials, yet plunging commodity prices don't appear to be acting as much of a cure-all on Japan's moribund economy.

"In the Great Depression, energy prices—all prices, in fact—were tumbling," says Paul Kasriel, director of economic research at the Northern Trust Corp. in Chicago. "That should have been a great stimulus. By all rights, things should have been booming in the Great Depression."

Regular readers will excuse my repetition on this subject. With the exception of Kasriel and a handful of others, no one considers why the price of oil is falling and what the implications of it are. (An economist friend of mine, who shall remain nameless, says it's the *pons asinorum*—literally "bridge of asses"—of economics. The *Oxford English Dictionary* defines pons asinorum as "the difficulty which beginners or dull-witted persons find in 'getting over' or mastering" a concept.)

ALL FALL DOWN

The price of a commodity can fall because of increased supply or reduced demand. Is OPEC pumping more oil? Hardly. While the countries that make up the Organization of Petroleum Exporting Countries cheat on their respective quotas, they have cut official production by 3.5 million barrels a day this year.

"The price of oil is falling because of a shift back in demand," Kasriel says. "Why is it good if this one price falls for that reason? Why isn't it good if all prices go down?"

When all prices go down, it's called deflation. Anyone reading the papers these days knows that deflation is as big a story as oil (and the subject of last Friday's column).

My exasperation with the way the oil story is being told—as a one-way street, with only winners and no losers—is not an argument against a pickup in the economy in the U.S. It's more a matter of being right for the wrong reason.

A history lesson is in order. Back in 1986, when OPEC was engaged in another price war, crude oil prices plunged in the first quarter of the year, giving rise to the same nonsense about a tax cut for the American consumer.

JUST THE FACTS

Specifically, crude oil prices fell from about $32 in November 1985 to $10 in April 1986, a 69 percent decline. Real gross domestic product rose 3.7 percent in the first quarter. With oil plummeting and the Federal Reserve aggressively easing monetary policy—the Fed lowered the discount rate by 200 basis points between March and August—there were great expectations of a boom in the April to June quarter.

Alas, second-quarter real GDP growth was less than half that of the first quarter: 1.7 percent. The postmortems on the results claimed that, ah, yes, lower oil prices wreaked havoc with the oil patch, those areas of the country, such as Texas, that rely on oil production and revenue as a source of income.

Anyone who thinks falling oil prices are unequivocal good news for an economy should do a refresher course on 1986.

Although consumption spending on energy goods accelerated from a 7.6 percent increase in the first quarter of 1986 to an 8.5 percent increase in the second quarter, overall consumer spending decelerated to 3.4 percent from 3.7 percent, Kasriel says.

WHAT ABOUT INVESTMENT?

Curious as to what could have been the source of the economy's tepid growth, Kasriel mined the data and found the answer at the wellhead. The hit to GDP came from falling investment: specifically investment in petroleum and natural gas structures, which fell 23.3 percent in the first quarter and 85.4 percent in the second. (It makes the 19.5 percent decline in investment in information technology in the third quarter of 2001 look like child's play.)

Despite the oil "tax cut" and Fed ease, the economy did not fare that well.

"Maybe the oil price decline, which slowed domestic business activity, affected GDP more than [increased energy] consumption helped," Kasriel says.

The repercussions from falling oil prices in 1986 should make people be somewhat circumspect when they declare falling oil prices to be an unconditional positive for the economy.

Then again, why ruin a good story with the facts?

Taking Some of the 'Shock' Out of Oil Prices
———— May 12, 2004 ————

IT DIDN'T TAKE LONG. No sooner did job growth disappear as a stumbling block to a self-sustaining economic expansion than oil prices spread a viscous slick on global growth.

"The track record of oil shocks is close to perfect," writes Stephen Roach, chief economist at Morgan Stanley. "In the United States, each of the five recessions since the early 1970s has been preceded by an oil shock."

Not so fast. Revisionist history of the first Gulf War is incorrect. Saddam Hussein invaded Kuwait on Aug. 2, 1990. Crude oil futures, which settled at a benign $20.69 on July 31, rose to $27.32 by the end of August, pierced $30 in September, and touched $40 briefly in early October before retreating as fast as they had climbed.

Oil prices slid back to $20 a barrel following the onset of hostilities in January 1991, when coalition forces ousted the Iraqi dictator from neighboring Kuwait.

The problem with attributing the 1991 recession to the spike in oil prices is the niggling matter of timing. The recession started in July, according to the National Bureau of Economic Research's Business Cycle Dating Committee. The rise in oil prices was neither coincident with nor causative to the July 1990 to March 1991 recession.

RESPONSE TO OIL

Even if you ignore the timing issue, linking recessions to oil prices ignores one not-so-small piece of the puzzle: how the central bank reacts.

The Fed pushed the federal funds rate up from 6.5–6.625 percent in March 1988 to 9.75–9.875 percent in February 1989. (There were ranges in those days because the funds rate target was a closely guarded secret.) The banking system was reeling under the weight of bad real estate loans, reducing financial institutions' ability to lend.

In spite of the Fed's subsequent aggressive effort to stimulate the economy—it lowered the funds rate from 9.875 percent in June 1989 to 3 percent in September 1992—the early 1990s witnessed the slowest broad money growth in history. The temporary jump in oil prices months after the recession started was the least of the economy's worries.

Oil prices hit $40 a barrel last Friday, a 52 percent increase from a year ago. However shocking the price is—remember the *Economist* magazine's "$5 Oil" cover on March 6, 1999?—it's hard to make a case for a supply shock when both OPEC and non-OPEC producers have been increasing production. (In an e-mail response to questions, Roach clarified that "$40 is high but the shock comes at $50.")

WHERE'S THE SHOCK?

A supply shock is a specific microeconomic phenomenon expressed by a shift inward (to the left) in the supply curve, which is upward sloping: The quantity supplied by producers is higher at higher prices.

"If there's no fall in the quantity, it's not a supply shock," says Bob Laurent, professor of economics and finance at the Illinois Institute of Technology's Stuart School of Business.

The implications of a rise in price coming from reduced supply are different from those coming from increased demand. A supply shock means higher prices and lower output. A demand-driven price increase augurs higher prices and higher output.

Total world oil supply rose to 82.1 million barrels a day in the first quarter of 2004 from 78.8 million in the first quarter of 2003, according to the International Energy Agency. OPEC output rose 1.3 million barrels a day over that time.

SPIGOTS OPEN

"Despite official announcements of OPEC production cuts and adherence to targets, OPEC members excluding Iraq produced close to 25.8 million barrels a day for the sixth straight month" in March, the IEA said in its monthly oil market report.

On Monday, Saudi Arabia, which produces a third of OPEC's output and is one of a handful of countries with excess capacity, encouraged OPEC to increase production quotas by 1.5 million barrels a day from the current 23.5 million. OPEC pumped 25.85 million barrels of oil a day in April, according to a Bloomberg survey.

Almost all of the commentary on the impact of higher oil prices on the economy restricts itself to one side of the equation: Higher oil prices impinge on consumers' discretionary income and raise companies' cost of production.

Never is any consideration given to who benefits: oil producers and their shareholders, many of whom are consumers.

WASTED ENERGY

"The U.S. consumes just under 20 million barrels of oil per day, so the increase from last year's average oil price of just over $31 to $40 would cost American households and companies some $65 billion over a full year," says Ian Shepherdson, chief U.S. economist at High Frequency Economics in Valhalla, New York. "That's about 0.6 percentage point of GDP."

But the hit to national income is less, Shepherdson says, because the U.S. produces about 30 percent of the oil it consumes.

"U.S. producers are enjoying a windfall benefit amounting to about $20 billion at an annualized pace," he says.

And that's not the end of it. Even the revenue sent overseas to buy oil imports doesn't disappear. It comes back to the U.S. in the form of purchases of goods and services or foreign direct investment. All is not lost from higher oil prices.

Besides, oil prices, like the prices of other industrial commodities, are highly cyclical.

"A cyclical rise in oil prices is normal," Shepherdson says. "You can't turn around and say it subverts the cycle."

ENERGY EFFICIENCY

China accounts for about 7 percent of total global energy demand but is responsible for most of the growth, according to the IEA. Demand from China surged 18 percent in the first quarter from a year earlier.

So U.S. consumers are being presented with higher energy prices that aren't the result of their own appetite. The rise in price still doesn't qualify as a supply shock.

And don't forget the increase in energy efficiency following the oil shocks of the 1970s.

"The quantity of crude needed to produce a dollar of real GDP has fallen by more than half since its peak in the early 1970s," Shepherdson says.

Oil prices aren't going to kill the economy, given the considerable stimulus and momentum already in place. When history is rewritten, don't be surprised if oil takes the rap for the next recession.

13

Rewriting History

THE LATE PHILOSOPHER George Santayana is best remembered for his observation that "those who cannot remember the past are condemned to repeat it."

Who needs to remember the past when rewriting it can be such a liberating experience?

Take the question of what caused the unexpected federal budget surpluses in the late 1990s during President Bill Clinton's administration, for example. The two parties have different "recollections."

The surpluses from fiscal 1998 through fiscal 2001 were either the result of the 1993 tax increase and spending constraints (the Democratic view); or they were a side effect of the economic boom, with the stock market bubble generating a windfall of tax revenue for the Treasury from soaring capital gains and options-generated income (the Republican stance).

Both parties—at least those familiar with budget dynamics—would probably acknowledge the effect faster productivity and economic growth had on the bottom line, raising tax revenues and reducing government transfer payments, such as unemployment insurance.

Budget history isn't the only thing that gets rewritten. Bad forecasts—of the economy, of the markets—are either forgotten or rephrased with appropriate caveats to make them look not so bad after all.

If Europe's common currency, introduced at the start of 1999, went down when it was expected to go up, why, analysts have a whole host of ready-made reasons—all of which existed a priori. They never made it into the forecast, but they work just fine in the retelling.

Bankers don't rewrite history as much as forget it. Chastened by losses on loans to a particular class of risky borrowers, they swear "never again," only to repeat the cycle a decade later—in some cases, to the same class of borrowers (emerging-markets countries, for example).

Caveat Emptor, or
How the Banks Got Taken Again

———————— Sept. 28, 1998 ————————

IT HAPPENS late in every business cycle. The characters are different but the themes are the same. It ends with promises of "never again" and calls for increased regulation.

Memory, unfortunately, is short-lived.

Long-Term Capital Management is just the last in a line of banking mistakes. The dream team of John Meriwether and his band of "quants" up in Greenwich, Connecticut, familiarly known as "Solly North," was such a proven moneymaker that banks and securities firms were willing to lend the fund huge sums of money at attractive terms without performing much due diligence.

"If you ever want to know where the next disaster is going to strike, always look where banks are making the most irresponsible loans," says Ed Bishop, president of Kestrel Technologies.

A loan is a covenant between two parties. Party A lends money to Party B. Party A demands something in return: namely, collateral. The collateral can be a home, in the case of a mortgage loan, or securities, in the case of securities loans.

It's the lender's job to analyze the underlying collateral and assess the credit risk. A mortgage lender uses the appraisal of the home and the financial statement of the home buyer as the basis for his decision. A counter-party in a securities-lending transaction is supposed to assess the value of the securities he is holding as collateral for the loan.

Now, Russia's default in August and the effect it had on other emerging markets weren't exactly normal events. For that reason, neither Long-Term's risk-management models nor Long-Term's lenders could anticipate the huge widening of the spread between U.S. Treasuries and everything else.

CREDIT HISTORY

But weren't the lenders supposed to require more or better collateral than the bonds of a government that, in hindsight, everyone knew was corrupt? Russia didn't pay lenders 70 percent for the use of their money for six months because it was a high-grade credit!

John Meriwether and his Nobel laureates were apparently considered such a gilt-edged credit risk that folks on the other side of his trades were willing to cut corners and make allowances for inadequate collateral. In fact, banks were tripping over one another to extend friendly credit terms just to get a piece of the action.

History is littered with examples of the banks overextending on a type of collateral, which, after a huge run-up in price, collapses, leaving the banks holding the bag: bad collateral and nonperforming loans.

Who can forget the aggressive lending to the oil and gas industry in the 1970s and early 1980s? Oil was a commodity that was in limited supply, everyone needed it, and the Organization of Petroleum Exporting Countries had a virtual lock on the price. Oil prices, it was thought, could only go up. The wildcatters putting up rigs in the Gulf of Mexico found easy credit terms to underwrite their ventures.

The price of oil collapsed in 1986. So did the loans to the oil patch.

NAME CHANGE

At around the same time they were making oil and gas loans in the 1970s, the banks were "diversifying"—making sovereign loans to Latin America. They came up on the short end of that stick, too. When the Latin American nations couldn't pay, the banks first forgave the loans, then restructured the bad loans into good bonds, known as Brady bonds.

Fast-forward 20 years: "Less-developed countries" have evolved into "emerging markets." But money flowed into them again, this time to Asia.

"Corporate memory is about 10 years long in every area," Bishop says. "The guys who made the loans are no longer there," and the cycle starts all over again.

REAL BAILOUT

In between their escapades in emerging markets, the banks had plenty of time to get into trouble in the real estate arena. Everyone wanted to capitalize on the soaring property market in the 1980s. The banks were right there, lending hand-over-fist to anyone who could sign on the dotted line—or else someone putting up a house on spec.

The collapse of the real estate market in the late 1980s and early 1990s was followed by a period that witnessed the highest rate of bank failures since the Great Depression. Eventually the federal government had to step in to ensure that depositors were paid off, good loans of insolvent banks assumed by solvent banks, and their bad assets sold off. The tab came to a cool $300 billion. Now that was a bailout. Even Bob Rubin wouldn't dare to say that it didn't cost the taxpayer a dime.

No, Long-Term Capital Management isn't a new story. Not coincidentally, it comes along after extended bull runs in financial asset prices. The banks were in there swinging with the best of them. In the last two years, banks' securities loans have risen 51 percent. The last time there was an increase of that magnitude was in 1978, according to Jim Bianco, president of Bianco Research. Repo loans at large banks are up a huge 65 percent in the past year alone, Bianco notes.

HELPING HAND?

The Federal Reserve, which is universally expected to lower interest rates tomorrow to relieve some of the stress the emerging markets collapse has brought on the financial system, bears some of the responsibility, says Paul DeRosa, former managing director of Eastbridge Capital and now a private investor. But not for brokering the deal to rescue Long-Term Capital.

"The Fed should have tightened more in 1996," DeRosa says. "Rates were too low, and capital set out in search of yield, creating an investment bubble in overseas markets."

DeRosa notes that foreign overseas private investment went from $50 billion in 1992 to $300 billion in 1996. Some of that capital wanderlust had to do with an extended period of low interest rates in the U.S., which was necessary so the banking system could heal from its previous bout of over-lending.

"The Fed's blunder was over-easing in 1995," DeRosa says. "There is a precedent for the consequences of monetary policy showing up not in the CPI but in asset prices: the 1920s."

CONFLICT OF INTEREST

Ironic, isn't it, that the cause—easy money—is the same as the cure.

Almost as ironic as the fact that Long-Term Capital's portfolio—soon to be owned by a consortium of 14 banks and securities firms—stands to depreciate even further if the Fed lowers interest rates. Many of Long-Term's bets reportedly stand to benefit if interest rates rise and Treasuries underperform other fixed-income assets, such as mortgage-backed securities.

Leverage, of course, is the bread and butter of Wall Street. Wall Street lives and dies by the mantra of borrowing short and lending long.

It seems the rate cut that Wall Street needs for its own profitability is at odds with the conditions required for the Meriwether portfolio's future profitability.

Talk about a conflict of interest.

As an Economic Historian, Al Gore Gets an 'F'

——————— Aug. 14, 2000 ———————

LOVE HIM OR HATE HIM, Bill Clinton wowed everybody with his ability to master complicated subjects and absorb the most minute details of any policy issue.

When the newly elected president was informed in 1993 by National Economic Adviser Robert Rubin that he couldn't propose a government "investment" program because it would raise long-term interest rates and hurt the economy, Clinton digested the information and fired back: "You mean to tell me that the success of the program and my reelection hinges on the Federal Reserve and a bunch of f—ing bond traders?"

Alas, Al Gore, who will be anointed the official Democratic presidential nominee this week at the party's convention in La-La Land, hasn't demonstrated the same flair when it comes to economics. To prevail, Gore will have to convince the voters that he has a better command of the subject matter than was evident in an interview with Fox News Channel's Jim Angle on Friday.

Fox: Now, you talk almost every day on the campaign trail about the recession from the Bush–Quayle years being the worst since the Great Depression.

Gore: No. No, the recession during the previous 12 years, during the time when we tried this prescription in the past. There was a triple-dip recession during those years, but in the early part of those years, the deepest recession since the 1930s was in '81–'82.

Fox: That wasn't Ronald Reagan's recession; that would have been Jimmy Carter's recession.

Gore: I disagree, because we had a new economic proposal that came in those years. And again, it's not about the individual, it's about the priorities.

Fox: But it is about which administration and which policies are responsible for the economy.

Ronald Reagan took office in January 1981 following a six-month recession, according to the National Bureau of Economic Research, the official arbiter of economic cycles. Inflation was running at 12 percent. The overnight federal funds rate (there was no funds rate target at the time—and a lot more volatility—because the Federal Reserve was targeting non-borrowed reserves) was at 19–20 percent. Three-month bill yields were close to 15 percent. Bonds yielded 12.40 percent.

In other words, Reagan inherited a holy mess.

Congress passed the Economic Recovery Tax Act in July 1981, slashing marginal tax rates by 25 percent, lowering capital gains tax rates to 20 percent from 28 percent and indexing tax brackets to inflation.

The tax cuts were phased in in three parts, starting in the fall of 1981 with the final installment in January 1983. No reasonable person, including Al Gore, could look at the tattered economic landscape at the time and blame it on Reagan's policies.

TEXTBOOK EXAMPLE

In fact, one of Gore's key economic advisers, Alan Blinder, cites the 1981–1984 Reagan tax cuts in his introductory economics textbook as an example of successful tax policy, compared with the failures of 1968 (tax increase) and 1975 (tax reduction), both of which were advertised as temporary. Not surprisingly, Blinder writes, consumers make decisions about their current spending on the basis of their expected income over the long term.

Incidentally, federal tax revenues doubled during the 1980s to about $1 trillion from $500 billion, even as the rich paid a larger share of the total, according to Stephen Moore, president of the Club for Growth.

The Reagan deficits, which Gore snidely denounces as a sign of profligacy now that the Democrats have found fiscal religion and surpluses, had nothing to do with the tax cuts. Instead they were the result of both parties' aggressive spending agenda: the Republicans on the military and the Democrats on social programs.

LOWER TAXES, HIGHER REVENUE

You won't hear this from Al Gore (it doesn't fit the party line), but some of the Clinton surpluses, projected at $232 billion for the fiscal year that ends Sept. 30, are a result of an explosion in capital gains revenue. The Clinton administration lowered the capital gains tax rate to 20 percent from 28 percent in 1997 (it was raised in the 1986 tax act), and revenues went from $62 billion in 1996 to an estimated $110 billion last year, according to Moore.

It was precisely the Reagan tax cuts in combination with the slaying of the inflation dragon, allowing the Federal Reserve to relax its vise on the economy, that sparked the decade-long boom following the 16-month recession from July 1981 to November 1982.

That was a deep recession, which Gore fatuously places at the feet of the Reagan-Bush administration after an artful segue from the 1990–1991 triple-dip recession—the mildest and shortest in postwar history, according to the NBER—which occurred during the Bush–Quayle administration. (Gore must think people will focus on his ready-for-prime-time newly capped teeth instead of what he says.)

BOB AND WEAVE

In the Fox News interview, Gore suggests that one of the failed policies of the Bush-Quayle years was the "huge tax giveaway primarily targeted to the wealthy."

Angle, thinking on his feet, reminds Gore about ol' George "read-my-lips, no-new-taxes" Bush, who was forced to take early retirement in Kennebunkport because of a broken promise.

President Bush "only increased taxes as part of two deficit reduction packages," Angle says. "In fact, one could argue that your administration did the same thing he did: raised taxes in an effort to lower the deficit."

Gore: "Never submitted a balanced budget."

Fox: "Didn't he inherit those from Ronald Reagan?"

Gore: "Well, he was part of that administration. But, look, it's not about the individuals, it's about the policy."

Huh? Who's on first? What's on second? If Gore expects to round the bases and cross home plate standing up, he's going to have to do a lot better on economic policy.

POSTSCRIPT: *The 2001 recession matched the 1990–1991 downturn in duration (eight months) and was even shallower in terms of lost output.*

Don't Confuse Fiscal Responsibility with Luck
——————— Feb. 14, 2001 ———————

THE NERVOUSNESS is palpable. As tax-cut fever gains broad public acceptance—the only unanswered questions seem to be how big and what kind—the Left is in a virtual state of panic.

What better way to harness the collective energy of the tired, hungry, huddled masses than to drag out its big gun, former Treasury secretary Robert Rubin, in the paper of record, the *New York Times*?

There he was, the aw-shucks self-effacing Trader Bob, occupying prime real estate on the op-ed page Sunday, lecturing us on the importance of fiscal responsibility and the inadvisability of a large tax cut.

That the U.S. federal budget swung from record deficit to record surplus during the Clinton–Rubin years is indisputable. Whether the 1993 tax increase was responsible for the government's sound fiscal health today is open to question.

I know of no economic theory that claims higher taxes are stimulative. In fact, the traditional Keynesian prescription for slowing a runaway economy is to raise taxes and cut spending.

What's more, the argument that lowering long-term rates through debt reduction produced a booming economy has no empirical basis.

THOSE PESKY FACTS

"The evidence is to the contrary," says Larry Kudlow, chief economist at ING Barings LLC. "There is little if any correlation between the volume of debt and level of interest rates."

Tell that to Federal Reserve Chairman Alan Greenspan, who yesterday reiterated his view that "the greater the budget surplus, the lower interest rates would be."

To his credit, Rubin did advise Bill Clinton in 1993 to forgo increases in government spending. He convinced him to raise taxes and cut spending instead to reduce the federal budget deficit, which hit a record $290 billion in 1992. In so doing, long-term interest rates would fall, stimulating investment and economic growth, Rubin argued.

Before revisionist history becomes the law of the land, let's look at the facts. The Clinton budget, featuring an increase in the top marginal tax rate to 36 percent from 31 percent, with a 10 percent surtax lifting the effective rate to 39.6 percent, passed the House and Senate on Aug. 5 and 6, 1993.

PRICE DISCOVERY

Long-term interest rates fell consistently from late 1990 through late 1993, troughing at 5.77 percent in October. Yields then soared to 8.17 percent, peaking on Election Day in November 1994, when the Republicans took control of both houses of Congress for the first time since 1952. Anyone wishing to ascribe a causal connection between interest rates and the tax increase would have to conclude that the direction of rates was up.

To be sure, there were other things going on at the time. The U.S. economy was stirring from its long post-recession slumber, with the pickup in growth reflected in rising commodity prices. The Fed was raising interest rates aggressively (300 basis points) during 1994.

Still, connecting the dots from a tax increase to lower long-term rates, which is what Rubin does, is as disingenuous as claiming higher taxes are responsible for the extraordinary prosperity the U.S. experienced in the late 1990s.

That the junior senator from New York, Hillary Rodham Clinton, who wants to redistribute everyone's income but her own, can use fiscal responsibility as a argument against tax cuts is nothing short of laughable.

STATIC VS DYNAMIC

The Democrats in effect stumbled onto budget surpluses and claimed fiscal responsibility as their mantra. The U.S.'s fiscal health is a result of rising productivity growth—a by-product of the private sector's investment in technology—which raised the economy's potential growth rate.

When U.S. economic growth soared to an average 4.5 percent rate in the final four years of the 1990s, tax revenue ballooned. The 1997 cut in the capital gains rate created another windfall for the Treasury.

Now that the Treasury's cup runneth over and the Congressional Budget Office expects total available public debt to be redeemed by 2006, the Democrats are apoplectic about the prospect of the government returning to the taxpayer what is rightfully his. The maintenance of fiscal discipline is furnishing them with a not-too-opaque cover.

The entire tax-cut debate relies on strict static analysis: $1.6 trillion of tax cuts costs $1.6 trillion.

That is unrealistic. Rather than be accused of resorting to voodoo— the 1980s deficits figure prominently in the Democrats' critique of tax cuts—the Republicans have been willing to play by the static rules.

FEEDBACK LOOP

The revenue feedback can't be ignored, however.

"As a rule of thumb, you get $1 back for every $3 of static revenue loss," says Stephen Moore, president of the Club for Growth. "It's unrealistic to assume that a $1.6 trillion tax cut [in marginal rates] will cost $1.6 trillion. That assumes zero feedback. The cost would probably be closer to $1 trillion."

The Democrats, of course, are going in the opposite direction, claiming the $1.6 trillion cut will cost $2 trillion because of additional interest expense (a result of reduced debt paydowns).

"[Treasury Secretary] Paul O'Neill is arguing that if the Democrats want to use dynamic scoring for debt and interest expense, they should allow the administration to use dynamic scoring to reflect the impacts of tax cuts on economic growth," ING's Kudlow says.

The much-maligned Reagan tax cuts produced a doubling of federal revenue between 1980 and 1990, Moore says. "There was no reduction in revenue once the economy started to grow."

BEYOND RUBIN

Rubin's op-ed was prima facie evidence at yesterday's Senate Banking Committee hearing, where Fed chairman Greenspan presented his semi-annual monetary report to Congress. The Democrats were hoping to get the anointed one to renege on his recent endorsement of tax cuts.

Like all good liberals, Rubin says the tax cut is too large, too late to act as fiscal stimulus, too imprudent given the unreliability of 10-year budget forecasts, and too weighted toward the rich. He does not, however, recommend a tax increase for the current malaise, which in his book stimulated the economy by lowering long-term rates.

Greenspan's support for tax cuts is based on necessity. If the U.S. doesn't lower taxes now, the exploding budget surpluses will put the government in the unsavory position of having to buy private-sector assets by 2006.

I've got a better idea. Once the available public debt has been redeemed, any surplus funds should be returned to individuals with the specification they be used to establish private retirement-savings accounts. The money would be redistributed—the right buzzwords would make it difficult for the Democrats to oppose—on the basis of payroll taxes paid.

Payroll taxes could be gradually cut, another idea that will appeal to the Democrats, who want to lower the burden on the poor. Individuals would be in a much stronger position owning their private accounts than relying on meager returns from Social Security. That would make the inevitable reduction in benefits or increase in taxes when the baby boomers retire easier to swallow.

What a sight to behold. The Democrats, denied a pile of surplus cash, would watch as their support base becomes increasingly independent. At that point, it would take a bigger gun than Bob Rubin to quash the move toward financial empowerment. Calling FDR!

Postscript: *I received three nominations for president based on my proposal for private retirement-savings accounts, all of which I declined. Four years later, the U.S. has no surplus and is no closer to a Social Security solution.*

A Space Traveler's View of the Political Landscape
———— March 17, 2001 ————

If you returned to planet Earth in the year 2001 from an extended intergalactic odyssey, you might be forgiven for experiencing a degree of political identity confusion.

The Democratic Party, traditionally the party of tax and spend, is now fiscally conservative, preoccupied with debt reduction *über alles*.

The Grand Old Party of Republicans, on the other hand, is now fiscally irresponsible in its determination to cut taxes when a cumulative 10-year $5.6 trillion federal surplus is only a paper projection.

Sitting down in front of the small screen, which is no longer small but enormous in some cases, you'd find class warriors Tom Daschle and Richard Gephardt, Democratic minority leaders of the Senate and House of Representatives, respectively, preaching fiscal discipline. (Yes, it's the same Dick Gephardt who was representing the Third Congressional District in Missouri when you left.)

"Our first priority must be to continue paying down the trillions of dollars in federal debt Washington ran up in the 1980s," Daschle said in the Democratic response to President George W. Bush's Feb. 27 address to the nation. "We can't just pass this debt on to our children, not when we have the ability to pay it off."

REVISIONIST HISTORY

As an aside, the Democrats will mention that a large tax cut will deprive their base of vital social programs. But the main thrust of their argument against Bush's $1.6 trillion plan is the experience of an across-the-board cut in marginal tax rates in 1981.

"Deficits skyrocketed. The national debt quadrupled. High interest rates choked American industries. Unemployment soared. Working families struggled to meet their mortgages, to pay for health care and save for college," Daschle said. (In case you read an article that portrays the 1980s in a positive light, it's important to see history through Daschle's filter.)

Because tax cuts caused all these awful things, the Democrats are fighting to save America from a rerun.

The debt-reduction bandwagon probably owes its origin to First Trombone Robert Rubin, who was secretary of the Treasury during the Clinton administration. Rubin advised incoming President Bill Clinton to forgo traditional fiscal spending to ignite the economy and instead to do Keynes in reverse: Raise taxes and cut spending to reduce the deficit, bring long-term rates down and stimulate economic growth.

HIPPOCRATIC OATH

The Clinton years saw the federal government's accounts swing from a deficit of $290 billion in 1992 (the final year of the Bush administration) to a surplus of $237 billion in 2000. Real GDP growth averaged 3.8 percent. Inflation was low. Productivity soared.

We'll never know if A caused B, C and D, or if A, B, C and D coexisted; there is no control study in real life.

Daschle and Gephardt, along with the rest of the Democrats, like to take credit for the economic boom. The Republicans, instead of acknowledging they were wrong when they predicted a long dark winter following the 1993 Clinton tax increase, came up with an ex post facto explanation: It was the Reagan tax cuts in the 1980s that were responsible for the 1990s economic boom.

I suspect the boom was a result of the checks and balances that ensured Clinton would "do no harm," or his incredibly good luck—being in the right place at the right time. The economy had been prepped for takeoff by an extended period of low interest rates in the early 1990s to allow the banking system to recover from the savings and loan crisis. (If Japanese business schools use the case-study method, this would be a good case study.) Without the tax increases, the economy probably would have done even better, given the technological revolution that was getting under way.

LIVE (DEBT) FREE OR DIE

How debt reduction became the Democrats' mantra is curious. If paying down the debt is a means to an end, then what's the end? There is no theoretical basis to suggest debt reduction contributes to a high standard of living, good job and income growth, prosperity or anything else we care about.

And if it's an end in itself, which it seems to have become, where was the national debate on priorities?

The publicly held debt is about 33 percent of U.S. GDP, the lowest in the industrialized world, and sinking. Life without a risk-free benchmark for the world's reserve currency may not be such a great deal, especially when the U.S. needs capital inflows to finance its current account deficit, which is 4.6 percent of GDP.

Besides, as Nobel laureate Milton Friedman said, the real burden of government on the economy is not taxes or deficits but the resources government is in control of: what it spends.

The Democrats never cared about reducing the deficit because it would have meant reducing spending. Now they want to keep the surplus in Washington, instead of returning it to the people in the form of tax cuts. In so doing, they maintain control of those resources.

Maybe the roles of the two parties aren't as reversed as it seems.

The Democrats want bigger government: Either deficit spending or surplus hoarding will suit their goal just fine.

And if the projected surpluses give way to deficits, the Democrats will abandon the fiscal-responsibility mantra.

For the space traveler returning to Earth 20 years hence, it will once again be easy to identify which party is which.

Pick a Reason, Any Reason, Why the Euro Is Weak

—————— Feb. 29, 2000 ——————

WITH THE summer travel season fast approaching, Americans should be looking to maximize the purchasing power of the dollar by visiting Europe, where the single currency slipped to a 14-month low of 93.9 U.S. cents yesterday.

"The euro suffered a momentary slip yesterday morning, that is Monday morning, because it was in thin Asian markets and it then recovered a value of 97 cents," French Finance Minister Christian Sautter told RTL radio. "I consider that the euro has a potential for appreciation because the markets are going to realize that euro-pessimism is finished."

The euro has had a potential for appreciation since it was issued on Jan. 1, 1999, at $1.1667. The problem is, it's had a tendency for depreciation.

The list of reasons for 14 months of what European officials fondly refer to as momentary lapses is long and varied:

The euro was new.

It was misunderstood.

It suffered at the hands of the market-unfriendly former German finance minister Oskar LaFontaine.

It was whipsawed by a bunch of bumbling Eurocrats who couldn't decide if they wanted the euro to be strong or weak.

It reflected weak economic growth on the Continent.

The U.S. dollar was too strong.

The yen was too strong.

Sterling was too strong.

The Chilean peso was too strong.

The U.S. economy was too strong.

Kosovo was too close.

Austria was even closer.

Brussels was closer still.

Anglo-Saxon speculators set out to destroy it.

The beef crisis.

The banana crisis.

The rotten heart of the European Commission.

No actual euros minted.

PR Disaster

This list is hardly comprehensive, but it does capture the euro's essence. There is always some reason why the euro is going down, not up.

At the outset, the euro was blessed with the overwhelming support of the major global financial institutions, intent on currying favor with their central-bank clientele. Economic research departments churned out reams of research on why the euro would be a strong currency, challenging the dollar for reserve currency status.

The hedge funds piled into the German mark as a proxy for the euro in the months leading up to its Jan. 1 kickoff. Japanese accounts were similarly engaged in buying a proxy for the euro to invest in European bonds. After all, European officials said the euro would be as strong as the mark.

Former Bundesbank president Karl Otto Poehl is probably drowning his sorrows in some dark corner of the local Hofbrauhaus. At the time of the euro's inception, $1 would have bought 1.6767 deutsche marks. Today it fetches 2.0225 marks, more than at any time since June 1989.

Good as Gold

Not only was the euro supposed to be akin to its forebearer, but also the European Central Bank was supposed to be Buba incarnate. Instead, any nascent confidence in the euro has been undermined by the authorities, according to currency analysts.

"When the euro went through parity [with the dollar], I don't think it was a crisis of confidence," says Tim Fox, currency strategist at Standard Charter Bank. "Now that it's breaking down even as signs of growth are becoming embedded, it appears to be a confidence issue."

Yesterday's trouncing in Asia, with the euro falling 3 cents and 4.5 yen in a matter of minutes, happened when the Japanese were literally at lunch. It's not clear whether fully staffed trading desks would have prevented the slide or exacerbated it.

Either way, the folks at the ECB aren't doing anything to help.

"Confidence was damaged by the euro's performance, and the ECB isn't doing anything to support it," says Chris Widness, an international economist at Chase Securities.

OTHER ILLS

ECB officials have been sending mixed messages about their intentions on monetary policy. Last Wednesday, bank vice president Christian Noyer said exchange-rate developments would be taken into account in the goal of price stability. The following day, he reversed himself, downplaying the idea that the bank was preparing the markets for an imminent rate hike. Bundesbank President Ernst Welteke and council member Klaus-Dieter Kuehbacher echoed the dovish Noyer line.

With annual inflation in the Euro-11 hitting the ECB's ceiling of 2 percent last month, traders and investors are understandably confused as to "how the ECB sees the trade-off between growth and inflation," Fox says.

What's even more important—and what may be the root cause of the euro's downward spiral—is why there is a trade-off when the U.S. has defied the notion that strong growth inevitably leads to higher inflation. If Europe does have an inflation threat after years of economic malaise and 9.6 percent of the euro-zone population unemployed, what does that say about its economy?

It says that Europe has serious structural problems, including high taxes, inflexible labor markets and excessive regulation. That these issues need to be addressed before capital flows into Europe rather than seeking attractive investment opportunities abroad. And that a single currency is not a panacea for a myriad of problems.

POSTSCRIPT: *The euro lost almost 30 percent of its value against the dollar in the two years following its introduction on Jan. 1, 1999, at $1.1667. It set a low of $.82 in October 2000, edged its way back to parity with the dollar in early 2003 and finally reached its value at inception a full 4½ years later. The euro hit an all-time high of $1.37 on Dec. 30, 2004.*

14

Men in Black

INANCIAL MARKETS are fertile breeding ground for conspiracy theories. Any time there's a significant yet inexplicable move—inexplicable, that is, to conspiracy theorists—the inference is the market's being manipulated by government officials and their chosen agents in the futures pits.

Stocks going up after a huge meltdown? It must be the Plunge Protection Team, a fiction loosely based on an actual working group created by the president following the 1987 stock market crash to ensure the smooth functioning of financial markets in a crisis. The conspiracy theorists turned a "what-if" discussion group into an active intervention agent.

Suspicious movements in asset prices elicit knowing nods and whispered references to the Trilateral Commission and Bilderberg Group, two private organizations created in the 1970s to encourage international coordination and mold public policy. To critics, the groups are elitist, sinister and a first step in the march toward one-world government.

From that point, it's a hop, skip and a jump to men in black in low-flying black helicopters coming to get you.

Don't laugh. The folks who believe this stuff aren't crazy. I'm the one who's naïve for not taking it seriously, according to some of my readers.

Nothing elicits more vitriol than attempts to dispel the notion that conspiracies are alive and well and operating in the financial marketplace. The e-mails in response to the columns in this chapter, some of which appear in chapter 19, kept me occupied for weeks.

Stocks Tanking? Call the Plunge Protection Team
—————— March 27, 2003 ——————

PERHAPS YOU'VE HEARD of the Plunge Protection Team. If not, let me acquaint you with this august group.

You know all those gut-wrenching dives in the Standard & Poor's 500 Index that mysteriously stabilize, then reverse into huge rallies into the futures close?

If you are a conspiracy theorist, the PPT is a select group of government officials and bankers who intervene from time to time to support the stock market.

According to some traders, pundits and a slick band of conspiracy theorists, the Federal Reserve—the same central bank that buys and sells government securities above the table in daylight hours—operates sub rosa in the stock market.

Never mind that the Federal Reserve's menu of what it can purchase doesn't include equities of any description. According to the 1913 Federal Reserve Act, which has been amended over the years, the Fed can buy U.S. Treasury and agency securities, foreign government securities, banker's acceptances, bills of exchange, certain municipal debt, foreign currency and gold.

Try and engage a conspiracy theorist on the subject, and the conversation stops and ends there. Talk about the reserve impact—if the Fed buys stocks, it adds reserves to the banking system, which would depress the overnight federal funds rate unless the Fed drained reserves through open market operations—and the CTs say the money comes from the Treasury's slush fund, officially known as the Exchange Stabilization Fund.

THE GROUP

Forget the technical inconsistencies. If the CTs are correct, and the Fed buys S&P futures contracts (purportedly its intervention vehicle of choice), there is a human being somewhere who executes the trade, clears the trade, and oversees the account.

That means someone somewhere could extort a bundle of money from the Fed to keep quiet or command a huge advance from a publisher to write a kiss-and-tell book.

The authors of articles on the Plunge Protection Team, striving for legitimacy ("Trust me, it exists!"), reference a *Washington Post* article of Feb. 23, 1997.

What's curious is that the *Post* story never mentions anything about buying stocks. *Post* reporter Brett Fromson outlined the creation of the President's Working Group on Financial Markets following the Oct. 19, 1987, stock market crash. The group, which includes the Treasury secretary, Federal Reserve chairman, chairman of the Securities and Exchange Commission and chairman of the Commodity Futures Trading Commission, was formed to ensure the smooth operation of financial markets.

METAMORPHOSIS

"The Working Group's main goal, officials say, would be to keep the markets operating in the event of a sudden, stomach-churning plunge in stock prices—and to prevent a panicky run on banks, brokerage firms and mutual funds," the 1997 *Post* article said.

The thrust of the article is officials' efforts to avert a liquidity crisis, which is exactly what the Fed did when it flooded the banking system with reserves following the 508-point plunge in the Dow Jones Industrial Average on Oct. 19, 1987.

How an effort to ensure adequate access to credit to prevent a domino effect in the event of a market meltdown morphed into a cabal to prop up the stock market is anybody's guess. For a window into the depths of the conspiracy theory, type "plunge protection team" into Google and see what comes up.

AUTHORITATIVE VOICES

Notice the authority with which the authors write.

"On November 24, [2000,] within minutes of the combined Fed and Goldman Sachs intervention, the Nasdaq was soaring, ending the day well above 3,100 for a daily rise of 5.7 percent," one anonymous Internet pundit wrote. "According to informed market insiders, had the Fed and Plunge Protection Team not stepped in, there would have been a full-blown systemic financial crisis which would have soon spilled over into a dollar crisis."

What's more, ever since the October 1987 stock market crash, Goldman strategist Abby Joseph Cohen "has been used to 'predict' a rebound every time the markets were threatened," the Web site says.

Look at all the people who are in on this deal. Not one of them wants to capitalize on this inside information to write a No. 1 bestseller?

According to a recent press report, the Fed has given up the stock index business in favor of picking individual stocks. Realizing the 30-stock Dow Jones Industrial Average "is much easier to manipulate," London's *Evening Standard* concluded on March 19 that the "huge volume in recent days" in 3M Co. was convincing evidence that the U.S. market was being rigged by the government in advance of war with Iraq.

No Guarantee of Success

Who's to say that the PPT's alleged intervention would succeed? Academic economists are still trying to determine whether currency-market intervention has more than a transitory effect.

If this group is so adept, why are stocks entering the fourth year of a bear market? With volume on the New York Stock Exchange averaging 1.43 billion shares a day during the past year, it would take some sizable purchases to reverse a market move.

Then again, maybe the PPT has hijacked the Strategic Petroleum Reserve and is quietly selling oil into the market at elevated prices, turning around and using the proceeds to buy stocks.

Come to think of it, no one's been able to trace the source of those fabricated moon landings.

Black Helicopter Theories Whir Through Markets

—————— June 15, 2004 ——————

IT MUST SAY something about fear and greed that normally sane people take leave of their senses to construct financial market conspiracy theories.

Some of these theories, embarrassing as it would seem, find their way into print. A recent conspiracy theory (CT) making the rounds concerns the surge in money supply growth and—watch the web being spun—the implication that "the Fed must know something."

According to this line of thinking, the Federal Reserve is flooding the banking system with reserves in the same way that it did following the Sept. 11, 2001, terrorist attacks—except this time it's anticipating the event.

Two weeks ago, Safehaven.com posted an alarming analysis on its Web site, warning of the "unprecedented, unheard-of pre-catastrophe M3 expansion" (unprecedented for a four-week period unless you count similar spurts in July 2003 and November 2002).

M3, the broadest monetary aggregate, rose $154 billion, or 22 percent annualized, from mid-April to mid-May. This suggested to the author (with a Ph.D. after his name) "a crisis of historic proportions coming, and the Federal Reserve is making sure that there is enough liquidity in place to protect our nation's fragile financial system.

"The Fed's actions mean they know what is about to happen," the posting went on. "They are aware of a terrible, horrific imminent event."

Is the Fed just acting irresponsibly? No, the author concluded, this isn't your garden-variety central bank printing party. "Something is up, bigger than we have ever seen in the history of the United States."

COVERT OPERATIONS

A chill came over me, but I managed to get on with life.

When I received yet another e-mail alerting me to the Fed's classified intelligence, I replied to the sender: "If the Fed knows something, maybe it ought to alert the Office of Homeland Security."

The 9/11 Commission found ample evidence of intelligence failure, some of it the result of bureaucratic infighting between the FBI and the CIA. You'd think if the Fed were onto another terrorist attack, it would be eager to alert the authorities.

Besides being loopy, this CT doesn't add up. If the Fed were providing the banking system with more reserves (the raw material for money creation) than banks are required to hold against certain deposits, the overnight federal funds rate would have plummeted.

That hasn't happened.

MAGIC WAND

Alas, this is the same pesky logic advocates of the "Plunge Protection Team" ignore when they assert that the Fed, the Treasury and a cabal of large investment banks step in to buy S&P futures contracts whenever the stock market is going into one of its swan dives.

The Fed doesn't have a slush fund (don't tell the conspiracy theorists). The central bank creates reserves out of thin air. If it were secretly buying stock index futures—how secret could it be with someone executing and clearing the trades?—there would be a reserve impact. The Fed would have to drain reserves, internally or through open market operations, to keep the funds rate steady.

The other CT being promulgated right now has to do with activity in the Chicago Mercantile Exchange's one-month Libor futures contract, which is hardly the vehicle of choice for speculating on short-term interest-rate movements. The contracts have 633,890 in open interest compared with 6.5 million in the three-month Eurodollar futures.

Open interest, or the number of outstanding contracts, for all of the one-month Libor futures contracts, was hovering roughly between 50,000 and 75,000 late last year. It "increased 10-fold in the last five months," said Jim Bianco, president of Bianco Research in Chicago, who brought this CT to my attention.

September Surprise

The talk at the Chicago Merc is that a futures broker is executing spread trades for a customer betting on a collapse in interest rates after August. These trades involve being long the October one-month Libor contract and short the August contract, among other permutations.

The idea is that something is going to happen after August— a September surprise?—to cause interest rates to plunge.

With interest-rate futures markets getting increasingly bearish on expectations for higher rates going forward, these trades aren't exactly working.

As conspiracy theories go, black helicopters are way out there. Silent black choppers are supposedly being used by secret agents of the New World Order—a conspiracy theory within a conspiracy theory of a United Nations plan to invade the U.S. and implement global totalitarian rule.

While the Fed is an endless source of speculation for financial markets —another popular CT says the Fed won't raise rates aggressively because it will hurt financial companies, which make up 20 percent of the S&P 500 Index—it can't hold a candle to black helicopters.

Wait a second. That money-dropping helicopter Milton Friedman used to talk about in explaining monetary policy to his students: Wasn't it black?

Postscript: Eight weeks after M3 growth peaked at 22 percent on a four-week annualized basis, the broad monetary aggregate was contracting at a 7.7 percent rate. I doubt the conspiracy theorists will ever admit their theory was flaky; the holes in it were evident at the time. Instead they'd probably say the Fed knows something isn't going to happen and is draining the liquidity.

15

No One Else
Would Write About This

THE TITLE of this chapter is an inside joke—at least it was an inside joke—between my longtime editor, Steve Dickson, and me.

While I enjoy the solitude of writing, I have a strong need to interact. I like to tell my editors what I'm working on. It's unclear whether I'm looking for approval, encouragement or human contact.

Sometimes I want actual input—when I'm having trouble with the structure of a column and need a midcourse correction before I submit it for final editing. Mostly, however, I just want them involved in the process.

One day, I had written a particularly geeky column on the problems in calculating owners' equivalent rent, the single largest component in the consumer price index. Because the purchase of a house is considered an investment, not consumption, in government statistics, the Bureau of Labor Statistics dropped the asset-price approach to measuring home prices in the early 1980s in favor of a rental equivalency measure (the imputed rental value of a home).

The subject is of limited interest, in other words—appealing to a coterie of economists and statisticians, not to mention conspiracy theorists, who are always eager to accuse the government of manipulating the inflation numbers for political purposes.

When Steve was done editing the column, I went over to his desk to discuss the proposed changes, as is our custom.

"So what did you think?" I asked hopefully.

"It's good. I mean, no one else would write about this," he said.

We both started to laugh at what sounded like a backhanded compliment. To this day, I'm not sure whether he intended to flatter me (What a unique approach to a fascinating subject!) or express his reservations (Who else would think this is remotely interesting?).

Either way, it's become a frequent refrain (sometimes I beat him to it), and we both get a good laugh.

This Old House Still Conveys New Information

————— March 29, 2000 —————

HOUSING MARKET indicators command a lot of attention on Wall Street, as well they should: As housing goes, so goes the nation.

Historically, the housing market peaks and troughs before the rest of the economy for the simple reason that it's more sensitive to changes in interest rates than other sectors. The lead time tends to be longer at the peak than at the trough, according to Michael Carliner, an economist at the National Association of Home Builders.

"Typically housing turns up three to six months ahead of the economy and turns down on average two years before the rest of the economy," Carliner says.

Mortgage rates have been on the rise for the last 1½ years, with only faint hints that they are curbing housing demand. Freddie Mac's weekly national average 30-year commitment rate has risen almost 200 basis points, from 6.5 percent in October 1998 to a high of 8.4 percent in mid-February before edging down to 8.23 percent last week.

The seeming failure of higher mortgage rates to damp housing demand has some economists flummoxed, prompting declarations that the economy is inured to higher interest rates for any number of dumb reasons.

Let's go to the numbers and see if this premise is correct. Housing starts stood close to a 13-year high in February; it's starts, not sales, that count in the computation of the residential construction component of GDP. (To the extent that home sales beget purchases of appliances and furniture, they contribute indirectly to growth.)

TWIN PEAKS

Even single-family starts, the most interest-rate sensitive of the bunch, performed well through December, hitting a 22-year high of 1.441 million (annualized) before sagging a cumulative 9 percent in January and February.

New home sales, which are the catalyst for housing starts, actually peaked in November 1998 at an annualized 995,000. A combined measure of new and used home sales was lower in February than at any time during 1998 or 1999, says Christopher Low, chief economist at First Tennessee Capital Markets.

Owing to huge builder backlogs as a result of shortages of skilled labor and materials, starts continued to climb even as sales ebbed.

"Last year, there was trouble everywhere keeping up with demand," Carliner reports. "Now there's regional variability," with only the Northeast and California reporting shortages.

With the NAHB's latest housing market index—a gauge of current sales, expected sales and traffic—showing a steep 8-point drop to 61 in March, the lowest in more than two years, Carliner expects to see softer sales ahead.

R & R

Some analysts cite the recent rise in the Mortgage Bankers Association's weekly home purchase index as an indication that sales won't slow anytime soon. The relevance of this series as a leading indicator is questionable. Intuitively, a mortgage purchase application should presage a home purchase. "Given how easy it is to apply online, and with no cost, the series is more confusing than helpful in forecasting home sales," Low says.

Housing is important to financial markets professionals for another reason: It accounts for the largest share—almost 40 percent—of the consumer price index. If housing acts up, the tame core inflation of recent years is history.

The largest component in the CPI's housing category is shelter, with a weighting of 30 percent (of the CPI). Within shelter, there's rent of primary residence (7 percent); lodging away from home (2.4 percent); owners' equivalent rent of primary residence (20.5 percent); and tenants' and household insurance (0.4 percent).

Taken together, the rental components account for more than one-quarter of the CPI. In 1999, the CPI rose 2.7 percent while owners' equivalent rent (OER) and residential rents (RR) rose 2.4 percent and 3.1 percent, respectively.

HOUSE NOT A HOME

These hybrid rent categories are not an attempt to measure home prices. A home is considered to be an investment; it goes into the "I" component of GDP. It also shows up as a personal consumption expenditure (the imputed rental value) and as personal income (the imputed rent received).

If the price of housing goes up, "it's not the same as the price of food or clothing going up," Carliner says. "It's not a higher cost for the homeowner."

Prior to 1983, the Bureau of Labor Statistics used an asset approach to home-ownership cost, including home prices, mortgage interest costs, property insurance and taxes, and maintenance and repair in the shelter component of the CPI, says BLS economist Pat Jackman.

Today's rent components are determined by a single sample survey of rental units, with different weightings assigned for each category.

For example, a rental unit in an owner-dominated area would get a high weight in OER and a low rate in RR. A rental unit in an area dominated by renters gets a high weight in RR and low weight in OER.

RETAINING WALL

Because the booming economy has enabled more renters to become first-time homeowners, the rental components of the CPI may be understating the inflation rate, according to Henry Willmore, chief U.S. economist at Barclays Capital Group.

"Vacancy rates have been on the rise because of the increase in the home-ownership rate," Willmore says.

Vacancy rates have crept up from 7.3 percent in 1993 to 8.1 percent in 1999. At the same time, home-ownership rates, "which were stable for a decade at 64 percent, rose 3 percentage points to 67 percent from 1995 through 1999," Willmore says.

Since the BLS uses rental units as a proxy for the owners' market, and rental demand has softened, the effect has been "to bias OER and housing down," he adds.

Housing costs as expressed in the CPI may be starting to catch up with what folks perceive is going on with housing in the real world. (Jackman says that over a 5- to 10-year period, rents correlate well with home prices. Carliner says rents aren't a good measure of home prices, even over a long period of time.) In the three months ended February, RR and OER rose at a 3.6 and 3.1 percent annualized rate, respectively.

Housing prices, as measured by a repeat-sales index compiled by the Office of Federal Housing Enterprise Oversight, rose 5.9 percent in the fourth quarter compared with the fourth quarter of 1998. This series bottomed in the fourth quarter of 1990 at 0.3 percent.

Fancy that. Right in the middle of the last recession!

As industries go, housing may be strictly Old Economy. In its ability to predict the future, it can hold its own against anything the New Economy has to offer.

Stuck on Hold? That's Inflation, Soviet-Style

———————— Oct. 12, 2000 ————————

EVERY TIME I open my long-distance telephone bill, I'm grateful for deregulation and lower rates. Every time I have to call the telephone company, I wish I had the option to pay higher prices for decent service.

Every consumer has horror stories about the serious shortfall in customer service when only 3.9 percent of the labor force is unemployed. Whether it's the trap of endless phone menus, real people who are as incompetent as the automated voices, problems that go unresolved for months, the lack of any follow-up, the loss of precious time, or the incredible amount of stress, we've all been there.

How do we quantify this phenomenon? Is this the dark side of the productivity miracle that isn't being captured in the data? Is it something else?

Federal Reserve Chairman Alan Greenspan, an early convert to the idea that the U.S. economy was becoming more productive as a result of technological innovations in information technology, probably doesn't have to wait on hold for tech support. Nor does he spend his time getting information and rates for long-distance carriers.

LESS LEISURE

Still, he must know that some of the increase in worker productivity is occurring because the consumer is doing more of the work. Remember when annoying salespeople used to follow you around the store, asking if you needed help? Now they're "sales associates," and they don't ask, don't know, don't care and don't sell.

It's a great deal for companies, which can boast higher productivity—more output per worker hour. For consumers, who do all the work to get the product or service desired, it stinks. Generally they have to "infringe on their leisure time, which reduces their net social welfare," says Bob Barbera, chief economist at Hoenig & Co. in Rye Brook, New York.

If things can't be accomplished during leisure hours, then they will impinge on work time. At some point, either the distraction during working hours or the stress from dealing with it outside work should start to manifest itself.

There's another context in which the increased burden on consumers isn't being measured, and that's in prices.

POOR SERVICE

"The consumer price index adjusts for quality improvements but not for service degradation," says Neal Soss, chief economist at Credit Suisse First Boston. "That's the form inflation is taking in a fully employed economy. Firms don't raise prices to ration users. They just degrade the quality of service."

For example, an airline ticket may cost the same today as it did a year ago, but the consumer gets less space, more delays, and a lower grade of service. Paying the same price for less is the same as paying a higher price for the same thing. In both cases, it's inflation.

The Bureau of Labor Statistics adjusts for quality improvements in goods. For example, when it compares the price of a rental unit at six-month intervals, it subtracts any upgrade in air-conditioning so that it compares apples with apples.

No such adjustment is made for service deterioration. The BLS, which produces the CPI every month, is aware of the shortcoming.

"We acknowledged as much in our response to the Boskin Commission report," says Pat Jackman, an economist at the BLS. "We just don't know how to implement it."

LESS ISN'T MORE

A congressional commission, headed by Stanford University professor Michael Boskin, a former chairman of the president's Council of Economic Advisers, determined that the CPI overstated inflation by 1.1 percentage points. More than half of the overstatement—0.6 percentage point—was due to a failure to make adequate adjustment for changes in the quality of goods and services people buy and to account for the value of newly available goods, the commission found.

A higher price for a computer or car that delivers more computing or horsepower isn't scored as a price increase but as a quality adjustment.

The BLS's adoption of a hedonic model was an attempt to deal with the quality-adjustment issue. These models "try to measure the value consumers place on various characteristics of a good," Jackman says.

With services, which account for 58 percent of the CPI, it's not so easy. In a June 1997 response to the Boskin Commission's final report, the BLS posed the question of service deterioration. Specifically, the BLS mentioned the "reduced convenience and comfort of air travel and deteriorating quality of higher education" as examples of quality decreases that are ignored in the CPI.

SOVIET MODEL

"Whereas the [Boskin] commission notes some service quality improvements, such as the introduction of automatic credit-card readers at gasoline pumps, the BLS often hears complaints about broad-ranging declines in the quality of customer service, which are equally difficult to incorporate in the CPI," the BLS study said.

There doesn't seem to be much research on this subject.

"The only literature on the phenomenon is that which pertains to a centrally planned economy," Soss says.

When the state controls the means of production and distribution, it sets the prices, too. Inflation in the former Soviet Union was zero.

But there were long lines to purchase goods, and the quality and selection were poor.

"As a practical matter, if you have to wait in line to get food, the length of the line is the form inflation takes," Soss says.

After years of dealing with lines, literally and figuratively, a little price inflation wouldn't be bad.

Give a Gift to IRS Along with Your Tax Return

————— April 15, 2004 —————

ASKED LAST MONTH if they would prefer balancing the budget to cutting taxes, Americans by an overwhelming majority expressed a preference for fiscal balance.

Sixty-one percent of 1,001 registered voters nationwide said they were in favor of balancing the budget, and 36 percent preferred lowering taxes, according to an Associated Press–Ipsos poll. (The opinion poll provided no options for supply-siders, who would respond in the affirmative to both: cutting taxes as a means to balancing the budget.)

How many of the folks who say they want to balance the budget actually do something about it?

Americans are charitable by nature, but most of us probably never think about making a second, voluntary contribution to the federal government after we've forked over a considerable chunk of our income on April 15.

The Treasury's Internal Revenue Service and Bureau of the Public Debt make it easy for willing donors to contribute to this worthy cause. Look no further than the IRS's instructions for filing a federal return, or 1040, to find out what to do.

Interested parties can write a check payable to the Bureau of the Public Debt and mail it to Department G, P.O. Box 2188, Parkersburg, WV 26106-2188. Alternatively, you can enclose the check with your income tax return. (Do *not* make the mistake of combining your gift with your tax payment, the IRS warns.)

The gift, considered a charitable contribution, is tax-deductible.

GIVING SEASON

The Bureau of the Public Debt's Web site is less intimidating than the IRS's and keeps a running total of year-to-date contributions. So far in fiscal 2004, which began Oct. 1, the Bureau has received $277,073, compared with $1,277,423.40 for all of fiscal 2003.

The gifts "come in all year round, several a week—small gifts mostly but some in the small four figures," says Pete Hollenbach, a spokesman for the Bureau of the Public Debt. "We get some bequests."

In other words, it's your average Janes and Joes who chip in, not billionaires like George Soros, who rant and rave about the deficit but who don't fork over a penny for the cause.

What if all these folks who want to reduce the deficit by raising taxes on the rich (themselves) put their money where their mouth is? If New Jersey Democratic senator Jon Corzine ponied up $1 for every word he utters on the subject, he could match the $10 million in gifts the IRS has received over the past 20 years.

CAMPAIGN GIMMICK

Massachusetts senator John Kerry, the presumptive Democratic presidential nominee, could be the standard-bearer. Instead of holding another celebrity-studded fundraiser, the Kerry campaign could enlist Hollywood's elite at a charity event. Who would contribute the most to debt reduction? Alec Baldwin? Barbra Streisand? Senator Kerry and his heiress wife?

Kerry could even donate one of his five homes—perhaps the ski house in Idaho or the beach house in Nantucket. The Bureau of Public Debt accepts donations of "real and personal property made only on the condition that the property be sold and the proceeds used to reduce debt held by the public."

There's one caveat. Under the statute that outlines the terms for charitable gifts for debt reduction, "the Secretary [of the Treasury] and the Administrator [of General Services] each may reject a gift under this section when the rejection is in the interest of the government."

Perhaps a large donation from a man who would be president wouldn't be "in the interest of government."

Citizen Soros isn't off the hook.

16

Love Affair

I NTEREST RATES move the economy. But what moves interest rates, at least those rates not set by the central bank?

In a macroeconomic sense, market interest rates are determined by a real rate (the real cost of borrowing) and inflation expectations.

Come down one notch to something less esoteric, and a whole host of variables go into pricing sovereign debt, such as U.S. Treasuries. The value of the nation's currency, the current and expected stance of monetary policy, fiscal policy (including tax rates and the budget deficit or surplus), the stability of the nation's political system and investor psychology all come into play in setting yields on risk-free fixed-income securities. (Corporate bond yields take into account perceived credit risk.)

On a day-to-day basis, you can throw most of these variables out the window. Bonds like nothing better than to find a host organism and form a symbiotic relationship.

Symbiosis, or "living together," refers to a close relationship between two organisms. Symbiotic relationships can be mutually beneficial, parasitic (one benefits at the expense of the other) or commensal (neither benefits and neither is harmed).

The bond market likes to sidle up to another asset class that seems to know where it's going.

In the days following the October 1987 stock market crash, if you asked bond traders why Treasuries were up, invariably they would say "because stocks are down."

Easy enough. A reflex response to another market removes the burden of having to make an independent decision.

In the 18 years that I've been following the bond market as a journalist, bonds have paired up with stocks, the dollar, oil, soybeans, the CRB index, crop reports and weather forecasts.

These couplings can last days, weeks or months. The nature of these on-again/off-again relationships can be loving (prices moving in the same direction) or antagonistic (prices going in opposite directions). And it can change without warning.

The only thing more challenging than finding reliable inter-market relationships is trying to explain them.

It used to be that rising oil prices were a negative for the bond market because of the inflationary implications. Last year, with crude oil prices soaring to $55 a barrel, Federal Reserve policy-makers and private economists decided the damping effect higher crude prices would have on growth outweighed any inflationary consequences. So bond prices rose when oil prices went up.

Bonds and oil aren't destined to be one of the great on- and off-screen romances, like Tracy and Hepburn, Bogart and Bacall, or Gable and Lombard.

But, hey, living together even for a while can be fun.

For Every Rule, There's an Offsetting Exception

——— Sept. 28, 1999 ———

HAVE YOU EVER CONSIDERED...

• Why a strong yen nailed Japan's Nikkei 225 index last week when a weak dollar had the exact same effect on U.S. stocks?

• Why expectations of higher U.K. interest rates are good for sterling while a U.S. Fed-on-the-move has been a negative for the dollar and rock-bottom interest rates are yen-positive?

• Why U.S. bonds rallied last week because of a decline in stock prices, yet stocks and bonds historically have a strong positive correlation?

"It all depends on the circumstances," says Ian Shepherdson, chief U.S. economist at High Frequency Economics in Valhalla, New York. "The only ironclad rule is that supply and demand always works."

Even when there is a presumed rule or paradigm that applies to a particular market in a particular country, it often reverses on a dime. For example, until a few weeks ago, Japanese policy-makers had eased up on their currency comments. At its high in mid-July, the Nikkei was up almost 40 percent from the start of the year, prompting Japan's officialdom to reconsider their verbal yen-bashing and foreign-exchange intervention.

After all, if a strong dollar is in the best interest of the U.S. and a strong dollar has underpinned a five-year stellar run in the U.S. stock market, maybe the Rubin doctrine is applicable to Japan as well?

That premise was good for a short time—until the stock prices of some high-profile Japanese exporters, including Sony Corp. and Toyota Motor Corp., started to sag, pulling the whole market down with them. Japan's tolerance for a strong yen went the way of the Nikkei.

GOOD NEWS, BAD NEWS

So in a very short period of time, a strong yen made a round trip from being bad for the Nikkei to good for the Nikkei to bad for the Nikkei. What does that say about hard-and-fast rules when it comes to markets?

It's an ever-changing cycle, it seems.

Often perceptions matter more than reality. The Japanese economy is hardly out of its misery, even though it has posted two back-to-back quarters of positive growth. Yet international fund managers, long underweighted in Japanese assets, started pouring money into the Japanese stock market this year. The indexes of small-capitalization, over-the-counter stocks are up more than 150 percent year-to-date.

"Once the perceptions about economic recoveries in other countries —Europe, Japan—improved, the prospective returns improved as well," Shepherdson says.

Why, then, has the euro been struggling since its inception on Jan. 1? This is increasingly perplexing since the Euribor futures contracts anticipate a 100-basis-point increase in three-month euro rates in the next year and 175 basis points in the next two.

Made to Be Broken

Aren't higher short-term interest rates supposed to be good for a currency?

They are, unless they're not. The yen has been appreciating against every single currency this year, and it's not because money market instruments offer an attractive return.

The same holds true for the current account. A country's international trade balance, including goods, services and financial transactions, indicates whether the country is a borrower from or lender to the rest of the world. If a country runs a current account deficit and is dependent on capital inflows to finance it, it can be a negative for the currency.

In the case of the U.S., whose current account is pushing $300 billion this year, that amounts to almost $1 billion a day going overseas to pay for goods and services. Those dollars have to be lured back to U.S. shores. The only issue is, at what price?

TBA

Although the current account deficit has deteriorated markedly in the past year—from $52.4 billion in the second quarter of 1998 to $80.7 billion in the second quarter of 1999—the dollar was still appreciating through midyear against a broad basket of currencies. (Even now, the dollar is only weaker year-to-date against a handful of world currencies, including the yen, the Canadian and Australian dollars and the Mexican peso.)

So the current account wasn't an issue, until all of a sudden it was.

Japan runs a current account surplus irrespective of whether the yen is weak or strong. In this case, the chronic surplus is a reflection of protectionist trade practices and closed markets more than anything else.

What's the bottom line? Unfortunately, there isn't one. This is a story without an ending, a fable without a moral, an analysis without a conclusion. It's about debunking myths rather than discovering any hard-and-fast rule of the markets.

✿   ✿   ✿

Can Stocks and Bonds Ever Reconcile?

————— April 16, 2003 —————

STOCKS AND BONDS have been moving in opposite directions for so long now that an entire generation of traders—those whose first experience of a bear market was in 2000—has no idea the two asset classes are former fellow travelers.

The positive correlation between stock prices and bond prices existed pretty much until the mid- to late 1990s. The reason was based on mathematics. Interest rates—usually a long-term interest rate—are used to determine what the future cash flows (dividends) of a company are worth today, otherwise known as their present value. When interest rates go up, a dollar today becomes relatively more valuable than a dollar received tomorrow, so the value of the future cash flows—and what an investor is willing to pay for them—goes down.

The bull market from 1982 to the mid-1990s "can be fully explained by the changes in interest rates and earnings," says Paul McCrae Montgomery, a market analyst who publishes *Universal Economics*. "After 1994, stocks slipped their moorings and rose exponentially unrelated to earnings or interest rates."

After three years of a bear market, much of the out-of-whack pricing in the equity market has been corrected, Montgomery says. The yield on stock earnings is more in line with the yield on Treasuries.

DOMESTIC DIFFERENCES

Specifically, at 3.9 percent the yield on the 10-year Treasury is 1.2 times the 3.2 percent earnings yield (the inverse of the price/earnings ratio) on the Standard & Poor's 500 companies, according to Tim Hayes, chief equity strategist at Ned Davis Research in Nokomis, Florida. That's close to the historical average of 1.4 since 1981.

By this measure, among others, stocks were "showing signs of risk from a valuation point of view when the 10-year Treasury yield exceeded the earnings yield by 1.5 times during 1998," Hayes says.

It got worse before it got better. During the second half of 1999 and early part of 2000, the bond/earnings yield ratio was over 2.

Investors weren't buying stocks for the yield then. And they aren't buying Treasuries for the yield now, either.

"They're buying them because one, bonds aren't stocks, and two, the prices are going up," Montgomery says.

SEPARATION AGREEMENT

Treasuries were and are a safe haven: a place to avoid the punishing losses of the stock market; a place to hide when tales of corporate malfeasance and accounting chicanery dominated the headlines; a place to run when geopolitical uncertainties took their toll on risk assets.

The mathematics of the stock/bond relationship and the psychology driving it are two different things. Mathematically, with earnings yields and bond yields back to a more normal relationship, "it makes sense for stocks and bonds to start moving together," Montgomery says. "Psychologically there is no evidence we have reached that point just yet. Market action is still being driven by a lower brain-stem function."

It's hard to remember the days when bond traders focused on more than the intraday moves in the stock market.

"The flip occurred sometime in 1997 and 1998 when bond traders recognized that the stock market was the most important economic indicator," says Jim Bianco, president of Bianco Research in Chicago. "Higher stock prices begat better economic activity, which was bad for bonds."

MISCOMMUNICATION

This message—that the stock market is the economy—is being reinforced each and every day in Washington, Bianco says.

"The centerpiece of the Bush economic stimulus plan is a cut in the tax on dividends," Bianco says. "It's supposed to get the economy moving again, but it's really about getting the stock market moving again."

I'd challenge his assertion. The elimination of the double taxation of dividends is good policy because it removes a distortion in the tax code. But to listen to some of Washington's sales and marketing, you'd be forgiven for being confused.

Will stocks and bonds ever take up with one another again? They went down hand-in-hand in the '70s and up as one in the '80s.

This should be the sweet spot of the business cycle, when the economy can grow fast without generating inflationary pressure (lots of unutilized resources) and earnings improve. Technically, there is nothing to prevent stocks and bonds from rallying.

REUNITED

Except for the minor point that both asset classes are expensive. According to Ned Davis Research's proprietary models, stocks are expensive on an absolute basis, with a price/earnings ratio of 28 for the S&P 500 Index compared with an historical norm of 15.6 since 1926.

Bonds are expensive based on "external indicators, such as nominal GDP, the CPI, and the budget deficit," NDR's Hayes says.

There's one option left if stocks and bonds are to reassert their positive relationship.

"We think that before this long-term bear market is done, there will be a period when both stocks and bonds go down together," Montgomery says. "Conventional asset allocators will have no place to hide."

Bonds Looking for Love in All the Wrong Places

———————— Sept. 24, 2004 ————————

OVER THE YEARS, bonds have hitched their wagon to various asset classes, forming an obsessive, monogamous relationship for a period of days, weeks or months.

Some of the pairings have been notable, some forgettable.

For the better part of the last century, stocks and bonds were fellow travelers. Their prices rose together or, to put it in terms that explain the relationship, stock prices rose when bond yields/interest rates fell because the discounted future cash flows (dividends) were worth more.

The positive correlation—correlation explains the movement of one variable in terms of the movement of the other without implying causation—broke down around the time of the Asian financial crisis in the fall of 1997. Bonds keyed off stocks in a myopic way, only in reverse: They went up (yields fell) when stock prices fell. Trading desks were left wondering why they'd spent so much money to hire "quants."

Emotional crises are bad for the stocks/bonds relationship. The long-time lovers become antagonists.

"The day after the stock market crash—Oct. 20, 1987—was the biggest up day for bonds in history," based on 3 p.m. closing prices, says Jim Bianco, president of Bianco Research in Chicago.

The Mexican peso crisis in 1995 and the near-collapse of Long-Term Capital Management in 1998, to name just two, caused stocks and bonds to go their separate ways.

FLIRTATIONS

Bonds have had long-term relationships (stocks) and short-term flings (soybeans). They've traded in lockstep with the dollar, commodities in general (the Commodity Research Bureau Index) and specific commodities (gold, oil). They've dallied with old corrugated boxes and freight-car loadings.

During the droughts in the summer of 1983 and 1988, bonds got hooked on beans (soy, not green). Bonds traded down when beans traded up, and up when beans went down. Eventually bonds got tired of their day-to-day love affair with beans; they wanted something they could count on in the future.

They fell in love with crop forecasts, then six- to 10-day weather forecasts, to get an edge on what bean prices would do next week or next season.

The bonds weren't the beans' first love. Soybeans had an on-again/off-again relationship with silver in the 1970s, when everyone was worried about inflation, says Paul McCrae Montgomery, president of Montgomery Capital in Newport News, Virginia, and author of *Universal Economics.*

OLD FLAME

Why the tight correlation between silver and soybeans when all commodities were hot in the inflationary '70s?

"Years later, someone told me that the two trading pits were next to one another," Montgomery says.

So much for the tortured fundamental explanations for the odd coupling.

(The Chicago Board of Trade couldn't confirm the layout of the trading floor in the 1970s.)

Bonds have recently taken up with one of their old flames, oil. But not in the way you'd think. In the old days, bond prices used to slide when oil prices surged because of the inflationary implications.

There is nothing inflationary about higher oil prices per se, to borrow a turn of phrase from Federal Reserve Chairman Alan Greenspan. Whether a relative price change morphs into an increase in the price level (inflation) depends upon what the central bank does. If the monetary authority creates enough money so that consumers don't have to cut back on their purchases of non-oil goods and services, then the price level will rise.

NEW RELATIONSHIP

Bonds and oil are back together again, but they've redefined their relationship for the new century. In the last four months, crude oil prices and 10-year note prices have moved in the same direction more than 80 percent of the time.

News stories infer causation from correlation. I read that Treasuries have been rallying because the jump in energy prices may weaken the economy and persuade the Fed to temper the pace of rate increases.

"Let me see if I can get this straight," Bianco says. "People think the Fed is willing to monetize the rise in oil prices?"

Because the Fed targets an overnight rate, not a stock of money, it passively provides all the reserves the banking system demands at that rate. With the inflation-adjusted federal funds rate still negative, it's hard to imagine why higher oil prices wouldn't filter through to the price level. The betting is clearly that the higher prices will kill the economy first.

CO-DEPENDENCY

So taken are bonds with oil right now, they've forsaken their old relationship with short-term rates. Traders who've been around for 30 years say they can't remember a time when long-term rates started falling before the first increase in the federal funds rate.

The yield on the 10-year Treasury peaked in mid-May and has been falling in earnest since mid-June. The Fed has raised rates three times for a total of 75 basis points since June 30.

Bonds demonstrate all the classic symptoms of co-dependency. They identify themselves in terms of some other asset class.

To observe this relationship is one thing. To explain it is something else.

It's really "a function of psychology more than an intrinsic connection between the fundamentals," Montgomery says. "Investment behavior is just a subcomponent of human behavior."

And we all know how many marriages end up in divorce.

17

Bumbling Bureaucrats

F OR AN INSTITUTION that outlived its purpose when foreign-
exchange rates were allowed to float in the early 1970s, the
International Monetary Fund sure was busy in the 1990s.

The IMF orchestrated bailouts for Mexico, South Korea, Thailand,
Indonesia, Brazil and Russia, to name just the high-profile clients that
won rescue packages when foreign capital took flight and central banks
depleted their foreign-exchange reserves trying to support currencies
that were tied to the U.S. dollar.

That these crises occurred at a time when the fund was beefing up its
"surveillance" suggests the early warning system was badly flawed.

The IMF has the unusual distinction of being a target of criticism
from the left and the right. The left accuses the fund of bailing out rich
lenders—those who made risky loans to developing countries—at the
expense of poor taxpayers. The right says the IMF imposes the wrong
medicine—currency devaluation, tax increases and spending cuts—
on developing countries, increasing the pain rather than alleviating it.
It also claims IMF bailouts encourage bad behavior—risky loans on the
part of lenders, bad policies on the part of countries—a phenomenon
known as "moral hazard."

Countries that can't finance their large current account and budget deficits have to make changes, with or without the IMF's assistance. Economists still debate whether IMF intervention, which buys
countries some time, encourages or discourages needed structural
reforms.

Some countries have been receiving IMF loans for three or four decades. A longtime IMF client, Argentina, defaulted on its debt in 2001, creating a crisis for both Argentina and the fund. (The fund can't lend to countries in arrears, and only three-quarters of bondholders have agreed to accept 30 cents on the dollar for Argentina's defaulted debt.) Is there any better argument for reevaluating the IMF's role and instituting some performance standards for financial assistance, be it loans or grants?

While it became popular during the 1997 Asian financial crisis to talk about "contagion effect," healthy countries don't contract the capital-flight disease from sick ones. Countries with large current account and budget deficits are predisposed to developing the condition on their own—which would seem to put the U.S. at high risk.

Central bankers have a more clearly defined role, and a better success rate, than the international lending agencies. While they may stray outside their field of operations—warning governments about bloated budget deficits, cautioning regulators against overzealousness—they do one thing, which is manage aggregate demand in the domestic economy.

That doesn't mean they always do it well. Sometimes central bankers ignore the lessons of history.

If the Bank of Japan had learned anything from the U.S. experience during the Great Depression, it might have avoided some of its policy mistakes of the 1990s, along with the economic hardship those actions produced.

With the benefit of hindsight, the Great Depression was compounded, if not caused, by a series of policy blunders: from the implementation of protective tariffs to tax hikes to an increase in banks' reserve requirements to an increase in interest rates to defend the dollar from speculative attack to a contraction in the money supply.

BOJ officials either missed that chapter in the history books or didn't see the relevance. Like policy-makers in the U.S. six decades earlier, Japan's central bankers saw low interest rates and concluded policy was easy. They failed to appreciate the effect a strapped banking system can have on an economy, even with deposit insurance. (For a long time, they failed to acknowledge the bad-loan problem, which made it impossible to address.)

Consumer prices fell continuously in Japan for almost six years from 1998 to 2004. Yet the BOJ was worried about ... *in*flation, or a rising price level.

Inflation would have been the least of its worries. For a central bank, it's not the hardest problem to fix.

Were Treasury and the IMF Really Dancing in the Dark?

——————— Sept. 22, 1999 ———————

THE CONGRESS of the United States has embarked on a series of hearings to determine who lost Russia. Or who got taken by Russia.

Allegations of Russian corruption, capital flight and money laundering through U.S. financial institutions—including a possible diversion of funds from the International Monetary Fund—produced a predictable response in Washington. U.S. officials were "shocked, shocked" to learn that all was not aboveboard in Russia.

The current hearings by the House Banking Committee, which will spawn a proliferation of others in coming months, aren't likely to produce a smoking gun.

"We've known about corruption in Russia for years," says Ian Vasquez, director of the Washington-based Cato Institute's Project on Economic Liberty. "The only reason the Treasury and IMF are looking at it now is because the authorities are looking at charges of money laundering."

The Treasury and IMF have little vested interest in getting to the bottom of the Russian scandal. All along, they chose to look the other way.

"Either they didn't know what was going on, in which case they are incompetent, or they did know, in which case they are negligent," says Janine Wedel, associate professor at the Graduate School of Public and International Affairs at the University of Pittsburgh, and the author of *Collision and Collusion: The Strange Case of Western Aid to Eastern Europe 1989–1998.*

According to Wedel, Russian press reports documenting the corruption are translated into English and readily available in the U.S. in publications such as *Johnson's Russia List.*

Press Pussyfooting

Until last month, when the *New York Times Magazine* penned a cover story titled "Who Lost Russia?" talking about high-level corruption in Russia in the same breath as U.S. institutions was off-limits to the mainstream media, Wedel says.

After the Bank of New York probe into money laundering became public in August, Treasury officials suddenly became fully cognizant of the problems associated with converting a huge command economy into a democratic, market economy when no rule of law, or institutions to enforce the law, existed.

In congressional testimony yesterday, Treasury secretary Larry Summers defended the U.S. policy of supporting conditional financial aid to Russia by international lending agencies and outlined a series of safeguards, including regular internal audits of the Russian Central Bank.

But there was no acknowledgment of the flawed design of the policies intended to help Russia.

"It was political aid under the guise of economic aid," Wedel says. "All the economic aid was channeled through the 'Chubais Clan,'" a small group of reformers led by longtime Boris Yeltsin aide Anatoly B. Chubais, the chief architect of Russia's economic reforms.

Architectural Accident

Thanks to the seal of approval from the Harvard Institute for International Development, a group of über-advisers on Russian reform, large sums of Western aid were concentrated in a few hands.

Any time there was a threat of a disruption in Western aid to Russia, the boys at Treasury went into action. Former Treasury secretary Robert Rubin and his then deputy Larry Summers bullied Congress into ponying up an additional $18 billion of funding for the IMF last year, threatening everything except the demise of Western civilization if Congress failed to approve the request.

In fact, the second mantra of Rubin states that the additional IMF funding would "not cost the taxpayer a dime." If that's so, why is Congress so intent on investigating an issue that is under the aegis of the Justice Department? Whose money is it anyway, Bob?

As for the IMF, the less everyone knows about it the better. The fund would be out of business right now if it confined its activities to what it was created to do, which is make short-term loans to countries experiencing temporary balance-of-payments outflows.

Tyrannosaurus Tendencies

In a world of floating exchange rates, the IMF is redundant, but instead of dying a quiet death, the fund reinvented itself in the image of a global lending agency, making loans to developing countries (the designated role of its sister organization, the World Bank); a macroeconomic adviser and conditional lender to countries in distress; and an unofficial watchdog of the global financial system.

Recently, the IMF assumed the role of the International Red Cross in providing disaster relief to Turkey in the wake of an earthquake last month.

The fund even provides macroeconomic forecasts, which is interesting since it didn't see the Asian crisis coming despite its enhanced surveillance facilities. Today, for instance, in its *World Economic Outlook,* the IMF commended the Bank of England for its "skillful management of monetary policy" while warning that the U.S. Federal Reserve may have to raise interest rates again to forestall inflationary pressures.

Just be glad U.S. monetary policy is in the hands of Alan Greenspan, not Michel Camdessus.

Don't Ask, Don't Tell

While the fund won't make the next payment on Russia's $4.5 billion loan until the conclusions of the congressional hearings on Russian money laundering, the notion that the IMF approved a new loan in July—even one to repay a previous IMF loan—is astonishing. At yesterday's House Banking Committee hearing, Summers testified that senior Treasury officials learned of the probe into Russian money laundering by the Bank of New York in April.

What, then, was the IMF thinking when it signed off on another $4.5 billion in July? It was insuring a continuation of its gilt-edged status as a lending agency. After all, why allow a debtor to default if you can roll over a loan and, in the process, justify your existence?

At this point, self-propagation seems to be the IMF's main goal. As for accountability, there is none.

"The IMF followed its own procedures" with the loans to Russia, Cato's Vasquez says. "The IMF does not know what happens to the money once it leaves Washington."

Don't ask, don't tell.

So Many IMF Critics, So Much Inertia on Reform
——————— April 17, 2000 ———————

ALMOST EVERYONE has a bone to pick with the International Monetary Fund and World Bank, the mothers of all international financial institutions.

They lend too much or they don't lend enough; they extend credit indiscriminately or they lend for the wrong reasons; they promote global capitalism or they support corrupt governments.

Clearly, the proper role for these institutions is a source of disagreement both inside the IMF and World Bank headquarters and outside in the streets, where protestors tried to disrupt the annual spring meetings over the past few days.

Congressional discontent with the IMF blossomed after Russia took the IMF's money and ran in 1998.

"It's surprising that an institution that has been around for a half-century does not have accounting procedures to monitor those funds," said Jim Saxton, a Republican congressman from New Jersey, at a hearing on IMF reform last week.

As a precondition for approving the Clinton administration's request for an additional $18 billion in U.S. funding for the IMF in November 1998, Congress established a bipartisan commission to recommend reforms of international financial institutions.

RX FOR REFORM

The International Financial Institutions Advisory Commission (IFIAC), chaired by Carnegie Mellon University economics professor Allan Meltzer, delivered its final report on schedule in March. The majority report, which was signed by eight of the 11 members, was premised on eliminating overlaps between the IMF and World Bank.

The commission recommended the IMF restrict itself to short-term emergency liquidity lending. It said the World Bank should replace its traditional system of subsidized loans with grants for infrastructure and social service projects, to be made to truly poor countries that have no access to capital markets.

The IFIAC also favored forgiving the debts of highly indebted poor countries.

Democrats, many of whom didn't bother to read the report, blasted the recommendations as partisan even though there was broad agreement between the commission's suggestions and reform measures proposed by Treasury Secretary Larry Summers late last year.

Summers's proposal for IMF reform, outlined in a speech to the London Business School on Dec. 14, called for longer-term IMF lending to be "phased out." The fund "should not be a source of low-cost financing for countries with ready access to private capital, or long-term welfare for countries that cannot break the habit of bad policies," he said.

IMF REINVENTED

Few would quibble with this prescription for reform, especially since the IMF has outlived the purpose for which it was founded. The IMF was created after World War II to provide short-term loans to countries experiencing temporary capital outflows. When foreign-exchange rates were allowed to float in the early 1970s, and imbalances resolved themselves through currency fluctuations rather than gold transfers, the need for the IMF was greatly reduced.

Instead, it got into long-term structural lending, a function previously reserved for the World Bank, and reinvented itself as a kind of global economic watchdog and über-adviser to wayward countries.

Saxton, vice chairman of the Joint Economic Committee of Congress, introduced an IMF reform bill (H.R. 3750) that would mandate increased IMF transparency and require the fund to lend at market interest rates (currently the rates are subsidized) for less than one year and only in the case of a crisis.

Sounds like as close to unanimity of opinion as you can get among Treasury, Congress and an independent advisory panel. Why, then, were the reform proposals that emerged from the weekend meeting of the Group of Seven industrialized countries buried among more of the same?

The G-7 communiqué devoted an entire annex to IMF reform. While the kernels of reform are discernible—the decision to release its operational budget on a quarterly basis was hardly an IMF initiative—they are presented as addenda to its existing functions, not as a new, limited role.

SLIM FAST?

The G-7 said conditional lending—loans in exchange for reforms— was still "an important tool" of the IMF, as was developmental lending to alleviate poverty. The IMF was widely criticized—most recently and publicly by former World Bank chief economist Joseph Stiglitz in the *New Republic*—for imposing harsh macroeconomic measures on Asian countries in 1997 and deepening the crisis.

Buried in point six of the annex was something about creating a "streamlined structure for IMF lending" that would provide "clear incentives" to implement crisis-prevention policies, address "short-run balance of payment imbalances," and allow the IMF to respond quickly.

Streamlining is probably not high on the IMF's priority list. No bureaucracy wants to slim down and sacrifice position and power.

"If the IMF were to adopt either the Meltzer Commission's or Saxton's proposals, they would have very little to do most of the time," says a congressional staffer, who requested anonymity. "It is not in the IMF's bureaucratic self-interest to streamline itself."

U.S. Is IMF

The U.S. is such a key player in the fund, contributing 18 percent of the capital and 26 percent of the usable funds, it's hard to imagine that it can't force the IMF to shed some of its excess weight. Unless, of course, the IMF serves as a slush fund for Treasury.

The Clinton administration, even more than its predecessors, "has used the international financial institutions as sources of readily available funds to support its foreign policy," Meltzer said in his JEC testimony last week. "If it could not make heavily subsidized long-term loans through these institutions to Russia, China, Mexico, Brazil and other countries whose policies the U.S. wishes to influence, the administration would have to change policy or ask Congress to appropriate the funds."

Saxton questioned the witnesses, all commission members, about Treasury's role in the IMF.

"If the U.S. wanted to shorten the term of IMF loans, reduce the subsidy and open the doors, is it doable?" Saxton asked.

"Not an agreement is made without the accord of the U.S. Treasury," said Adam Lerrick, senior adviser to the chairman of the IFIAC. "Treasury has veto power."

"Do you think this will happen?" asked Saxton, referring to the reinventing of the IMF as a short-term-only, emergency lending facility.

"I light a candle," Meltzer replied.

The BOJ Consults the
Fed's Guide to the Great Depression

——————— July 12, 2000 ———————

IF THE RISING decibel level of the voices is any guide, the Bank of Japan is preparing to engineer a small increase in interest rates at its policy meeting next Monday.

What's the rush? To be sure, some of the economic data have been looking up. The Japanese economy expanded at an annualized 10 percent rate in the first quarter after a two-quarter contraction; surely no one believes that double-digit growth is an emerging trend.

The closely watched Tankan survey, a quarterly poll of business sentiment released last week, showed improved business conditions among large manufacturers in the second quarter. In fact, the index registered its first positive reading, of +3, in almost three years.

Still, anyone who believes that stabilization in the financial system is a necessary condition for issuing Japan a clean bill of health will be unconvinced that the time is right for an end to its near-zero interest-rate policy.

Judging by its vital signs, Japan's banking system is nowhere near functional. Bank lending has been contracting on a year-over-year basis for almost four years. Growth in Japan's broad money supply, M2 + CDs, has decelerated dramatically in the past year, from a year-over-year 4.3 percent increase last June to 1.9 percent now. These are not the signs of a financial system that can support an economic expansion.

HISTORY REPEATS ITSELF

If we learned anything from the Great Depression in the U.S. in the 1930s and the savings and loan crisis in the late 1980s and early 1990s, it's that when your banking system isn't functioning, your economy is down for the count.

Bank of Japan governor Masaru Hayami had set two preconditions for abandoning its zero-interest-rate policy. One was signs of a self-sustaining economic recovery, which, if one quarter suffices as an adequate observation, satisfies his terms. In the first quarter of 2000, the contribution to GDP growth came entirely from the private sector.

The second precondition was an end to deflation. Where's the evidence of that? Japan's consumer price index fell 0.7 percent in May from a year earlier. In only a handful of months in the last 13 years—all of them within the last six months—has deflation been worse. (The fact that wholesale prices are falling at a slower pace than they were last year seems to be the source of the contention that deflation is ending.)

Like the Federal Reserve in the 1930s, the BOJ is worried about phantom inflation when it should be focusing on ending the deflation.

FED'S FOUL-UP

Following the Great Depression in the U.S., banks were holding huge amounts of excess reserves in an effort to assuage depositors' concerns and forestall any more runs against the banks. The Fed viewed the war chest of excess reserves as potentially inflationary; that is, the reserves were the raw material for lending and spending.

So the Fed raised statutory reserve requirements. Guess what the banks did? They went out and rebuilt their excess reserves, in the process causing a contraction in the money supply and a recession in 1937–1938.

Japanese policy-makers already nipped one recovery—in 1997—in the bud by raising the value-added tax. Are they really dumb enough to do it again?

The reasons the BOJ is purportedly so antsy to raise rates, if only by a pinch, are to force companies to restructure and to create some breathing room in case there's a need to lower rates in the future.

Huh? Let's start with the first notion. The idea that keeping interest rates at zero is promoting lending to losing operations, if I understand it correctly, is preposterous.

"The stupidity of that idea is that it sounds as if lenders don't care if they get repaid their principal," says Bob Laurent, professor of economics and finance at the Illinois Institute of Technology's Stuart School of Business.

MORE IS BETTER

If higher interest rates are the means toward restructuring, why raise the overnight rate to 0.25 percent? Why not push it up to 5 percent and get some m-a-j-o-r restructuring?

The central bank's role is macroeconomic, not microeconomic, management. It's not supposed to direct money to certain institutions and businesses and away from others, which is something Japan's policy-makers have yet to grasp.

The second reason for raising interest rates—to give the BOJ room to lower them—is even dumber, although the logic behind it was evident in the U.S. in the early 1990s as well. Between 1989 and 1992, the Fed lowered the overnight federal funds rate by almost 700 basis points to 3 percent, where it sat without spurring much sign of life in the economy. With each notch down, economists advised against further cuts on the grounds that the Fed needed "to keep its powder dry."

In other words, if and when things got really bad, the Fed would need several rounds of ammunition in its holster.

Do Some Good

Unfortunately, monetary policy is not like fine wine. It doesn't age in the bottle. It needs to be uncorked to have any effect.

If the BOJ thinks things may get worse, necessitating a rate cut, why raise rates now? In fact, the BOJ should be pumping more reserves into the banking system by buying all those Japanese government bonds the Ministry of Finance is issuing to finance massive fiscal spending.

This is another area where the BOJ doesn't get it.

Finally, policy-makers like to fall back on the argument that an increase in the overnight call money rate to an expected 0.25 percent from 0.02 percent won't do any harm.

Instead, why not do something that has a chance of doing some good?

18

The 2004 Election

WITH ARMIES of lawyers from both parties mobilized, Americans went to the polls on Nov. 3, 2004, uncertain whether their votes or judicial action would determine the next president of the United States.

The period of early voting leading up to Election Day was characterized by Democratic accusations of voter intimidation and Republican charges of voter fraud. Those who were neither intimidated nor committing fraud were more concerned about the potential for a nasty post-election legal battle than about the defeat of their chosen candidate.

In the end, President George W. Bush was reelected with 51 percent of the popular vote to John Kerry's 48 percent. The Electoral College tally was 286–252. The GOP picked up seats in both houses of Congress. There were no court challenges.

It was a decisive victory in a closely contested election.

Now comes the hard part. Bush has set himself an ambitious second-term domestic agenda, in addition to prosecuting the war in Iraq. He wants to reform the tax code and put Social Security on sound footing by allowing workers to divert part of their Social Security taxes into private retirement accounts.

It's a tall order for any president. Bush's predecessors were afraid to touch the "third rail" of politics, convinced it would mean certain death. And real tax reform, with a couple of exceptions (the Tax Reform Act of 1986, for example), remains elusive.

There are so many entrenched special interests benefiting from loopholes in the tax code that the stiffest opposition to reform is apt to come from big business, not ordinary working folks.

Freed from the burden of facing the electorate again, Bush has an opportunity to focus on good policy at the expense of good politics. The president could do a lot worse than leaving as his legacy a simple, fair tax system and a retirement system that's as secure as its name implies.

Hard Choices for Election Day and the Elected

Nov. 2, 2004

THE FINAL campaign ads have been aired, the final opinion polls have been conducted, the final campaign rallies are under way.

All that's left is for Americans to go to the polls today and hope that they, not the lawyers, get to decide the next president of the United States.

Amid all the mudslinging of this highly charged, negative campaign, one thing stands out: We don't have great choices.

And I don't just mean the two candidates.

Whoever is elected, be it incumbent president George W. Bush or Democratic challenger John Kerry, the next president will have to make some unpopular decisions.

On the domestic front, the federal budget deficit will require more than a laissez-faire approach. Both candidates promise to cut the budget deficit in half. Each side accuses the other of fuzzy math—and in this case, both are correct.

In the fiscal year that ended Sept. 30, the federal deficit reached a record $413 billion, or 3.6 percent of gross domestic product. As a share of GDP, the 2004 deficit was below the high of 6 percent in 1983.

Aside from promises of fiscal responsibility, sacrifice and hardship are nowhere to be found in this presidential campaign. On the campaign stump, it's pretty much a question of what your country can do for you or give to you, not what you can do for your country. Wednesday morning is time enough for that.

Big Spender

In his four years in office, Bush has distinguished himself as a big-government conservative, presiding over the largest increase in government spending since Lyndon Baines Johnson's Great Society in the 1960s. For more than half his term, the GOP controlled both houses of Congress, so blaming spendthrift legislators isn't an option. Bush's veto pen has yet to be uncapped.

Increased spending on homeland security following the Sept. 11, 2001, terrorist attacks accounted for only part of the explosion in government spending.

"Between fiscal 2001 and fiscal 2005, the administration expects total outlays to rise by 31 percent," says Veronique de Rugy, a research fellow at the American Enterprise Institute, a conservative think tank in Washington. "Clearly no trade-offs are being made in the budget as evidenced by the 42 percent increase in non-defense discretionary spending in the same four years."

Not Credible

Bush proposes to deflate the rise in government spending by holding the increase in discretionary spending outside of defense and homeland security to 1 percent.

Spending in those two categories "amounts to less than $350 billion in a $2.4 trillion budget," de Rugy says.

Holding the growth of 15 percent of the budget to 1 percent is not going to rein in total spending growth. And the real problem going forward isn't discretionary spending, or those expenditures subject to annual congressional appropriations. The big problem is mandatory spending for Social Security and Medicare.

In the next decade, as the baby boomers start to retire, the costs of the two programs will consume an ever-larger share of GDP and command a growing portion of federal revenue. According to the 2004 annual report of the trustees of the Social Security and Medicare trust funds, the annual cost of the two programs will more than double to 15 percent of GDP by 2040 and rise to 20 percent in 2078, "at which time it would exceed total federal revenues at their historic share of 19 percent of GDP."

Privatization vs Avoidance

Bush has proposed letting workers invest a small portion of their Social Security taxes in private accounts, which will compound over their working lives. He has not talked about how he would finance the transition to a partially private system, estimated at a cost of $1 trillion to $2 trillion.

Kerry has accused Bush of scheming to cut Social Security benefits. His contribution to the debate has been to propose nothing to ensure the solvency of the system.

When it comes to discretionary spending, it's hard to find much fiscal restraint in Kerry's agenda other than the verbal promises. Kerry will make permanent the middle-class tax cuts, including a larger child tax credit, a reduction in the marriage penalty and lower marginal tax rates. He will provide tax credits for health care, child care and education. He will have the government subsidize health care. And he will pay for all this by closing corporate loopholes and raising taxes on the wealthiest households.

Bush may not be credible on spending, de Rugy says. "But Kerry is worse. No matter what area he mentions—the war in Iraq, homeland security, education—Kerry always says that whatever Bush is spending, it's not enough."

REPARATIONS

The war in Iraq will put a huge drain on the U.S. Treasury in the next four years. It's not clear why European countries such as France and Germany would cough up any money to clean up a mess they didn't make in a war they didn't support.

France and Germany have said they will not send troops to Iraq, even if the internationalist Kerry is elected.

After the election, the U.S. is going to have to shift gears in Iraq: either clean it out or get out. The current conduct is unbecoming.

That holds true for President Bush or President-elect Kerry.

Postmortem: Kerry Could Have Been Somebody

Nov. 3, 2004

THE 2004 presidential election was always John Kerry's to lose.

And lose he did, by a margin of 3.5 million votes.

Incumbent president George W. Bush won a 51 percent majority to Kerry's 48 percent. Bush amassed more than the 270 Electoral College votes needed for victory.

So what went wrong? The Democratic senator from Massachusetts was running against an unpopular president conducting an unpopular war in Iraq that's not going swimmingly.

The U.S. economy has failed to create enough jobs, even in the face of solid growth, to convince the voters that the country is headed in the right direction, according to various opinion polls.

The stock market posted no gains this year through Election Day.

Front-page stories revealed the Bush administration's suppression of intelligence that cast doubt on Iraq's possession of weapons of mass destruction. Last week's jihad accused the Bush administration of letting a cache of explosives disappear from a munitions storage facility after the U.S. invaded Iraq in March 2003.

Yet Kerry managed to lose the election. While the pundits from both parties will be writing the postmortems for the 2004 presidential election for days and weeks, herewith are my seven contenders for why the Massachusetts senator lost:

1. Anybody-but-Bush had to be somebody as well.

The vitriol directed at President Bush made it seem as if any Democratic candidate, short of being a complete boob, could walk away with the election.

That turned out not to be the case. The anybody had to be somebody. It's not enough to be not-somebody-else.

John Kerry never defined himself except as an antidote to President Bush. "A fresh start" is better suited for a deodorant commercial than for a campaign slogan.

Other than posing as the anti-Bush and dwelling on how bad things are in the country, Kerry failed to present a vision for America that was more compelling than the status quo.

The U.S. is a young country. Except for a short tour of duty under King George III of Britain, all we've known is freedom and democracy. While the Republicans are notoriously bad at selling big ideas, the Democrats proved to be no better at the vision thing.

2. George Bush is not the British pound.

Billionaire investor George Soros thought he could run Bush out of the White House in the same way he pushed sterling out of the Exchange Rate Mechanism in 1992.

He was wrong.

Soros, chairman of Soros Fund Management LLC, spent $26.5 million to defeat Bush, more than any other single donor or political action committee.

"I'm really proud of what I have done," Soros said on Oct. 28 at the National Press Club in Washington.

His investors wouldn't be happy with that kind of return.

In 1992, Soros bet $10 billion that the British government would not be able to defend the trading band for sterling and would be forced to let it fall.

He was right. He made $1 billion, or a 10 percent return on his investment.

All he has to show for his bet on Kerry is a goose egg. Democratic minister-without-portfolio Soros will have to wait four more years to be a player again.

3. The European press can stay home.

Most newspapers in Europe endorsed John Kerry. That's probably the biggest kiss of death for a candidate next to a blessing from Al Gore.

I can't recall the editorial pages of the U.S. press coming out in support of a candidate for chancellor of Germany or president of France.

Europe has yet to find something better than its stagnant-growth model. My advice to the Euro press: Devote your efforts to encouraging and endorsing leaders who bring new ideas to Old Europe and let us worry about our own.

4. Buying the Senate isn't as easy as buying a Senate seat.

New Jersey Democratic senator Jon Corzine spent an estimated $60 million of his own fortune to buy himself a Senate seat in 2000. As head of the Democratic Senate Campaign Committee this year, Corzine was reportedly a whiz at raising money. Unfortunately, he led his party to defeat.

The GOP increased its Senate majority to 55 seats from 51. The Democrats have 45 seats, down from 49. (Jim Jeffords of Vermont is an independent.)

The biggest blot on Corzine's record was the defeat of Senate minority leader Tom Daschle, who lost to John Thune. It may have been only one seat in sparsely populated South Dakota, but it was a big symbolic victory for the GOP.

5. Let them pitch Botox.

Hollywood and the music world came out in force for John Kerry. Bruce and John (Springsteen and Kerry) shared the stage at some high-visibility events over the past week, two millionaires united in their struggle for the little guy.

I could never understand why anyone would care what the folks in La-La Land think about anything except the best Beverly Hills plastic surgeon.

I finally found an opinion poll (not in this election cycle) that validated my suspicions: Americans don't pay any attention to what the beautiful people think about substantive issues. That never stopped them from trying.

6. Even the Clinton team needs good raw material.

In an attempt to breathe some life into his campaign, Kerry hired Clinton wunderkinds James Carville and Paul Begala. Kerry is no Clinton. Clinton's appearances at the Democratic National Convention in July and with Kerry in the last week drove that point home.

The best strategists can't spin straw into gold.

Kerry's loss means Hillary doesn't have to wait until 2012 for her presidential bid. Carville and Begala have four years to figure out how to turn some of the red states blue, which is a tough assignment with the deep-blue Hillary.

7. Cave dwellers don't influence the U.S. electorate.

Osama bin Laden came out of his cave last week for a pre-election video performance. Everybody said Sheik Osama looked mah-vel-ous in his gold robe, what with the color restored to his cheeks.

The chattering classes said it would help Bush (a reminder of the terrorism threat) or it would help Kerry (a reminder that the al-Qaeda leader is still at large).

The lectern is a great look for academics. It's less effective for terrorists, whose punch lies in deeds, not words.

Osama failed to stage any terrorist attacks at the Summer Olympics in Greece. He was MIA at the Democratic and Republican national conventions in Boston and New York, respectively. And his experiment at influencing elections has been limited to Spain so far.

It sure seems like "Osama's bin losin'," writes Claudia Rosett in her "Real World" column for the *Wall Street Journal's* OpinionJournal.com.

19

Readers Write Back at You

I N THE ELECTRONIC AGE, readers aren't shy about letting you know what they think about your work, your ideas and, for that matter, you as a person. We live in a no-holds-barred, let-'er-rip, ready-shoot-aim world.

"You are an idiot," a reader wrote me in response to nothing in particular.

"Thank you for your response," I replied. "Please feel free to express your views in a letter to the editor. Don't forget to include your full name and affiliation."

That usually shuts them up.

I've learned a few things over the years about people who fire off personal attacks. One, they never expect to hear back from you. Two, they're taken aback if they do, which often elicits an apology for their rude behavior. And three, even if they do apologize, it's still not worth engaging because they aren't really interested in an exchange of ideas.

I've also learned to be wary of e-mail correspondents whose user names aren't their real names. Readers who go by "metallica," "abraxas" or "freaklemon" probably are up to no good.

Among more serious readers, some have trouble differentiating between news and opinion, which is odd since every Bloomberg News column features a triple disclaimer at the top:

"Commentary. Caroline Baum is a columnist for Bloomberg News. The opinions expressed are her own."

Commentary, columnist, opinions: Which part don't they understand?

Then there are readers who acknowledge my prerogative to express an opinion yet warn me against exercising it.

> *A game that is played with 100% accuracy: Pick the author of an article by just looking at the title. One can never fail to guess right on yours. They are always dripping with a heavy bias of personal opinion which you are in a perfect position to express. But be aware that not everybody shares your views and that your one-sided approach is offensive to some.*

I get plenty of adoring fan mail as well.

> *I read every one of your columns but I don't want to become an email stalker, so I write to you when your topics make me want to reach into my computer and just hug you.*

Flattery is generally the best approach. It grabs my attention and ensures a warm response.

> *Ms. Baum,*
> *Many years ago I had a job that came with a Telerate on my desk. Someone with your same name published morning and evening commentary about the motive forces propelling the bond market that day. I learned many things from that column that I credit for my failure to blow up my company or to get fired for mishedged losses. From your picture, you appear far too young to be the same person, but nevertheless, don't ever leave me again. I was very pleased a year or so ago to find your columns on Bloomberg. You eloquently and concisely express exactly the sort of fact-based uncommon sense that is absent from nearly all the rest of the media. Today's [Feb. 4] column is another example of the truth that we'll never hear on the evening news.*

Then there are notes that I read, reread and savor, the ones that make it all worthwhile.

> *Dear Ms. Baum,*
> *I have a Ph.D. in economics (1970), but have been a trader for the past thirty-one years. I am also an avid reader of your columns. I mention these two facts to lend credence to the following opinion. In my*

opinion, you write the best commentary on the economy available on an ongoing basis. Others may write better articles now and then, but not on a steady, consistent basis. The reason, I think, is pretty simple. Aside from the fact that you have the ability to write well, you understand the basic principles by which the economy works and, equally important, do not fall for the latest fad in commentary or analysis.

Getting back to the hate mail, readers who disagree with your views tend to fall into three basic categories. Those who call you names and leave it at that. Those who drop names to support their view and prove you are wrong. And those who are impressed by names, such as the schools you went to, the degrees you earned, and the jobs you've held.

Ridiculous column. Maybe you could share with us your credentials for such insight on economic policymaking? The degree from Tufts, the economics powerhouse, is in what? You have made how much money positioning yourself in the bond and equity markets?

The writer, a woman from Citigroup, was responding to a column on the symbolism of Bob Rubin, chairman of the executive committee at Citigroup, Inc., sitting next to Teresa Heinz Kerry at the Democratic National Convention in July 2004. (See chapter 7, "Rubin's Choice Seat Is a Reminder and an Omen.")

Usually people have to be challenged personally before they get so defensive. Traders are quick to put you in your place should you dare to contradict them. "You're just a journalist *writing* about the markets; I'm a *player* in the markets."

Sometimes, criticizing popular public figures (politicians, business leaders) is enough to get you into trouble.

Caroline,

I wish you would not have done it. I was hoping we could be friends forever. But you just cannot attack Robert Rubin. It's blasphemy. The guy is god. And most people know that.

Most people, that is, except for me.

[Paul] Krugman is a nationally respected economist, and his views are shared by such luminaries as Bill Gross and the IMF, for starters.

Multiple name-dropping is the equivalent of calling you dumber after they've already called you dumb.

Then there are the readers who clearly hate whatever you write but can't seem to give up the habit.

> *I have been reading your commentary for some time now; from your ridiculous historical accounts of Thanksgiving (who wrote your high school history textbook?) to your often awkward, and always misguided economic analysis. After your commentary today, I can't resist a reply. I am shocked and appalled that you would even attempt an argument based on "common sense" or even historical fact patterns. Didn't your Econ 101 professor teach you that historical results are a poor predictor of economic trends.*

This was in response to a column arguing that higher marginal tax rates don't necessarily produce more revenue for the federal government. The historical fact that appalled this reader was the observation that the federal government's tax receipts have been fairly constant at 18 percent of GDP over the last half-century even as the top marginal tax rate ranged from 91 percent to 28 percent.

I've been called a left-wing limousine liberal and right-wing extremist—in response to the same column! Readers occasionally complain to Bloomberg News Editor in Chief Matt Winkler when they find my response inappropriate. Once a reader copied Mike Bloomberg, founder of Bloomberg L.P. and mayor of New York City, on his note to me, apparently hoping to escalate his complaint to someone who could really put me in my place.

Nothing brings readers out in force as much as columns on conspiracy theories. Some of the responses are so off the wall, I find myself looking over my shoulder on the way home from work.

Sometimes it's tough to differentiate the truly wacko from the simply sarcastic in e-mail correspondence. Here are three excerpts from e-mails I received in response to a column on conspiracy theories (see chapter 14, "Black Helicopter Theories Whir Through Markets.")

Ms. Baum,

> *Yes, Caroline, there are black helicopters and the day of pecuniary recompense for the filthy idolaters of usury is at hand. Right now, even as I type, the reptilian mercenaries from Cygnet 61 and Zeta Reticuli*

are emerging from their underground base camps to lay siege to the money houses of Wall Street ... Pay close attention, should you share a meal with one of these money captains, the quick almost lizard-like movements of their tongues as they feast. Soon, you'll start to notice iguana-like chalky stool droppings in banks and financial offices all over Wall Street. That is the sign it's time to get out of town and head for the nearest subterranean shelter in any rural area outside of a 50-mile radius of the city. You have till August to get a clue and get to a safe haven. Just consider yourself one of the lucky ones.

☼

Give me a break Ms. Baum. You're poking fun at what is allowed by the US code. The central bank/welfare state cabal will do ANYTHING to ensure the survival of their power. Why is it I get the feeling that if you were critical of perceived manipulation, your editor would get a call and your column would be shutdown?

☼

The sad truth be told ... politicians, government, Wall Street, "expert" analysts, attorneys all have conspired to strip the hard-earned capital away from the only income producing people in this country ... YOUR READERS !! For you to write such an unknowledgeable and biased article based on all your "expert" research is ridiculous. Perhaps you and your "expert" analyst pals had a "STRONG BUY" on Enron in 2001? Or were you old enough to have heard of Enron? Truth be told all us hard-working, taxpaying citizens of the USA gave up all our "We the people" power the day Nixon signed away the gold standard. Look around you and take a serious look ... what's better for it? Do you really believe the US dollar is worth anything? Print what you want but look in the mirror if you want to see a "truly duped" conspirator! The black helicopter you hear ... it is coming for you Caroline.

I like to share the feedback from readers with my editors. At the suggestion of Bill Ahearn, a great newsman who is responsible for all the Bloomberg columnists, I wrote a column about the response to a column, "Higher Oil Prices Are Not Like a Tax. Really." You can find the original in chapter 4 and the follow-up below.

Readers Revolt, React to Idea Oil Is Not a Tax
———————   May 27, 2004   ———————

IN AN AGE of instant information, when the entire life cycle of a news event is condensed into 24 hours, it's unusual to still be hearing from readers three days after a column is published.

My Monday column on why higher oil prices aren't a tax on the consumer clearly struck a nerve. It's as if I challenged people's fundamental belief system—the existence of God, for example.

In a nutshell, my argument was that a demand-driven rise in oil prices, which encourages more output, is nothing like a tax. A tax drives a wedge between the price buyers pay and the price sellers receive. The result, in that case, is reduced output.

Generally when you challenge an ingrained precept, the first reaction is to lash out.

"You must work for the oil companies," one reader wrote.

"Go ride a bike," another said.

"Hullo!" wrote a third, implying I was so hopelessly clueless as to make the prospect of enlightenment through constructive dialogue unthinkable.

An alternative reaction to such perceived heresy from someone without a Ph.D. is to seek safety in numbers and big names. One "energy expert" went so far as to marshal a list of Nobel laureates in economics—Robert Solow, James Tobin, Milton Friedman—all of whom he said were in the oil-prices-are-a-tax camp.

If these folks think higher oil prices are tax, then I must be smoking something.

SUPPLY AND DEMAND

A Nobel laureate confusing a shift in the demand curve with a 1970s-style supply shock? I wasn't buying.

"If there's an exogenous increase in oil prices—from a monopolist—then you could view it as an excise tax," Solow said in a phone interview. "The extra revenue stays outside" the U.S., although even that's only a first-round effect.

All signs point to the current oil price rise as "a demand-side-driven increase," Solow said. As such, there aren't a lot of negative implications for growth.

"Growth is a supply-side phenomenon," he said. "We're seeing an increase in world aggregate demand."

The Paris-based International Energy Agency estimates world demand at 80.6 million barrels a day in 2004, the highest in 16 years and a 2-million-barrel-a-day increase from 2003.

INCOME RISING

Substantive reader challenges to my thesis fall into two basic categories. The first is that higher gasoline and heating oil prices act like a tax in that consumers have to allocate a higher proportion of their household income to them. That leaves less discretionary income to spend on other goods and services, reducing demand for the latter.

That's an entirely reasonable assumption if income is constant: More money for gas means less money for Wal-Mart. Prices of those other goods would presumably fall in response, enabling consumers to purchase the same quantity of goods as they did before.

But income isn't constant. Oil prices are rising because global growth—and oil demand to fuel it—is accelerating. Real GDP growth is rising at the fastest pace in 20 years. The U.S. is producing more; someone gets the revenue from that output. National income can be measured by output (gross domestic product) or by the income (wages, profits, rents) generated by that output.

"We're not producing more and getting poorer," wrote one reader, defending my analysis. "Why is it people think if we buy more of something the price should never rise?"

China, as it turns out, is a big consumer of raw materials, not just a provider of cheap consumer goods to the rest of the world.

LOST DOLLARS

The other major criticism has to do with the revenue paid to foreign oil producers that seemingly disappears into a deep hole in the ground to gurgle with the crude.

Unless a foreign producer literally wants to put dollars in the ground or under the mattress, the dollars that go overseas to purchase goods and services come back here either in the form of foreign direct investment (factories, real estate) or to purchase securities. (Sometimes they never leave the country, or the bank: The deposits are transferred from the buyers' accounts to the sellers'.)

If those dollars are used to purchase bonds, interest rates fall. If they buy stocks, shareholder wealth increases.

BACK TO THE '70S?

In economic terms, the current account is the mirror image of the capital account. The only issue to be determined is the price at which foreigners want to hold dollars.

The economy has changed a lot since the 1970s. Entire industries have been deregulated, trade barriers have fallen, and vast chunks of continents (Russia, Eastern Europe and China) have been liberated and integrated into the world community.

Alas, when it comes to oil prices, attitudes are hopelessly stuck in the 1970s oil-embargo/supply-shock model. Strange, since that was a decade most folks would rather forget.

This column, in turn, inspired a second round of feedback: comments on the comments on the first column.

Dear Caroline,

There is a wise saying that "when your opponent starts dropping names rather than ideas, he must have run out of good substantive arguments." This is especially true when he mobilizes the list of the Swedish Nobel Committee.

"What a great saying," I wrote back to the reader, whom I know professionally. "What's it from?"

"I just made it up," he replied, "when I saw the responses to your column."

I plan to invoke his saying the next time some "expert" disagrees with me and harnesses names, not arguments, in support of his point of view. Who knows? I may even attribute the quote to some dead Nobel laureate.

Index

About Bloomberg

Bloomberg L.P., founded in 1981, is a global information services, news, and media company. Headquartered in New York, Bloomberg has sales and news operations worldwide.

Serving customers on six continents, Bloomberg, through its wholly-owned subsidiary Bloomberg Finance L.P., holds a unique position within the financial services industry by providing an unparalleled range of features in a single package known as the Bloomberg Professional® service. By addressing the demand for investment performance and efficiency through an exceptional combination of information, analytic, electronic trading, and straight-through-processing tools, Bloomberg has built a worldwide customer base of corporations, issuers, financial intermediaries, and institutional investors.

Bloomberg News, founded in 1990, provides stories and columns on business, general news, politics, and sports to leading newspapers and magazines throughout the world. Bloomberg Television, a 24-hour business and financial news network, is produced and distributed globally in seven languages. Bloomberg Radio is an international radio network anchored by flagship station Bloomberg 1130 (WBBR-AM) in New York.

In addition to the Bloomberg Press line of books, Bloomberg publishes *Bloomberg Markets* magazine.

To learn more about Bloomberg, call a sales representative at:

London:	+44-20-7330-7500
New York:	+1-212-318-2000
Tokyo:	+81-3-3201-8900

About the Author

Caroline Baum joined Bloomberg News as a columnist in February 1998 after eleven years at Dow Jones. Her widely read column on the U.S. economy and bond market is distinguished by a lively wit and no-nonsense approach to markets.

For years, Baum had a weekly slot on the Financial News Network and she now appears on Bloomberg TV and radio. From March 2002 through August 2003, she hosted her own weekend radio talk show, *No Nonsense.*

In addition to her real-time column, Baum's work has appeared in *Barron's, The National Review, Bloomberg Markets, Bloomberg Personal Finance* and *The International Economy.* In April 1996, *Worth* magazine profiled Baum as "The Merry Mistress of Bonds."

The National Headliners Club recognized Baum's work with consecutive first-place awards in 2004 and 2005 for wire service/commentary. She won the Newswomen's Club of New York first-place award in 2001 for commentary/wire service.

Prior to joining Telerate in 1987, Baum spent six years selling municipal bonds to individual investors. She holds a BA in political science from Tufts University and an MA in cinema studies from New York University. Her postgraduate education includes courses in nonfiction writing, economics and technical analysis.

She divides her time between New York City and Martha's Vineyard.

Made in the USA
Lexington, KY
05 April 2011